QUEEN VICTORIA
AND THE
ROMANOVS

About the Author

Coryne Hall is an historian, broadcaster and consultant specialising in the Romanovs and British and European royalty. Her books include *Little Mother of Russia: A Biography of the Empress Marie Feodorovna 1847–1928*, *Once a Grand Duchess: Xenia, Sister of Nicholas II* (with John Van der Kiste), *Imperial Dancer: Mathilde Kschessinska and the Romanovs*, *Princess Olga: A Wild and Barefoot Romanov* (With H.H. Princess Olga Romanoff) and *To Free the Romanovs: Royal Kinship and Betrayal*. She is a regular contributor to *Majesty* magazine, *The European Royal History Journal*, *Royal Russia*, *Sovereign*, and *Royalty Digest Quarterly*.

QUEEN VICTORIA
AND THE
ROMANOVS

SIXTY YEARS OF MUTUAL DISTRUST

CORYNE HALL

AMBERLEY

*To the memory of my parents Peggy & Ernie Bawcombe,
always in my thoughts.*

This edition published 2022

Amberley Publishing
The Hill, Stroud
Gloucestershire, GL5 4EP

www.amberley-books.com

British Library Cataloguing in Publication Data.
A catalogue record for this book is available from the British Library.

ISBN 978 1 3981 0909 4 (paperback)
ISBN 978 1 4456 9504 4 (ebook)

Typesetting by Aura Technology and Software Services, India.
Printed in the UK.

Contents

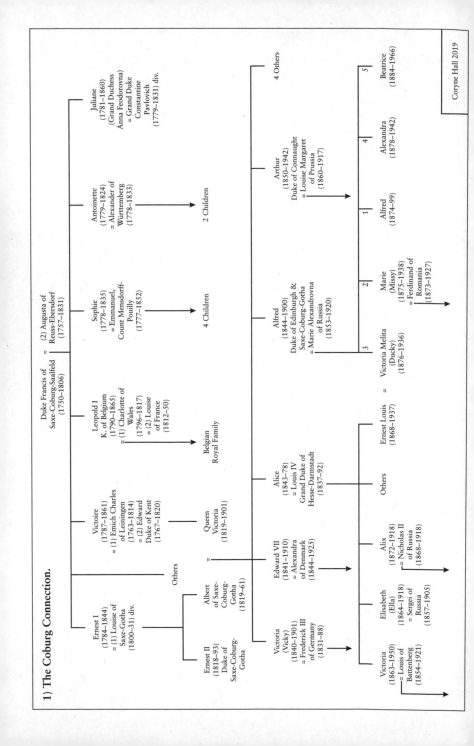

1) The Coburg Connection.

Coryne Hall 2019

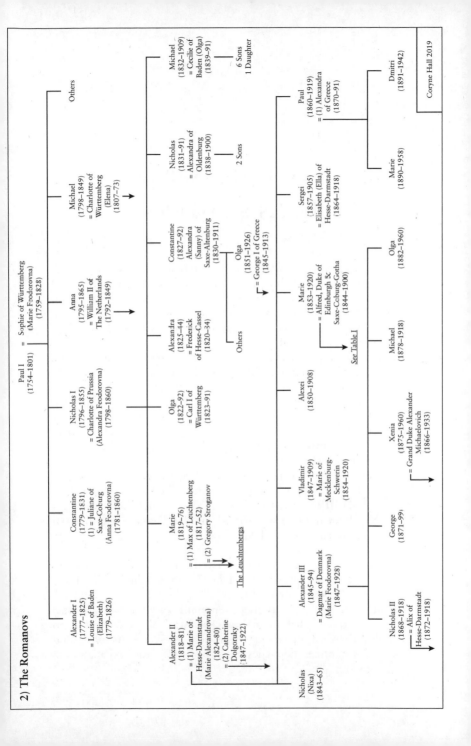

2) The Romanovs

Paul I (1754–1801) = Sophie of Württemberg (Marie Feodorovna) (1759–1828)

Alexander I (1777–1825) = Louise of Baden (Elizabeth) (1779–1826)

Constantine (1779–1831) (1) = Juliane of Saxe-Coburg (Anna Feodorovna) (1781–1860)

Nicholas I (1796–1855) = Charlotte of Prussia (Alexandra Feodorovna) (1798–1860)

Anna (1795–1865) = William II of The Netherlands (1792–1849)

Michael (1798–1849) = Charlotte of Württemberg (Elena) (1807–73) →

Others

Alexander II (1818–81) (1) = Marie of Hesse-Darmstadt (Marie Alexandrovna) (1824–80) (2) = Catherine Dolgoruky (1847–1922)

Marie (1819–76) = (1) Max of Leuchtenberg (1817–52) = (2) Gregory Stroganov → The Leuchtenbergs

Olga (1822–92) = Carl I of Württemberg (1823–91)

Alexandra (1825–44) = Frederick of Hesse-Cassel (1820–34)

Constantine (1827–92) Alexandra (Sanny) of Saxe-Altenburg (1830–1911)

Nicholas (1831–91) = Alexandra of Oldenburg (1838–1900)

2 Sons

Michael (1832–1909) = Cecilie of Baden (Olga) (1839–91)

6 Sons 1 Daughter

Olga (1851–1926) → George I of Greece (1845–1913)

Others

Nicholas (Nixa) (1843–65)

Alexander III (1845–94) = Dagmar of Denmark (Marie Feodorovna) (1847–1928)

Marie (1853–1920) = Alfred, Duke of Edinburgh & Saxe-Coburg-Gotha (1844–1900) → *See Table I*

Sergei (1857–1905) = Elisabeth (Ella) of Hesse-Darmstadt (1864–1918)

Paul (1860–1919) (1) = Alexandra of Greece (1870–91)

Nicholas II (1868–1918) = Alix of Hesse-Darmstadt (1872–1918) →

George (1871–99)

Vladimir (1847–1909) = Marie of Mecklenburg-Schwerin (1854–1920) →

Xenia (1875–1960) = Grand Duke Alexander Michaelovich (1866–1933) →

Michael (1878–1918)

Olga (1882–1960)

Marie (1890–1958)

Dmitri (1891–1942)

Alexei (1850–1908)

Coryne Hall 2019

A Note on Names, Dates and Titles

Russians used the old-style Julian calendar until 1 February 1918. This was twelve days behind the West in the nineteenth century and thirteen days behind it in the twentieth century. Dates have been used according to the western Gregorian calendar, which Queen Victoria would have used, although occasionally both sets of dates have been inserted for clarity.

The titles emperor, empress, tsar and tsarina are all correct and are used interchangeably. The eldest son of the tsar was the tsarevich, other sons were grand dukes. Daughters were grand duchesses. The wife of the tsarevich was the tsarevna. From 1886 the title of grand duke/duchess was limited by Alexander III to the sovereign's children and grandchildren in the male line only; great-grandchildren of the sovereign were prince or princess.

Russians have three names – their Christian name, patronymic (their father's name) and their surname. The sons of Nicholas I and Nicholas II had the patronymic Nicolaievich; the daughters were Nicolaievna. The sons of Alexander II and Alexander III had the patronymic Alexandrovich; the daughters were Alexandrovna.

The members of the Romanov family dealt with in this book were all descended from Tsar Paul I, whose children had the patronymic Pavlovich or Pavlovna.

Apart from the senior branch (represented by the reigning tsar) there were three other main branches, who all descended from Nicholas I's sons: the Constantinovichi (descendants of Grand Duke Constantine Nicolaievich, 1827–92); the Nicolaievichi (descendants of Grand Duke Nicholas Nicolaievich, 1831–91); and the Michaelovichi (descendants of Grand Duke Michael Nicolaievich, 1832–1909). The Dukes of Leuchtenberg were descendants of Nicholas I's eldest daughter Grand Duchess Marie Nicolaievna (1819–76).

List of Illustrations

Acknowledgements

There have been many books on Queen Victoria and no doubt there will be many more but no one has ever looked in depth at her relationship with Russia and the Romanovs. Queen Victoria had an ambivalent relationship with Russia and its ruling family but the reasons why have never been understood. *Why* did she fear and distrust Russia so much? *What* were the consequences of the queen's attitude to the Romanovs? *How* did her legacy help to destroy the Russian Empire that she so feared and distrusted? These were the questions which I sought to answer.

This is not a biography of Queen Victoria. I have looked purely at her relationship with the Romanovs through her personal correspondence and meetings with members of the family. The main sources for Queen Victoria are her copious letters and journals, which run into many millions of words. In this connection I would first of all like to thank Her Majesty Queen Elizabeth II for permission to publish material from Queen Victoria's diaries held in the Royal Archives at Windsor.

This book could not have been written without the help and support of many dear friends. First of all, a huge thank you to Ian Shapiro, who has gone way above anything I ever expected, supplying photocopies of documents in his possession (many of them unpublished), giving me ideas, helping with illustrations and also introducing some valuable contacts. I owe him an immense debt of gratitude.

Special thanks must also go to the following people to whom I am extremely grateful for help with research material, photographs, advice and general support. I cannot thank you all enough for the immense contribution you have made and without it the book could never have been completed:

Arturo Beéche, for permission to use photographs from the large Eurohistory archive; Darin Bloomquist, formerly of Sotheby's; Stefan Boller at the Statsarchiv, Berne; Julie Crocker at The Royal Archives; Lauren Dolman, Assistant Librarian at Balliol College Oxford; Tom Fell at Spinks, London; Margaret Guyver, for reminding me about the Finnish war memorial; Katherine Harrington, Assistant Archivist at Kew Gardens; Innes Israelsohn, for generously permitting me to reproduce the drawing of the 1844 Windsor Review and having it specially photographed for me; Joe Little at *Majesty* magazine for encouraging me to write the book; Barbara Merchant of Lewes History Group; Dr Nadja Muller; Stephen Patterson, The Royal Collection Trust; Karen Roth-Nicholls, who has helped me so much over the last twenty years and who put me on the trail of Anna Feodorovna in Switzerland; John van der Kiste for so promptly providing a wedding photo of Alfred and Marie; Katrina Warne for sending me much interesting material; Marion Wynn; Charlotte Zeepvat for valuable photographic advice; and Simon Zwygart at Schosshaldenfriedhof in Berne. Thank you too to Mark Chambers of Team Knowhow at Currys PC World, for his expert help with my computer. My thanks also to everyone at Amberley, especially Shaun Barrington and my editors Cathy Stagg and Alex Bennett for all their hard work in seeing the book through to completion.

Extra special thanks go to my long suffering husband Colin, who has yet again read and corrected the drafts and supported me in so many ways. I often tease him by saying that without his constant interruptions the book would have been completed in half the time – but the truth is, without his help and support throughout the innumerable complications of the past couple of years it would never have been finished at all.

Every effort has been made to trace all copyright holders. We will be happy to correct any errors and make suitable acknowledgement in a future edition.

My interest in imperial Russia began in childhood, when I discovered that my great-grandmother was born in St Petersburg and was an almost exact contemporary of Nicholas II. Her father, my great-great-grandfather, went to Russia as a teacher in 1859. The story fired my interest and I have always wondered what the family's life there was like only three years after the end of the Crimean War when relations between Britain and Russia were recovering from their lowest ebb. It was this that led to the idea of exploring Queen Victoria's attitude to Russia and the Romanovs.

I am always delighted to hear about families who had connections with the Romanovs and I welcome people getting in touch. I can be contacted via my website www.corynehall.com

Introduction

In November 2018 the exhibition Art, Russia and the Romanovs opened at the Queen's Gallery, Buckingham Palace, emphasising the cultural links between the British and Russian royal families back to the reign of Peter the Great. Yet it is the reign of Queen Victoria that provides us with the most fascinating window into this complicated association.

Queen Victoria had an ambivalent relationship with Russia and its ruling family. Certainly her remarks about the Romanovs were not always complimentary. 'A sovereign whom she does not look upon as a gentleman'[1] was her comment about Alexander III. In return, he described her as a 'pampered, sentimental, selfish old woman.'[2] According to Alexander's daughter Grand Duchess Olga, Victoria 'was always contemptuous of us' and was only really fond of her German relations. 'She certainly didn't like us,' the grand duchess maintained. '... She said that we possessed a *"bourgeoiserie"*, as she called it, which she disliked intensely.'[3] The feeling was mutual. Grand Duke Nicholas Nicolaievich once asked Carl Fabergé to fashion a jadeite caricature of the queen.[4]

Selfish, demanding, obstinate and prone to bouts of self-pity the queen may have been but her ancestors had ruled (with one short break) for nearly a thousand years. Victoria considered the Romanovs, who had only been on the Russian throne since 1613, as upstarts, not to be compared with the British royal family and certainly not to the great German houses of Brunswick, Saxony and Hohenzollern. The Russians, she pronounced on another occasion, were 'wolves in sheep's clothing'.[5] Russia was also an absolute autocracy and, as a constitutional monarch, the queen thought that this was wrong and that it 'was bound to end in tears'.[6] In that respect Victoria would be proved right.

She did have some good words to say about Nicholas II once she got to know him, and she had a good rapport with Alexander II in their youth – but the underlying suspicion and distrust was always there. As Victoria's views on the Romanovs fluctuated, her empire and country would always come before family connections.

Her attitude is all the more significant as her godfather was Tsar Alexander I and she was christened Alexandrina in his honour, although they never seemed to have met. Queen Victoria was the daughter of Edward, Duke of Kent (the fourth son of King George III), and his wife Princess Victoire of Saxe-Coburg-Saalfeld. In 1814 after the abdication of Napoleon, Victoire's brother Prince Leopold of Saxe-Coburg-Saalfeld entered London with the Allied Sovereigns as a general in the tsar's army. It was his friendship with Alexander I which allowed Leopold to meet and marry Princess Charlotte, only daughter of the Prince Regent (later George IV), heiress to the British throne, in 1816. By this time the Duke of Kent was deeply in debt but a marriage would ensure a settlement by parliament. Alexander I financed his trip to Germany to meet a prospective bride, the tsarina's sister Princess Katherine Amelia of Baden. Alas, she proved to be a forty-one-year-old spinster, so at the urging of Prince Leopold, Edward turned his attentions to the prince's widowed sister Princess Victoire. She had previously been married to Prince Emich Charles of Leiningen, by whom she had two children, Charles and Feodora, and she saw no reason to marry a portly man twenty years her senior. She turned him down.

The death of Leopold's wife Charlotte (George III's only legitimate grandchild) in 1817 left the British monarchy in crisis. Prince Leopold urged his sister to reconsider. Any children she and Edward had would be close to the throne and Leopold saw a chance of regaining some of the power he had lost with Charlotte's death. The widowed thirty-one-year-old Victoire married fifty-one-year-old Edward in 1818. *The Times* reported on 9 October that at a ball attended by the tsar at Aix-la-Chapelle, the Duchess of Kent 'attracted particular attention by the richness of her dress and the splendour of her jewels'. Soon afterwards, Victoire realised she was pregnant.

As Edward's younger brothers raced to marry and provide an heir to the throne, the Duke of Kent won when Princess Alexandrina Victoria was born on 24 May 1819, at that time fifth in line to the throne. Her parents wanted to call her Georgiana after Edward's brother George the Prince Regent, but a message came from the Russian Embassy that the tsar wished to stand as sponsor (godfather). The Regent, who had fallen out with Alexander when the tsar visited London (and proved far more popular with the crowds) declared that his own name could not possibly follow that of the Russian emperor. So Alexandrina she became, with Victoria (after her mother Victoire) added as an afterthought after an argument between Edward and his brother at the font. Yet the tsar's goddaughter remained resolutely anti-Russian all her life. This probably would not have mattered if she had not been destined to become queen but the deaths of both George III and her father Edward in 1820, followed by the childless Duke of York in 1827 and George IV in 1830 left only King William IV between Alexandrina Victoria and the crown.

Many people believe that her dislike of the Romanovs stemmed from the horrors of the Crimean War but there is evidence that her aversion predates this conflict by some years. The reasons for her attitude were both political *and* personal.

The political centred on the historical British distrust of Russia. Although there was a reasonably good relationship in the fields of trade and diplomacy Russophobia had been rife in Britain since the rapid expansion of the Russian Empire under Catherine the Great, followed by the military might displayed by the imperial army against Napoleon. There was always an underlying apprehension in Britain, even though the countries had been allies during the Napoleonic Wars. Later, fear of Russia's intentions towards India, disgust at the brutal Russian suppression of the Polish uprising and sympathy for the Turks during the period around the Crimean War all fuelled the fire. In Europe 'the Russian menace', whether or not it ever existed, was seen as very real.

The personal reasons centred on the bad treatment of Queen Victoria's maternal aunt Princess Juliane of Saxe-Coburg-Saalfeld by her Romanov husband Grand Duke Constantine, brother and heir presumptive of Alexander I. The queen's mother the Duchess of Kent was a sister of Juliane, who became Grand Duchess Anna Feodorovna of Russia on her marriage in 1796. Six years separated Victoire, born in 1787, from her elder sister and they had not met for many years but Queen Victoria's journal shows that from 1833 she was in contact with Juliane, whom she referred to as 'Aunt Julia' or 'Aunt Julie' and always remembered Juliane's birthday on 23 September. If Constantine and Juliane had not divorced and he had not renounced his rights, she could have been Empress when Alexander died in 1825, which would have put a Coburg on the throne of Russia.

Alexander I remained fond of Juliane and her brother Prince Leopold. Without the tsar's backing would Leopold's marriage to Charlotte, and that of Victoire and Edward, have been possible? Juliane's marriage to Constantine allowed the impecunious Coburgs to reach undreamed of heights. It was a major coup and a chance they seized with both hands.

Queen Victoria remained in regular contact with her Uncle Leopold, who after the Duke of Kent's death stayed in England and became a father figure to her, and the Coburg connection was to have a great influence on the queen's outlook towards the vast Russian Empire. Yet Victoria was soon forced to realise that, like it or not, at some point she would have to come face to face with the Romanovs. During her long reign she met all four of the tsars whose sovereignty coincided with her own – Nicholas I, Alexander II, Alexander III and Nicholas II. What she did not envisage was the fact that some of the Romanovs would eventually marry into her own close family and that one of her granddaughters would occupy what she described as 'this thorny throne'.[7]

So did she succeed in mending fences with the Russians, and how did she deal with this new situation?

1

The Queen's Unfortunate
Aunt Julie

'The rise of the Coburgs began with her.'[1]

According to Queen Victoria, it was her Aunt Julie who 'unfortunately has been the cause of the [Russian] emperor's unfriendliness towards our family'.[2] The treatment of her maternal aunt by Grand Duke Constantine also influenced Victoria's own views on the Russian imperial family, and those views would last the whole of her long life and reign. It is therefore with Aunt Julie that our story must begin.

In the summer of 1795 the Hereditary Prince Francis of Saxe-Coburg-Saalfeld and his wife Augusta were commanded by Catherine the Great to bring their three eldest daughters to St Petersburg. Seventeen-year-old Antoinette, sixteen-year-old Sophie and fourteen-year-old Juliane (called Julie or Julia by her family) were to be considered as prospective brides for the empress's sixteen-year-old grandson Grand Duke Constantine Pavlovich. After travelling across Europe, the girls and their mother arrived at Strelna on the Gulf of Finland on 6 October. As Augusta and her daughters alighted from the carriage Catherine watched them carefully and picked out Juliane as the most suitable.

The following day, after staging a grand reception at the Winter Palace for the Minister Plenipotentiary from the Grandmaster of the Knights of Malta, the empress awarded the prestigious Order of St Catherine to the three Coburg princesses. One of those present judged the girls 'very tolerable', but while he found fault with Antoinette and Sophie, he praised the beauty of Juliane 'who, however, he feared would soon grow fat'.[3]

Augusta's first assessment of the prospective bridegroom was favourable. 'Not in the world is there a more spiritual and moral young man,' she exclaimed.[4] Others were less complimentary. Grand Duke Constantine was the second son of the heir to the throne Grand Duke Paul but he and his elder brother Alexander had been brought up by their grandmother the Empress Catherine. One contemporary described him as having 'the same eccentricities, the same passions, the same severity and the same turbulence', as his father.[5]

Various entertainments were laid on for the visitors during which fair-skinned, auburn-haired Juliane flirted vivaciously. Louise of Saxe-Gotha (who knew her in later life after she married Juliane's brother Ernest) described her as 'pretty, lively and friendly', while the empress certainly considered her the best choice for her grandson. After only six days' acquaintance the grand duke was ordered to choose a bride. Constantine allegedly said that if he had to marry any of 'these ugly creatures', then he would take 'the smallest and the youngest',[6] fourteen-year-old Juliane, because he liked her sense of humour. He called her 'the little monkey'.[7] Countess Barbara Golovina thought that he did not want to marry.

There is another, most probably apocryphal, story that he chose her based on the way the three sisters alighted from their carriage when they arrived in Russia. Sophie fell over her long train as she got out; Antoinette saw this and crawled out on all fours; and only Juliane managed to alight gracefully.

Juliane, of course, was given no choice in the matter of her marriage. After a formal meeting with Augusta, the grand duke demanded the hand of her youngest daughter. By 14 October the decision was made and the dye was cast. Constantine and Juliane sat together at dinner that evening and opened the ball afterwards with the Polish minuet. The formal proposal came on 25 October. That evening, 5,655 people were invited to a public promenade at the Winter Palace.

As for Sophie and Antoinette, they did not wait to witness their sister's triumph. Showered with diamonds, they left to visit Tsarskoe Selo and Gatchina before returning home. The empress sent them 50,000 roubles each, plus a further 60,000 roubles for their mother. When her family departed, Juliane was left alone in Russia to prepare for her conversion to Orthodoxy and marriage to a man she barely knew. Juliane's mandatory (at that time) conversion took place on 2 February 1796. She took the name of Grand Duchess Anna Feodorovna. 'She was also awarded a diamond solitaire ring for 20,000 roubles, six spicated diamonds for 11,000 and a diamond band for 15,000.'[8] The official betrothal took place the following day. The wedding, postponed for two days because Juliane suffered a bout of fever and toothache, took place on 15/26 February.

Juliane's marriage saved her family from bankruptcy. She sacrificed herself so that the 160,000 gold rouble payment from Catherine the Great would not have to be refunded. Thanks to Juliane's marriage, Coburg was now under the protection of Russia, which prevented it from later being annexed by Napoleon.

But if the marriage was a masterstroke by Augusta, giving the Coburgs new standing in Europe as well as connections at the highest levels, on a personal level it was a disaster. Catherine the Great gave the newlyweds the Marble Palace on the Neva Quay in St Petersburg. This vast, cold building, which took its name from the thirty-two shades of marble used in its construction, was built for Gregory Orlov, one of Catherine's lovers. It is said that on the wedding night Constantine failed to perform his conjugal duties and instead spent the night railing against some guards who had committed a minor breach of regulations. It was not a good omen for things to come. Constantine seemed to prefer the parade ground to the bedroom, was sadistic and treated his young wife 'like a slave'.[9] Although he had received a good education, and was fluent in Russian, Polish and French, he was violent and subject to sudden fits of temper. He was not averse to suddenly firing his gun inside the palace or stuffing his young wife into one of the palace's massive Chinese vases, from which she could not escape without help. Juliane was very young and he had no idea how to treat her. 'He forgot all propriety and decorum so much,' a shocked contemporary recorded, 'that he, in the presence of his coarse officers, claimed condescensions [sic] from her, as her master, such as can scarcely even be hinted at.'[10] He also subjected her to beatings. The empress soon moved the couple into the Winter Palace so that she could keep an eye on things.

* * *

In November 1796 Catherine the Great died and Constantine's father became Emperor Paul I. The following year Paul gave his son the palace of Strelna, near Peterhof, which had wonderful views over the Gulf of Finland. However, this did nothing to improve Juliane's situation. Although she was now the rising star of the

Russian court, contemporary memoirists alleged that Constantine was jealous and treated his pretty, vivacious wife as his own property. He forbade Juliane to leave her room and if she did have the chance to emerge, he took her away. He was even jealous of his elder brother Alexander. 'The eccentricities, fits of passion, the brutalities, and the savagery of Constantine so terrified and alienated the poor girl that she refused to live with him not long after their ill-fated marriage,' wrote a contemporary chronicler.[11]

Paul's wife Empress Marie Feodorovna did not support Juliane, even though her brother Alexander of Württemberg had married Juliane's sister Antoinette in 1798 and later settled in Russia. In fact the Romanovs preferred Antoinette, who became 'a great favourite with them' until her death in 1824.[12] Juliane's brother Prince Leopold of Saxe-Coburg maintained that things would have turned out better if Constantine had chosen Antoinette, who 'would have suited that position wonderfully well'.[13] He blamed the failure of the marriage on the meddling of Empress Marie.

Constantine, now promoted to Inspector General of Cavalry, loved the army and was regarded as a good military strategist but 'his irregular way of life, licentiousness and numerous affairs' caused the marriage to fail.[14] Juliane's association with Constantine's army colleagues caused him to be accused of coarsening her, while older women at court branded her an airhead. The couple had no children.

Juliane's only friends were Tsarevich Alexander, with whom she had openly flirted since her marriage, and his wife Elizabeth, another German princess, to whom she became close. Elizabeth helped Juliane to accustom herself to court protocol and they spent a lot of time together, speaking in German about their native land when their respective husbands were away on military duties. They were each other's only consolation. Both girls complained that Marie Feodorovna treated them like ladies-in-waiting.

The artist Elizabeth Vigée le Brun, who arrived in St Petersburg from revolutionary France, painted Juliane twice in about 1797. She described the young grand duchess as 'not as outstandingly beautiful as her sister-in-law [Elizabeth], but still very pretty. She must have been about sixteen and the most lively exuberance shone through her features.'[15]

***

In March 1799 Juliane left St Petersburg and travelled south to Karlsruhe to take a cure. Grand Duke Constantine joined the tsar's army to fight against Napoleon. With Constantine away at war, Juliane told her family she did not want to return to her husband but wanted a divorce. Her parents Francis and Augusta, fearful of a scandal, refused to let her stay in Coburg and persuaded her to give the marriage another chance. She returned to Russia in the autumn of 1799.

Then in March 1801 Emperor Paul was murdered in a palace coup. Juliane was said to have been present at the dinner party which took place shortly before the deed was done. There were also rumours that she was somehow involved in the murder, or at least had prior knowledge of it.

On the accession of Alexander I, Constantine became heir presumptive to the throne. Although Alexander and Elizabeth had a daughter Maria, born in 1799, she died the following year; a subsequent daughter called Elizabeth was born in 1806 and died in 1808. (Both were ineligible to succeed according to Emperor Paul's Laws of Succession of 1797, which required the emperor to have a male heir.) In 1801 Juliane was thus in line to be the next Empress of Russia. Sadly, her marriage did not improve. Countess Barbara Golovina described Juliane's life as 'hard and impossible to maintain'. Only the friendship of Empress Elizabeth was able to 'smooth things out between the frequently quarrelling spouses'.[16]

During that year Augusta (whose husband had succeeded as Duke of Saxe-Coburg-Saalfeld in 1800) went to Russia to visit her daughter. Juliane then persuaded both her mother and the tsar that she needed to take a cure in Germany. Alexander agreed that she could go but once out of Russia she refused to return and asked Constantine for a divorce. He refused. 'You write to me that you were allowed to go into foreign lands because we are incompatible and because I cannot give you the love that you needed,' he told her. 'But humbly I ask you to calm yourself in consideration of our lives together, beside all these facts confirm in writing, and that in addition to this, other reason you don't have.'[17]

Juliane flatly refused to return to Russia. The official version is that in 1801 she went back to Coburg where she remained for a while, becoming a companion to her unmarried sister Victoire until the latter's marriage to Prince Emich Charles of Leiningen (widower of her maternal aunt Princess Sophie of Reuss-Ebersdorf) in 1803. But there is another scenario, proposed by the Hungarian author Laszlo Vajda, that when Juliane left Russia in July 1801 ('fled' according to German documents; 'sent home' according to the English version) she was pregnant and that the father was Tsar

Alexander I. With her went a Court Marshal and several ladies, including Countess Catherine Vorontzov who had been exiled by Tsar Paul in 1796 and was now a firm supporter of Alexander I. This version says that Juliane did not go to Coburg; instead she went to one of the properties owned by the Koháry family in Hungary, probably Schloss Szentantal, where she gave birth to a son. (Her great-uncle Prince Josias of Saxe-Coburg-Saalfeld was military governor of Hungary from 1791.)

On 18 May 1802 Queen Louise of Prussia wrote to her brother George in Mecklenburg-Strelitz: '... [Grand Duchess] Anna has had a healthy birth, the child was sent to Franconia [which became part of Bavaria in 1803] into a village. What a destiny for an emperor's child and grand ducal child, he [presumably Tsar Alexander] should do something – along with others – be part of this.' The boy, named Alexander but called Sandor, was brought up as the son of Joseph Vajda and Catalin Csontas at Mártonfalva, the estate of the asset manager of the Koháry family in Upper Hungary. Laszlo Vajda is a descendant of Sandor but, until other evidence comes to light, this claim remains unproven. Juliane continued to receive funding from the Russian court. She was received by Queen Louise of Prussia in 1804, but according to Vajda there is no other definite record of her until she hosted a reception at Castle Fantaisie, the Württemberg property near Bayreuth, in 1805.[18]

***

Juliane's marriage was so far the only spectacular union the Coburgs had made and it lay in ruins. Constantine was always considerate towards Juliane's relatives and they had done well in terms of patronage and advancement, with the Coburg sons in particular reaping the benefits of her marriage. Her brother Leopold had been enlisted in the Izmailovsky Regiment of the Imperial Guard at the time of Juliane's wedding, when he was only five years old. Soon he was an honorary captain; later he was made a colonel. In September 1806 Napoleon's army took possession of Coburg. Leopold fought with the tsar against Napoleon and finally became a Lieutenant General in the imperial Russian army. Despite the failure of his sister's marriage he remained a favourite with both Alexander I and Grand Duke Constantine, to whose staff he had been attached.

Shortly after the royal family were forced to flee Coburg, Juliane's father died. Her eldest brother Ernest was away fighting the French but it was thanks to Juliane's connection with the Romanovs that when Alexander I met Emperor Napoleon at Tilsit in 1807, he persuaded him to reinstate Ernest as duke and restore his rights of government. In return Ernest agreed to become a member of the Confederation of the Rhine, which operated under Napoleon's presidency.

The following year there was another scandal. Ernest was betrothed to the tsar's sister Grand Duchess Anna Pavlovna but the imperial family then learnt about his liaison with Pauline Panam, a young Franco-Greek beauty who followed him to Coburg and was living hidden in a farm at Esslau. (Juliane had been introduced to her.) She bore Ernest a son and confronted his mother in a painful scene. The Romanovs broke off the engagement and in 1816 Anna married the Prince of Orange. The Coburgs were now anxious to avoid further scandal and a total breach of relations with the powerful Romanovs. There was no formal separation from Constantine; Juliane kept her rank and title, remaining Grand Duchess Anna Feodorovna.

Constantine had apparently suggested as early as 1803 that his marriage should be dissolved. The reason was that he wanted to marry Princess Janetta Chetvertinskoy (sister of his brother Alexander's mistress, Princess Marie Naryshkin). The Dowager Empress Marie Feodorovna was horrified and forbade the union. He then lived with a French actress, Mlle Friedrichs, for several years.

Following Napoleon's retreat from Moscow, Alexander I and his army entered central Europe in triumph in 1813. In the wake of this there were several attempts to effect a reconciliation between Juliane and Constantine. The tsar asked Juliane to meet him in Bohemia and in 1814 he ordered Constantine to visit her in Coburg. Was there still 'a spark of affection' from him towards Juliane, as author Dulcie Ashdown supposes?[19] Or were the imperial family trying to tempt Juliane with an offer of the imperial crown? After all, Alexander and Elizabeth were childless and Constantine remained next in line.

After this meeting Constantine was ordered by his mother to visit Juliane's home in Switzerland. He was accompanied by her brother Leopold, who always had an eye to the main chance. Juliane would hear no talk of reconciliation with her husband. 'Julia amiably declined all his advances,' Grand Duchess Augusta wrote. 'I cannot blame her for refusing to resume a life of brilliant misery.'[20]

Leopold was horrified at his sister's separation. He later said that Constantine 'felt her hesitation showed revulsion for him.

And he is totally mortified. For my own part, I didn't think her reasons were very good ... youth can excuse much. She'd have to shut her eyes to certain things, and he'd do the same.' These certain things included the illegitimate children that both Constantine and Juliane now had.[21]

Although Juliane and Constantine's marriage had produced no issue, he had at least one child by Mlle Friedrichs, a son called Paul born in 1808. Also that year Juliane retired to live at the Villa Diodati in Coligny, near Geneva, and gave birth to a son, Eduard Schmidt-Lowe (born in Kaiserstuhl, Switzerland and christened on 30 October at Traub, near Berne), believed to be by Jules-Gabriel-Emile de Seigneux, a divorced Swiss nobleman and Prussian officer who had killed a man in a duel (although some, including the genealogist Jacques Ferrand, say that Alexander I fathered this child). De Seigneux became the head of her household and had a great hold over Juliane, but he was rude and arrogant and treated her no better than Constantine.

Having rid herself of de Seigneux, in 1812 (in Siemau, a village near Coburg) Juliane gave birth to a daughter, Hilda-Aglaë, who was adopted by Jean-Francois d'Aubert and his wife. The child's father was Dr Rodolphe-Abraham de Schiferli, the professor of obstetrics she had consulted during her preceding pregnancy. He had previously worked for Grand Duke Constantine's brother-in-law Grand Duke Frederick Louis of Mecklenburg-Schwerin. Schiferli was intelligent and good-looking, but he was also a married man with two sons. In 1811 he replaced de Seigneux as head of Juliane's household and remained her devoted friend and faithful assistant until his death. Hilda-Aglaë married Eduard Dapples in 1834 and died giving birth to her second child.

After Eduard's birth Juliane spent Christmas with her family in Coburg and in the summer visited her brother Ferdinand in Prague. In the autumn of 1810, while living near Lake Lausanne, she was received by the Empress Josephine.

Eduard, who was later ennobled by the King of Saxony as von Löwenfels, became an official at the Court of Coburg. He spent holidays with Schiferli and his family and visited Juliane, who officially was known as his patron. In 1835 he married Bertha, the illegitimate daughter of Juliane's brother Duke Ernest.[22] Eduard became close to Bertha's half-brother Prince Albert, who five years later would marry Queen Victoria.

* * *

In 1813 Alexander I sent Ioannis Antonios Kapodistrias to Berne to prepare the Russian participation at the Congress of Vienna. The tsar's support of Swiss neutrality was said to be largely thanks to Juliane, who urged it in her letters to him. After the Congress, Grand Duke Constantine was appointed Commander-in-Chief of the Polish army in Warsaw, eventually gaining Vice-regal powers. Juliane settled permanently in Switzerland.

In 1814 she bought an estate on the banks of the River Aare to the south of Berne called Brunnaderngut, which she purchased from Gottlieb A. Jenner. Situated near the Russian Embassy, it was on the site of a former convent and monastery, with gardens, fruit trees and abundant sources of water. Juliane rebuilt the country house in the Empire style and renamed the estate The Elfenau ('Elves' Meadow'), a name that was officially registered in 1816.

The landscape gardener Joseph-Bernhard Baumann (1775–1859), a native of the Alsatian village of Bollwiller, was commissioned to design the first English landscape park in Berne, containing flowers from all over the world, including exotic trees from Kew Gardens. Plants were ordered from Kew by Juliane in April 1817 and ten years later more plants were sent to Baumann.

Between 1820 and 1830 Juliane bought more land to the east, commissioning Rudolf Samuel von Luternau to design servants' quarters and an orangery in which to receive guests. Juliane loved music and she participated in the artistic life of Berne. She had a subscription to the *Hôtel de Musique* and entertained musicians and artists from all over Europe. The Elfenau soon became a cultural meeting place for the grand duchess's visitors, including her mother, brother Leopold, sister Victoire and the Duke of Kent (who visited her on their way to England after their marriage) members of the Russian colony and local society. She was invited by the Federal State to all the important social events and many foreign diplomats also flocked to her salon.[23]

She also had an Orthodox Chapel consecrated in 1817, which was directly dependent on the Russian Legation in Berne. This led eventually to the building of the first Russian Orthodox Church in Switzerland, situated in Geneva and constructed with funds left by Juliane.[24]

On 20 March 1820 her marriage was annulled by decree of Alexander I. Juliane remained Russian Orthodox, was given a generous allowance and retained her rank and title. To the outside world she remained Grand Duchess Anna Feodorovna but Duchess

Augusta disapproved of her daughter's scandalous lifestyle and worried about her fate.

* * *

Meanwhile Grand Duke Constantine had contracted a morganatic marriage with the Polish Countess Joanna Grudzińska on 14 May 1820. He renounced his rights to the Russian throne and in 1823 Alexander I signed a manifesto which appointed as his successor his next brother Grand Duke Nicholas. This manifesto was never made public.

When Alexander I died in remote Taganrog on 1 December 1825 Nicholas had no idea that he was now tsar. For two weeks there was an interregnum while Nicholas and Constantine batted the crown back and forth to one another. When Nicholas finally acknowledged his right to the throne an uprising, later known as the Decembrist revolt, took place in St Petersburg. It was led by officers at the head of some 3,000 men, who were alarmed that Grand Duke Constantine had seemingly been overlooked. The revolt was successfully put down, five of the Decembrists were hanged and the rest were sent off to Siberia.

It was thus Tsar Nicholas I with whom Victoria would have to deal when she became queen. Over the next sixty years Queen Victoria would have many dealings with the Russians and, to her horror, live to see her son and two of her beloved granddaughters marry into the Romanov family.

But before that happened, before she was even married, Victoria found herself bowled over by a handsome Russian grand duke.

Bowled Over by a Grand Duke

'How dreadful it would be if the Queen were to fall in love with him! For actually he is the only man whom she could not possibly marry.'

– Lady Cowper, 1838.

On 20 June 1837 King William IV of England died and was succeeded by his eighteen-year-old niece Princess Alexandrina Victoria of Kent. For the first nine years of her life she had been called Alexandrina, or just 'Drina', after her godfather Alexander I. When it became evident that she would one day become queen the name Victoria was substituted because it sounded more English.

She had endured a lonely childhood at Kensington Palace, her every move dictated by her widowed mother Victoire, the Duchess of Kent, and starved of companionship of people her own age. As soon as she learned of her accession, the new queen threw off the duchess's tutelage (and that of her mother's Comptroller Sir John Conroy) and moved into Buckingham Palace determined to lead an independent life at last.

Her Uncle Leopold remained a father figure who offered good advice, even though he was no longer living in England. On 4 October 1830 the Belgian people declared independence from Holland, deposed King William I and elected Prince Leopold of Saxe-Coburg as king of newly independent Belgium in 1831. He corresponded regularly with Victoria, although he was disappointed to be relegated to the role of loving uncle while her

Prime Minister occupied the premier place. Yet Leopold remained in conflict with Russia.

This was awkward on two fronts. King William's daughter-in-law the Princess of Orange was the former Grand Duchess Anna Pavlovna of Russia, Tsar Nicholas I's sister. The tsar, who was also King of Poland, had intended to send a force of mainly Polish troops to crush the Belgian rebellion and help the Dutch sovereigns but Belgium was saved from Russian intervention by a revolution in Poland, where Nicholas's brother Grand Duke Constantine Pavlovich (who died in 1831) was Viceroy. When Polish rebels voted for the dethronement of Nicholas and secession from Russia, Polish troops were overpowered by the Russians. The former Kingdom of Poland was incorporated into the Russian Empire and the throne of the Kings of Poland was taken to the Kremlin. Polish exiles flocked to France, Britain and Belgium, where they were welcomed as heroes fleeing the repressive rule of the tsar. Many officers joined the army of the new King Leopold I of Belgium and remained under his protection.

Tsar Nicholas would have liked to become reconciled with Leopold but said it was impossible as long as men he considered Polish 'rebels' remained in the Belgian army. Leopold now had his own axe to grind and his own reasons for disliking the land of the tsars. He encouraged his niece Victoria's suspicions of Russia. Leopold's liberal outlook and vehemently anti-Russian sentiments would have a great influence on the new queen.

* * *

On 19 July 1837 Count Orlov arrived at Buckingham Palace to present Emperor Nicholas I's compliments to the young Queen Victoria upon her accession. He also brought a letter from Empress Alexandra Feodorovna and the Order of St Catherine, (the highest female Russian order, instituted in 1714 by Peter the Great in honour of his wife) set in diamonds, together with a scarlet sash. This could only be bestowed by the empress or the dowager empress with the approval of the emperor.

The British Foreign Secretary Henry Temple, Lord Palmerston, was anxious that when Count Orlov returned to Russia he did not take with him any suggestion that the tsar might be invited to England. Lord Palmerston saw Russian expansion as a threat to the British Empire and was determined to prevent Russia from establishing a hold on the Bosphorus. It was believed that the tsar wanted his eldest son Alexander to see Europe and that Nicholas desired to accompany him to England. A visit by the tsar, Palmerston explained, would not be desirable and any reference to the fact that the queen was not acquainted with Nicholas should therefore be avoided. He advised the queen to assure the count that she wished to cement and maintain the friendly alliance between their countries and to say also that she took much pleasure in receiving someone who so fully possessed the emperor's confidence.

That evening the queen sat next to Court Orlov at dinner, proudly wearing the Order of St Catherine, 'which is a very handsome and a very distinguished Order; it was instituted by the Empress Catherine the 1st, [sic] Count Orlov told me, when she saved the Russian army from the Turks. Count Orlov is *the* favourite of the emperor, and is a clever man.'[1] This was Queen Victoria's first direct encounter with the mighty Russian Empire.

Nicholas I had not expected to become tsar and by 1837 he was beginning to sink under the weight of governing such a vast expanse of land. Catherine the Great had expanded her empire into the Crimea, the Caspian Sea, the Caucasus, Siberia and Turkey. The tsar's domains now covered one-sixth of the land surface of the earth; as the sun set at one end of the empire it rose again at the other. It was a land of strange contrasts. To the north-west was St Petersburg, the new capital built by Peter the Great; to the east lay the frozen wastes of Siberia, stretching up towards the Arctic. Over 75 per cent of the population were peasants, who lived in small isolated villages and worked the land for six months of the year. When the snow lay thick on the ground, they huddled, starving, inside their log huts. One-third of them were serfs, who could be bought, sold and mortgaged like cattle. The gulf between rich and poor was tremendous.

Keen to learn more about this mysterious country, Victoria spoke to Louisa Lambton, the Countess of Durham, one of her ladies of the bedchamber whose husband John, 1st Earl of Durham, had recently been ambassador to Russia. Louisa was therefore able to tell the queen more about the Russian court. She said that Nicholas I spoke French, German and English as well as his native Russian, was a keen horseman and soldier who enjoyed military drill and felt more at home among the troops than in the drawing rooms of Europe. He liked order and discipline and his favourite foreign country was Prussia, a liking increased by his marriage to Princess Charlotte of Prussia, who on her marriage and conversion to Orthodoxy took the Russian name of Alexandra Feodorovna. The countess told Victoria how the empress was 'excessively fond of dress, and how often she changed her dress in the course of the day', mainly to please the emperor, and how she even noticed what other ladies were wearing.[2] Victoria had heard from her Uncle Leopold (who made no secret of his dislike for Nicholas) that the emperor was severe towards his eldest son, while her half-brother Prince Charles of Leiningen said that Empress Alexandra was haughty.

The home of the Russian court was the Winter Palace in St Petersburg, which made the perfect setting. Built by Rastrelli for Empress Elizabeth in the eighteenth century, this massive building stretched for a third of a mile along the banks of the River Neva. The interiors of the palace were destroyed by a devastating fire in December 1837, which left it as a smoke-blackened shell, but it was rebuilt and restored immediately afterwards on the emperor's orders. Some of Victoria's descendants would come to know it well. The new Winter Palace of Nicholas I, which was ready for occupation in 1842, was said to have 1,050 rooms, 117 staircases and 1,786 windows. Behind 40-foot-high wooden doors inlaid with gold, the State rooms – St George's Hall, the White Hall, the Malachite Room and the Small Throne Room – were decorated with gold, silver, onyx, malachite, lapis lazuli and marble. Huge chandeliers were suspended from the ceilings and the light from thousands of candles was reflected in the mirrors and the parquet floors. The Nicholas Hall was 180 feet long, its gilded walls set off by two rows of colonnades. The rooms were filled with priceless paintings, *objets d'art*, gold and silver plate and richly carved furniture, with gold inlay, which luckily had been saved from the fire. Among the 1,200 servants were scarlet-shirted men who polished the parquet floors by skating along with a hard brush attached to one foot; exotic Circassian chiefs in chain armour; and Arabs in oriental dress.

On 31 December the queen had a long conversation about the Russian imperial family with her Prime Minister. For the first three years of her reign this was William Lamb, Viscount Melbourne, who in 1839 became the brother-in-law of Lord Palmerston. Aged fifty-eight to the queen's eighteen, he was worldly wise with a fount of knowledge and an irreverent wit which could always make her laugh. Melbourne, Victoria told King Leopold, was a man she could trust and within a short time he possessed her full confidence. Elizabeth Longford has called their partnership 'one of the romances of history'.[3]

Melbourne and the queen spoke about how the grand duchesses never converted from their Orthodox religion when they married, but 'if anyone married any of the grand dukes they were obliged to change.' Melbourne then explained the differences between the Russian Orthodox and the Roman Catholic religions. Victoria said her Aunt Julie had been obliged to change, 'her having only been fifteen when she married'. She told Melbourne how her aunt disliked it, and spoke about 'her temper; the Grand Duke Constantine having been a terrible man; [and] Aunt Julie's unhappy situation now'. Grand Duke Constantine, Lord Melbourne said, used to insult people. They then went on discuss the emperor's brother Grand Duke Michael Pavlovich, 'a violent, disagreeable man'. Victoria said she 'thought these Russian people were all rather savage', a comment with which Lord Melbourne agreed.[4]

Aunt Julie's unhappy situation to which the queen referred was probably in connection with her illegitimate children, whom she was unable to raise herself. '... Aunt Julie was not well thought of...' Victoria told Lord Melbourne, presumably referring to her aunt's somewhat disreputable private life.[5]

***

By 1838 Tsar Nicholas was anxious to solve The Eastern Question – the fate of the decaying Ottoman Empire which linked the Mediterranean, Aegean and Black Seas. Under the influence of the Turkophile British Ambassador at Constantinople, Viscount Ponsonby, Britain had been co-operating with France to keep Russia out of the Mediterranean. Consequently, the British government saw every Russian action in the most sinister light. Sultan Mahmud II was now anxious to reduce dependency on Russia and on 16 August an Anglo-Turkish commercial treaty was concluded and the sultan leased the port of Aden to Britain.

In search of an entente the tsar turned towards Britain. On 5 March Lord Melbourne informed the queen that they expected any day to officially hear that the Emperor of Russia would be sending his eldest son Alexander to London that summer. Victoria and the tsarevich were, in fact, related. Queen Charlotte, Victoria's paternal grandmother, was the aunt of Alexander's maternal grandmother, Queen Louise of Prussia. The formal notification arrived in early May but the tsarevich caught a cold in Copenhagen, which turned to bronchitis and he was forced to convalesce in Italy. The planned visit to England was postponed.

***

Tsarevich Alexander was born in the Kremlin on 17/29 April 1818 and was thus a year older than Victoria. He was courteous, honest, bright and naturally generous. In 1834, at the age of sixteen, he became the first Romanov to take an oath of allegiance to the ruling tsar at a ceremony in the Small Church of the Winter Palace. After finishing his formal education his father sent him off on a tour of Russia that lasted seven months. Uninterested in the usual round of hospitals, factories, schools and churches laid on for imperial visitors, Alexander sought out the poorest people in peasant huts to see how they lived. Then he set out on a European tour to find a bride. After convalescing in Italy, he found her while touring Germany in March 1839 – fourteen-year-old Princess Marie of Hesse-Darmstadt. Not even rumours that Grand Duke Louis II was not her real father could dissuade Alexander, and when he left to visit his aunt Anna, the Princess of Orange, in The Hague, he was wearing a locket containing some of Marie's hair. After a month in The Hague he planned to visit England.

In April Queen Victoria was informed that he would arrive between the twelfth and fifteenth of that month. Victoria was bored by the whole idea of his visit, especially as she would be required to entertain him. Also, many of her relatives had quarrelled with Russia, so what on earth could she talk about with him? The British Ambassador to Russia, Lord Clanricarde, was anxious for her to invest the tsarevich with the Order of the Garter (which the tsar had been given by George IV in 1827) but Lord Melbourne and the queen disagreed. Melbourne thought it inappropriate, while Victoria said that her Uncle Leopold would never forgive her. Melbourne was anxious that the queen be extremely civil to her visitor, especially as there was trouble with Russia over Persia. 'The emperor is very susceptible; he's half a savage, a Kalmuk, a Tartar, but they've a great deal of feeling,' he told her.[6]

By 1 May, after at least one postponement, Alexander's arrival in London was imminent. Melbourne wanted the queen to receive him on the Saturday. Victoria was annoyed – it was opera night and she didn't want to miss the performance. She was certainly not looking forward to meeting him but, as she told King Leopold, 'I shall put myself out of my way in order to be very civil to such a great personage.'[7]

This would be the young queen's first meeting with the Romanovs.

* * *

On Friday, 3 May the grand duke finally arrived on an unofficial visit to England. (Although he was actually the tsarevich, both the queen and many contemporary accounts refer to him as the Grand Duke Alexander.) He was accompanied by his cousin Prince Henry of the Netherlands and Count Orlov. For propriety's sake they stayed at Mivart's Hotel (now Claridge's) in London.

Alexander was described by a contemporary as resembling his father in build. He had big blue eyes and in public his face was not expressive but 'when the grand duke was with his family or close friends and allowed himself to be himself, his face radiated kindness, and his welcoming and tender smile made him truly sympathetic.'[8] The Russian Ambassador Count Charles Pozzo di Borgo was 'filled with admiration for [Alexander's] bearing, his reserve, his easy manner and, at the same time, his kindness, which proclaimed itself in every word and in all his manners'.[9]

The day after his arrival Alexander, accompanied by Prince Henry, Count Orlov and Count Pozzo di Borgo (whom Victoria had met several times before her accession) was received by the queen at Buckingham Palace. They conversed in French and later she recorded her impressions of the tsarevich in her journal: 'he is tall with a fine figure, a pleasing open countenance without being handsome, fine blue eyes, a short nose, and a pretty mouth with a sweet smile.' Prince Henry was not so impressive, an 'ugly and stupid looking and timid young man, very like his eldest brother Prince William'.[10] In return, Alexander recorded his impressions of Victoria. '[She] is very small [barely 5 feet tall], her figure is bad, her face plain, but she's very agreeable to talk to.'[11]

At dinner that evening Victoria sat between Alexander and Prince Henry. 'I found the grand duke exceedingly agreeable, so good-natured, natural, and merry. He is just a year older than I am.' She was again less impressed with the Dutch prince. 'Poor Prince Henry is very heavy, but very good-natured, and talks English perfectly; he is not quite nineteen.' Victoria was a man's woman and was obviously quite taken with Alexander. '... I like the grand duke extremely,' her diary entry concluded, 'he is so natural and gay and so easy to get on with.'[12]

The following day was a Sunday and he was surprised to learn that, unlike many places on the Continent, in England there were no theatres open on the Sabbath. Victoria had arranged to lend him carriages and horses, so they went riding in Hyde Park accompanied by the queen's gentlemen. Alexander, the queen noted, was very pleased with the horse lent to him.

Although there were tensions between England and Russia in the East, during Alexander's visit the British press stopped attacking Russia and Russian foreign policy. Emperor Nicholas was pleased with his son's reception. 'From the queen and the upper classes right down to the lower orders, everyone is receiving him with incredibly kind attentions,' the tsar wrote to his brother-in-law William, the Prince of Orange, in The Hague on 11/23 May. Alexander had already chosen his bride and the tsar could only hope that the 'pretty English girls' would not prejudice plans for the marriage with Princess Marie.[13]

It was not the pretty English girls who were the problem though – it was the queen. At the ball on 10 May, the queen 'danced the first and the last dance with the grand duke'. Writing to Lord Melbourne the following day, Victoria said that she made him sit near her 'and tried to be very civil to him, and I think we are great friends already and get on very well; I like him exceedingly'.[14]

Once he got to know Victoria better, Alexander found her 'charming, intelligent and witty'. He liked her complete independence and freedom of expression in her opinions. 'He could be free and easy around her, which he could not be at the court of his father.'[15] The historian Alexander Tarsaidze says that Alexander 'fell in love with the queen, and the queen responded'. Tarsaidze cites the Soviet historian A. N. Savin who, writing in 1926, stated that 'many pages and sentences of the czar's [Alexander II's] correspondence of the period have been excised', presumably so that details of this youthful fling would not be known. Dormer Creston, in the book *The Youthful Queen Victoria* published in 1952, also 'mentions it rather casually'.[16]

In a pleasure-loving mood and always susceptible to male beauty, the queen found herself falling in love with her handsome visitor and soon became very jealous of her popular younger cousin Princess Augusta Caroline, elder daughter of the Duke and Duchess of Cambridge, who was gaining his attention. Many years later Augusta told her niece, by then Queen Mary, about 'a scene I had with the queen at a small ball in the Gallery during the Tsarevich Alexander's stay in London, when he was more attentive to me than to her'.[17]

Nevertheless, the tsarevich's tutor Colonel Simon Yourievich confided to his diary that on the day after the ball Alexander 'talked openly about the queen. She impressed him with her youthfulness, her charm and sense of humour. Alexander was her constant partner ... and I believe she also derives a pleasure from his company. Indeed, together they are a perfect pair.'[18]

The visit took place during a political crisis, caused by Victoria refusing to accede to the demand of her new Prime Minister Sir Robert Peel that she dismiss her Whig ladies-in-waiting after the recent change of government and appoint Tory ladies in their place. The queen won that battle and to her great delight Melbourne and the Whigs remained in power. Victoria explained the situation to the tsarevich during an interval of the opera. Although they sat in separate boxes for the sake of propriety, during the interval Alexander entered the queen's box and they spent half-an-hour alone behind the velvet curtains. She told King Leopold that 'he was shocked at ... Peel's proposal [that she should dismiss her Whig ladies], thought his resignation on that account absurd, and was delighted at the continuance in office of my present government.'[19]

Colonel Yourievich was now becoming seriously worried. Alexander 'confessed to me that he loves the queen and that he is convinced that the feeling is mutual. I begged him to give me a few days to consider the situation.' The following day Alexander confronted Yourievich again and was told that such a marriage would be impossible. 'He will have to renounce his future crown,' Yourievich wrote, 'and, I added, that his conscience will not permit him to do that. He agreed with me, but it was apparent he was suffering. He was sad and pale.'[20] Yourievich reported the situation immediately to Count Orlov.

In desperation, Yourievich then approached Victoria's former governess Baroness Lehzen, now the queen's Lady Attendant and her closest confidante. She said that the queen had confessed her feelings for Alexander, and '... that he is the first man she ever fell in love with. She is happy in his presence, is fascinated by his looks and charm. "I am afraid," said the baroness, "she would accept this proposal".'[21]

Yourievich now had no doubt that if Alexander were to propose to the queen, 'she, without hesitation, would have accepted him.'[22] A despatch was immediately sent to St Petersburg. It was becoming imperative that Alexander leave England as soon as possible. In an effort to keep the couple apart, the tsarevich was sent to pay calls on the queen's relatives, visit the Bank of England and Newgate Prison and view a model of the Battle of Waterloo. He paid several visits to Westminster, saw the British Museum and dined with members of the aristocracy. He visited Oxford University, where at Brasenose College he was awarded a Doctor of Law degree, and at a London banquet arranged by the Russian Merchant Company in his honour, responded to their welcoming speeches by replying in fluent English. He gave the enormous sum of £20,000 to charities, particularly for the release of the debtors he saw in prison, and scattered orders, medals, snuff boxes and rings in all directions to members of the queen's court.

Victoria's twentieth birthday on 24 May was celebrated with another ball at the palace. The evening finished with a traditional country dance, in which she partnered Alexander. Although he had never danced it before, he appeared to enjoy the experience. 'We flew down the middle, and he is so strong that he can twist you about just as he pleases...' she recorded with pleasure.[23] By the time Victoria left the ball at half-past three the next morning she was complaining of a very bad headache.

* * *

The court moved to Windsor, where Alexander and his suite joined the queen a few days later as part of a large house party. From her window, Victoria saw him arrive. He looked up and bowed. There is speculation that because it was inappropriate for the unmarried tsarevich to stay under the same roof as the unmarried queen, he may have stayed at Frogmore Cottage. In 2018 *The Times* published a report that one of the tsars had scratched his name with a diamond on the porch window. Who it was remains unknown.

At dinner in St George's Hall, 'which looked beautiful', the queen sat between Prince Henry and the grand duke. Afterwards there was more dancing. 'I really am quite in love with the grand duke; he is a dear, delightful young man.' Among the dances was the Polish mazurka, full of quick and sprightly steps. Alexander asked Victoria to partner him, which she did, although she had never danced it before. 'The grand duke is so very strong, that in running round, you must follow quickly, and after that you are whisked round like in a valse, which is very pleasant...' Their high rank did not permit either the queen or the tsarevich to waltz, so the mazurka was the nearest Victoria would ever get to whirling around the floor with this strong, handsome young man.

The ball concluded with a German country dance called the *Grossvater*. Although Victoria had never even seen it before, when Alexander invited her to dance she agreed. 'We had such fun and laughter... It begins with a solemn walk round the room, which also follows each figure; one figure, in which the lady and gentleman run down, holding their pocket-handkerchief by each end, and letting the ladies on one side go under it, and the gentlemen jump over it, is too funny.' It is clear that Victoria was quite bowled over by this young man. 'I never enjoyed myself more. We were all so merry; I got to bed by a quarter to three, but could not sleep till five.'[24] When King Leopold heard about this he wrote a disapproving letter to his niece.

The following day the queen and her guests set off in an open carriage for the races at Ascot. Alexander was both pleased and amused by the racing and had a bet with the queen which Victoria won, saying she would keep his gold sovereign as a souvenir. He also donated £300 to the Jockey Club, who named a race 'The Cesarewitch' in his honour. (The race is currently run at Newmarket every October.) By this time the queen was sorry he would soon be leaving. She wanted to dance again and decided to try and persuade him to stay longer.

At dinner that night Alexander spoke warmly of the very fine reception he had received in England, which he said he would never forget. She recorded his words in her diary: '"These are not only words, I assure you, madame," he said, but that it was what he felt, and that he never would forget these days here, which I'm sure *I* shall never also, for I really love this amiable and dear young man, who has such a sweet smile; his shake hands [*sic*] was always so warm...'

The dancing began after supper, and Victoria was delighted when Alexander asked her to partner him. 'The grand duke is so strong that when he took me round the waist to give that finishing turn, I felt lifted from the ground; then I took a turn with Prince Henry – who does not do it so well; then with the grand duke, who runs along so fast...'[25]

The queen took a liking to Alexander's little black and white spaniel called Fancy, which he said had been with him for seven years. She looked after Fancy while the grand duke attended a military review the following day, and then arranged for Alexander to be shown over the castle before they took a drive through the park to Virginia Water. It was his last day. The emperor was becoming concerned about his son's apparent fondness for the young English queen. He ordered him back to St Petersburg.

At dinner in St George's Hall that night Victoria said 'how grieved' she was, 'as I really was', that this was their last dinner. Alexander agreed that departures were terrible. The *Gay Loisir*, the favourite quadrille of the queen and grand duke, was played and Alexander told her he would take the music back to St Petersburg. When it was played, he said, it would always remind him of these days at Windsor. Later they exchanged autographs before there was time for one last mazurka and then the *Grossvater*, which that evening was livelier than ever. '... the jumping over the pocket-handkerchiefs [was] delightful; Prince Henry never clearing one jump properly – but always pulling down the pocket-handkerchief; so that the grand duke split his sides with laughter; there is another very funny figure, in which everybody holds up their pocket-handkerchiefs across, and you have to dance under it, which we did creeping along, so that the grand duke caught his head in my wreath.'

As the evening ended, Victoria felt extremely sad that her delightful young visitor was leaving and that there would be no more lively mazurkas and *Grossvaters*. She could only think of his handsome face and the masterful way he piloted her around the room. During her secluded upbringing at Kensington Palace Victoria had never experienced anything like that.

When Alexander came to say goodbye he kissed Victoria's hand and she kissed his cheek, a gesture he then returned. He was pale and his voice faltered as he told the queen that he lacked the words to express what he really felt. He said 'how deeply grateful he felt for all the kindness he met with, that he hoped to return again, and that he trusted that all this would only tend to strengthen the ties of friendship between England and Russia...'[26] Victoria felt as if she was taking leave of a dear relative rather than a stranger. 'I felt so sad to take leave of this dear amiable young man, whom I really think (talking jokingly) I was a little in love with...' she confided to her journal on 29 May.

Yet Victoria had experienced strange, new sensations and it is clear that she was certainly not joking.

* * *

The next morning Victoria was surprised to discover that she felt very flat. Her attitude towards the Russians had also changed. Initially reluctant to meet the tsarevich, Lord Melbourne now noticed that she could not stop talking about him and her eyes were wet with tears. She consoled herself by showing Melbourne some books of prints, one of which showed Alexander as an eleven-year-old boy. They both agreed it still looked so much like him. Her Uncle Leopold did not approve of her sudden affection for Russia. He hated the Russians, the queen told Melbourne, 'which I said I never did – but of course still less now, from knowing them all'.[27]

The tsarevich had been equally upset at leaving, but he had to attend the wedding of his sister Marie to Maximilian de Beauharnais, 3rd Duke of Leuchtenberg, on 2/14 July. 'Last night,' Yourievich wrote on 30 May, 'we said goodbye to the English court. When the tsarevich was alone with me, he threw himself into my arms and we both wept. He told me he will never forget Victoria. On parting, he kissed the queen. It was his happiest and saddest moment of his life...'[28]

Queen Victoria was always susceptible to a handsome man but the visit of the tsarevich had raised her standards. Life felt very dull after the departure of the Russians. Everything that reminded her of their visit to Ascot was now 'delightful'. When *Gay Loisir* was played she went into rhapsodies, declaring it was just like 'old times'.[29]

Many years later in her memoirs, Victoria's granddaughter Princess Alice, Countess of Athlone, called Alexander 'Grandmama Victoria's first beau'.[30]

Although it was impossible for the queen to even contemplate a marriage with the heir to the Russian throne, there would be a surprising development later in the lives of their respective children.

***

In June the tsarevich's cousin, twenty-year-old Duke Charles-Alexander of Saxe-Weimar, arrived at Buckingham Palace as a possible potential suitor. Although his mother was Nicholas I's sister Grand Duchess Marie Pavlovna, the heir to the Grand Duchy failed to impress. 'The young grand duke is just the same age as *the* grand duke; is not at all good-looking, but has a fine, tall figure and seems gentlemanlike; but after the other grand duke, no one is seen to advantage,' Victoria wrote in her journal on 3 June. She still missed the Russians, who were so jolly and ready to do anything. During dinner the queen sat next to Charles-Alexander, who she thought 'good natured but too talkative' and certainly not as handsome as his cousin. He spoke about the tsarevich, who Victoria praised saying that one must love him. Charles-Alexander then asked if he could repeat that, and on receiving Victoria's assent told her that he often corresponded with Alexander and would write to him. Afterwards there was dancing, but somehow for Victoria it was just not the same.[31] Charles-Alexander left Buckingham Palace without making a favourable impression on the queen. In 1842 he married Princess Sophie of the Netherlands.

Then in mid-June a letter arrived for the queen from Tsarevich Alexander. Victoria drafted her answer but, of course, Lord Melbourne had to be informed of its contents before it could be sent. 'That will do very well indeed,' he told Victoria, adding cautiously, '*ought* you, however, to say *bonne soeur*?' worried that it sounded inappropriate. 'He wrote *bon frère*,' Victoria replied. Lord Melbourne agreed that the queen could therefore do no less.[32]

At the end of June a rumour reached London that Alexander was shortly to become betrothed to Princess Marie of Hesse-Darmstadt. The princess was still very young and her health was causing concern, so it seemed that the marriage would not take place for some time. Victoria told Lord Melbourne that she thought it hard that Alexander should have to marry so young. The British Ambassador's wife Lady Clanricarde had recently returned from Russia. Victoria summoned her and heard many interesting things about Russia and the emperor's family.

On 2 September an enormous green malachite vase arrived at Windsor Castle. Standing almost 6 feet tall, it was probably made by the Imperial Lapidary Works at Peterhof around 1836 and had originally been in The Hermitage in St Petersburg. It was a present from Emperor Nicholas I to thank the queen for her hospitality to his son whose visit to England, despite Russian concerns about security, had passed off without incident. It was placed in the Grand Reception Room at Windsor, where it still stands. In 1842 he sent her a Siberian wolfhound, a dog that was very rare and expensive in Britain.

Beside Tsarevich Alexander, Victoria's cousin Prince Albert of Saxe-Coburg, whom she had met in 1836, paled into insignificance. He was extremely good-looking but hated late nights, rich food and took no pleasure in the balls and parties which so delighted the queen. Although Victoria had told King Leopold in 1836 that Albert possessed every quality that would make her happy, when it was now suggested that Albert and his brother Ernest should pay another visit, Victoria realised what was afoot. She could not, she told Lord Melbourne, think of marrying for another three or four years. The queen valued her independence. She knew Albert was intended to be her husband and teased him in a letter in June, telling him about the tsarevich's recent visit and saying how much she liked him. Now she wanted to cancel Albert and Ernest's visit.

Lord Alfred Paget, one of her handsome young gentlemen, had been regaling her with stories about the emperor, empress and grand duchesses romping in the garden. It all seemed such fun to the lonely young queen.

* * *

The visit of the tsarevich, who had so impressed everyone by his kindness and easy manner, had eased the tensions over the Eastern Question, aided by the truce in the British press. Britain had succeeded in counterbalancing Russia's influence in Constantinople; the sultan had been freed from his sole dependence on Russia and was now able to manoeuvre between the Russians and the British. He was determined to reconquer Syria from Egypt but the defeat of his armies in Syria caused new tensions between Britain and Russia. With neither country completely dominating the Ottoman Empire, it now seemed an opportune moment for Tsar Nicholas to sound out the British with a view to mutual co-operation in the Near East. In this atmosphere, the tsar sent Baron Philippe de Brunov, one of his most competent diplomats (who later became Russian Ambassador to the Court of St James's), to London with a number of concessions and instructions to 'invite the British government to tell us candidly what it thinks, what it wants and where it wishes to go'.[33]

In October the queen had a frank discussion with Lord Melbourne about the Eastern Question, which she recorded in her journal. Melbourne told her that Russia proposed to act with England but without France (unless of course England wished France to be included). 'If the Egyptian Pasha marched on Constantinople then it should be allotted to *them* to defend Constantinople; but *no* other fleet to come up the Dardanelles. Russia is bound by the Treaty of Unikiar Skelessi to defend Constantinople.'[34]

Against opposition from almost the whole cabinet, Melbourne and Palmerston were in favour of accepting de Brunov's propositions. Melbourne told the queen that he thought that Turkey would now fall into the hands of Russia, although her tenure, which would be insecure, would not constitute any real power. The Duke of Wellington, however, thought that Russia would become a very formidable power if she gained access to the Black Sea alongside the ports she already possessed on the Baltic.

Baron de Brunov told Lord Palmerston that if he valued the Ottoman Empire's existence, he should 'leave Russia in peace, respect the closure of the Dardanelles, and do not force our emperor to seize them. For, mark my words well, on the very day that you force a passage through the Straits [the 125-mile passage from the Black Sea, through the Sea of Marmora to the Dardanelles and the Mediterranean], Russia will set her armies in motion and the final hour of the Ottoman Empire will have struck.'[35] With this warning, de Brunov returned to his post as Russian Ambassador in Stuttgart.

In mid-December de Brunov returned to London, where a convention had been convened comprising Britain, Russia, Prussia and Austria. France was excluded, a move that caused resentment in Paris. The tsar was impatient, and with no agreement reached by May 1840 he announced that if nothing had been settled within the next month 'I will think of other measures for the decision of this matter in accordance with our dignity.'[36]

Not until 3/15 July 1840 did representatives of England, Russia, Austria and Prussia sign the London Convention. Lord Palmerston, alarmed by French influence in Egypt, made no attempt to supplant it with British influence. Instead, he supported the Sultan of Turkey and co-operated with Russia against France. The Egyptian pasha was offered terms, which he rejected and after several months the sultan was eventually persuaded to recognise him as ruler of Egypt. The sultan's hopes for an Arab empire were lost and it also constituted a defeat for France.

The Straits Convention of 13 July 1841 between the sultan and five European powers further increased Russia's security. The Unikiar Skelessi treaty of 1833 was not renewed. This was not the end of the affair and misunderstandings festered until they eventually came out into the open in the Crimea.

* * *

Meanwhile, the queen had been distracted by other, more personal, matters.

On 10 October 1839, at the urging of King Leopold of Belgium, Prince Albert of Saxe-Coburg-Gotha and his elder brother Ernest arrived at Windsor. The princes were the sons of the disreputable Duke Ernest of Saxe-Coburg-Gotha, the eldest brother of the queen's mother Victoire Duchess of Kent, Aunt Julie and the queen's uncle King Leopold. Albert, born on 26 August 1819, was a serious, sensitive young man who had seemed dull and frail to her when they first met in 1836. His mother Louise, who as heiress had brought the duchy of Gotha to the Saxe-Coburg family, had separated from her philandering husband when Albert was only five and died young in 1831 having never seen her children again. Long after their divorce Duke Ernest married his niece Marie of Württemberg (daughter of his sister Antoinette). King Leopold of Belgium was now determined that the Coburgs would sit on the throne of England and, with his own influence starting to wane, had been grooming Albert for the role of consort.

Victoria was instantly smitten by tall, blue eyed, handsome Albert, who looked so much better now than when they met three years earlier. She immediately decided that this was the man she wanted to marry. Five days later, and in accordance with royal protocol, the queen proposed and Albert, of course, accepted.

When news of the intended marriage reached Russia it did not go down well with the tsar. Nevertheless, as a wedding present he sent copies of the portraits of his daughters Grand Duchess Marie and Grand Duchess Olga, both of whom Victoria would later meet. Victoria had discovered shortly after her engagement that Albert also disliked the Russians and thought the emperor was 'so cruel'. The queen discussed Russia's reaction with Lord Melbourne. He had already told her that the Russians hated the Coburgs and she realised how angry the tsar would be at this marriage. Tsar Nicholas had once replied to a question about the Duchess of Kent by saying, 'I do not know her ... but she comes from a family who I do not like, a family who likes money, it is vile, it is low.' Melbourne and Victoria also discussed the queen's Aunt Julie and her turbulent marriage to Grand Duke Constantine, and what a difference it would have made if the couple had not remained childless. Lord Melbourne told the queen about Constantine's love of insulting people, saying, 'he insulted ladies whom he made love to.'[37] Lord Melbourne's remarks did nothing to alter her opinion that, on the whole, the Russians were savages. By January 1840 the queen was telling Melbourne that she disliked Russia as much as did her Coburg relations, especially King Leopold who had a particular aversion to Russia and still had no diplomatic relations with the tsar.

On 10 February Queen Victoria married the handsome Prince Albert at the Chapel Royal, St James's Palace and in November gave birth to her first child, Victoria (Vicky), created Princess Royal the following year. As for Tsarevich Alexander, he had completely forgotten the English queen. His engagement to Princess Marie of Hesse-Darmstadt was formally announced in April 1840 but, because of her extreme youth, they did not marry until 16/28 April 1841.

* * *

In the summer of 1841 the queen's mother the Duchess of Kent was travelling in Germany, where she met her sister Juliane for the first time in twenty-four years. The Coburgs had done well out of Juliane's disastrous marriage. In 1816 her brother Ferdinand married Antoinette, heiress of the extremely wealthy Koháry family; twenty years later their eldest son Ferdinand married Queen Maria II of Portugal and became King Consort. Leopold sat on the throne of Belgium and Victoria (with another Coburg at her side) on the throne of Britain.

Queen Victoria continued to keep in touch with her Aunt Julie. Sending good wishes for her birthday that September, Victoria wrote: 'I am very grateful for the kind letter you wrote me some time ago, for the very pretty brooch, and for all the good kind messages you sent me for Mama, who was so happy to see you ... and so sad to have to leave you again. The stay at Coburg, and at Gotha, and at Reinhartsbrun must have been most agreeable. It is so sad to see this happy family gathering break up...' The Princess Royal was now ten months old and, the queen added, she 'is making great progress: she suffers a little sometimes with her teeth, but much less than children ordinarily do...'[38]

The birth of the Princess Royal was followed in November 1841 by the birth of a son, Albert Edward, Prince of Wales. The choice of King Frederick William IV of Prussia as one of his sponsors caused mutterings of discontent in Russia. In April 1843 a second daughter, Alice, was born.

In September 1843 the queen and Prince Albert visited King Leopold of Belgium at Laeken. He was uncle to both Victoria and Albert and had made a second marriage in 1832 to the much younger Princess Louise, daughter of King Louis Philippe of France, with whom the young Victoria had formed an intimate bond when they first met in 1835. Queen Louise of Belgium had become almost like a big sister and Victoria always referred to her as 'dearest Louise'.

Waiting with Leopold when the queen and prince arrived was Aunt Julie. It was the queen's first meeting with the aunt she had heard so much about. Victoria thought her 'very like Mama, only taller & slighter. She is quite wonderful for her age, sixty-two.' A series of family deaths, including that of Schiferli and Hilda-Aglaë in 1837, had severely weakened Juliane's health. . '.... In her ways, & *"tournure"* [turn of phrase] she puts me so in mind of mama,' Victoria continued, 'though she is livelier.'[39] The party spent three delightful days sightseeing in Belgium, including a trip to Antwerp to view the art exhibition in which Albert took a particular interest.

On 20 September the queen and Prince Albert had breakfast with Juliane, who presented Victoria with a ring. Then it was time to leave. 'Aunt Julie was so sorry to take leave of us so soon after having just made our acquaintance. She is so cut off from her relatives, her position is so painful & unfortunate, that I feel most deeply for her. We saw them all get into the barge & watched them till they landed at Lifkenyók, where they were to embark on a small steamer to return to Antwerp,' she recorded that evening. 'Sad, to feel that the happy *"séjour"* was over.'[40]

Thanking King Leopold for his hospitality, Victoria told him that 'the delightful souvenir' of the visit would remain with her. 'To leave my dearest Louise too was so painful and also poor Aunt Julie, so immediately after making her acquaintance; pray tell her that, for me.'[41]

Having heard the story of Juliane's disastrous marriage, the queen's sympathies lay entirely with her aunt who she realised was lonely. 'Dearest Louise seems much pleased with Aunt Julie, which I am glad of, and I rejoice that poor Aunt has had the happiness of making my beloved Louise's acquaintance, for it will be a happy recollection for her in her solitude,' Victoria told King Leopold.[42]

'This Greatest of all Earthly Potentates'

'The Crimean War was all the fault of one man.'
— Queen Victoria.

'We expect the Grand Duke Michael here this afternoon,' Victoria told her Uncle Leopold in early October 1843 'He is to stay till Friday.'[1]

Grand Duke Michael Pavlovich was the Emperor Nicholas's brother. An officer in the imperial army, he was unhappily married to Princess Charlotte of Württemberg, who had taken the Russian name of Grand Duchess Elena Pavlovna on her marriage. The couple had three surviving daughters, none of whom was endowed with good health. Michael and Elena had no common interests. He was bored by his wife's intellectual pursuits; she disliked his love of military life. To get away from his wife Michael began to travel around Europe.

On 3 October he arrived at Windsor. 'He is very military looking and talks loud, is very tall and broad and aged about forty-five,' the queen wrote in her journal. He brought with him a Russian-style shirt for the two-year-old Prince of Wales which, the queen recorded proudly a few days later, he appeared in during lunch. (In fact he was to wear a loose shirt many times, usually during the appearance of a visiting member of the imperial family.)[2]

The following morning after breakfast the queen and her guests went for a walk to Adelaide Cottage and the kennels before Albert took the grand duke for a tour around the castle and St George's Chapel. It was a lovely warm day, so after lunch Albert rode out with Michael while Victoria and her half-sister Princess Feodora (who had married Prince Ernest of Hohenlohe-Langenburg in 1828 and was on a visit from Germany) followed in a pony phaeton.

Dinner that night was in the Waterloo Gallery. The queen sat between Grand Duke Michael and Albert's brother Prince Ernest of Coburg. She was impressed with the grand duke, who she found 'very agreeable and amiable – talking very pleasantly'. Albert thought him 'very reasonable and moderate in his views'.[3]

Michael spent his time riding or going shooting with Prince Albert. He attended a review, visited the military college at Sandhurst and also Eton College. He told Victoria and Albert about Moscow, spoke about his army life and explained the difference between the Russian Orthodox Church and the Roman Catholic Church, saying the former was more severe. 'Their fasts are much more rigorous,' the queen recorded. 'On Wednesdays and Fridays in Lent, they are not allowed even to eat fish, and no butter or cream, and towards the end of Lent they are hardly allowed to drink at all. On great Feast Days, like Good Friday, Easter, and Xmas the service in the morning lasts four hours, and two in the evening. The music is very fine; all men's voices, unaccompanied, which must have a splendid effect.'[4]

One morning at breakfast he began discussing the French retreat from Moscow in 1812 and praised the bravery of the French general. Coincidentally, the queen and prince had recently been reading *1812: ein historischer Roman* by Ludwig Rellstab, and Victoria was gripped by the account of the Battle of Borodino and the fire in Moscow. She had also received a first-hand account from the French side.

Victoria admired Michael's brown and white dog called Dragon, which was large, like a Newfoundland. She praised it to King Leopold, saying it had 'the most expressive eyes imaginable and [is] *si bien dressé* [so well trained]'.[5]

On 7 October news arrived of the birth of a first son to Tsarevich Alexander, the queen's former *beau*, and his wife Tsarevna Marie Alexandrovna. This next direct heir to the Russian throne, born on 8/20 September, would be baptised Nicholas but known as Nixa. Victoria and Grand Duke Michael then discussed the links between their families. Michael, the queen wrote in her journal on 6 October, 'spoke several times with great affection' about her mother's sister Princess Antoinette of Saxe-Coburg, who married Michael's uncle Duke Alexander of Württemberg. Victoria also noted that her father's sister Charlotte, the Princess Royal and daughter of George III, had married King Frederick I of Württemberg, another of Michael's uncles, and, of course, 'poor Aunt Julia married the Grand Duke Constantine, and I think she unfortunately has been the cause of the emperor's unfriendliness towards our family'.[6]

The grand duke left on 31 October, extremely gratified with the reception he had received. On parting, he gallantly kissed and pressed the queen's hand. 'I must say he is very amiable and civil,' she wrote to King Leopold.[7]

In Russia, Tsar Nicholas wrote to his sister Queen Anna of the Netherlands that 'it appears that the queen welcomed [Michael] very kindly.'[8] At the end of the year, addressing Albert as '*Mon Frère et Cousin*' Nicholas sent him the Order of St Andrew, which according to Victoria, only King Louis Philippe of France had so far received. 'This conferring of the Order is meant as a return for our civility to the Grand Duke Michael,' she noted. Albert was happy to accept this token of Nicholas's friendship and regard. It was also the tsar's way of recognising Albert's position and status at the British court.[9]

* * *

Grand Duke Michael's stay paved the way for an even more important visitor. On 14 April 1844 the queen learnt that the tsar, suspicious of a recent visit paid by Victoria and Albert to King Louis Philippe of France whom he disliked, wished to come to England. The Russian Minister Baron de Brunov (the post was downgraded from Ambassador in 1844) had been informed by Count Nesselrode, the tsar's Chancellor and Minister of Foreign Affairs, that the monarch wished his visit to be incognito and conducted with the same simplicity as that of his brother. He would be in England for no longer than a fortnight. It would be the first visit of a Russian tsar since that of Alexander I in 1814.

The Foreign Secretary Lord Aberdeen thought that for security reasons he would be unable to visit London. Nevertheless, a formal invitation was issued, saying that the queen would be happy to receive him in late May or June. Although the Prime Minister, Sir Robert Peel, told Baron de Brunov that the queen and prince were pleased at the thought of entertaining the emperor, Victoria was reluctant and troubled. Not only was Nicholas still in conflict with King Leopold over the Polish exiles, but he wished to restore the monarchies deposed in the revolutions in France and Belgium in 1830, including that of his sister Queen Anna and his brother-in-law King William (whose father had lost part of his Dutch Kingdom to Leopold). Victoria had no wish to upset her uncle but eventually was persuaded by Prince Albert that the tsar's visit would help to mend the fractured relations between the monarchies of Europe. 'We are still threatened with a visit from the Emperor of Russia, which alarms me somewhat,' she wrote in her journal on 7 May.[10]

The Emperor Nicholas had fond memories of his previous visit in 1816, when as a young grand duke he had attended a 100-course banquet with the Prince Regent at Brighton Pavilion, met the Duke of Wellington and been a great hit with the ladies of London society. The success of this earlier four-month stay instilled in him the belief that the English monarchy and aristocracy were his allies. He now wanted to discuss foreign policy with the queen, not appreciating the limits placed on her as a constitutional monarch.

Emperor Nicholas's public persona was described by a contemporary: 'No one was better created for the role of autocrat. He had both the appearance and the necessary moral qualities. His impressive and majestic handsomeness, his regal bearing, severe perfection of the Olympic profile, commanding gaze, everything down to his smile of a condescending Jupiter – everything about him breathed of an earthly god, omnipotent ruler, everything reflected his unshakeable belief in his calling. The man never felt a shadow of doubt in his power or its legitimacy.' Lady Londonderry, who met him in 1836, described him as a 'magnificent looking being'.[11]

The queen was expecting her fourth child in the summer and hated receiving people in what she called 'my present condition'. Another problem was that King Frederick Augustus II of Saxony (who owed his crown to Napoleon) was also due to arrive on 1 June and this would cause complications about precedence. As the queen pointed out, 'no one yields to the other in rank in spite of the greater size and power of the kingdoms.' The visit of the tsar now was therefore not particularly convenient on all counts. 'But it cannot be helped, disagreeable as it is. He will only remain a week,' she noted in her journal on 30 May.[12] By now, to her surprise, she had learnt that the emperor was on his way. Count Carl Nesselrode had informed the British Ambassador Baron Bloomfield that the monarch had left St Petersburg on 24 May. He could arrive at Buckingham Palace as early as 3 June.

* * *

The sudden news of his imminent arrival on 1 June therefore threw Buckingham Palace into a panic. The rooms set aside for the emperor were hastily freshened up and Russian pictures, including one of the Empress Alexandra, were hung on the walls.

King Frederick Augustus of Saxony had already arrived and, with little warning of the tsar's arrival, many events had to be improvised.

At ten o'clock that night Nicholas arrived at Woolwich wearing a large grey travelling cloak and grey cap. He was travelling as Count Orlov to avoid the attentions of Polish nationalists who might want to assassinate him in the wake of his brutal suppression of the 1830 uprising. With a large community of Polish exiles living in London, there were very real fears for his safety. Even Baron de Brunov was not told of the exact time of his arrival. As it transpired, their concern was justified. An armed Polish man was apprehended at Windsor Castle during his visit.

The tsar lodged with Baron de Brunov at the Russian Embassy at Ashburnham House, Westminster, and immediately sent a note to Prince Albert asking to see the queen at the earliest opportunity. In order not to inconvenience the heavily pregnant Victoria the emperor also said that he would not stay at the palace before the court left for Windsor on 3 June.

The country the tsar arrived in was like nothing he had known before. Now a great and powerful country, England was smaller than many provinces in his own empire, yet 'its friendship was to be desired and its enmity to fear.'[13] Unlike his visits to the small German courts, there would be no anxiety here to win the emperor's favour.

On 2 June Prince Albert conducted Nicholas to Buckingham Palace, where Victoria greeted him at the door of the Grand Hall. He was dressed, she recorded, *'en grande tenue'*, in the red uniform of the *Chevaliers Gardes,* with high boots and the Garter Star on his breast. He chivalrously kissed the queen's hand and she embraced him. Although he was already forty-eight Victoria thought his appearance striking – 'handsome, very tall and with a very good figure'. They sat talking in the rooms prepared for the emperor, then they had lunch before he and Albert left to call on the Duke of Wellington, leader of the House of Lords, and on members of the royal family. The Duchess of Kent, however, was not in London; she was travelling in Europe where her itinerary included a visit to her sister Juliane, the tsar's former sister-in-law.

At dinner that night Victoria sat between the King of Saxony and Tsar Nicholas, who was in civilian evening dress. She noticed a slight defect in one eye, which gave him a rather terrifying stare. 'There is a strange expression in the emperor's eyes, one might almost say wild, which is not prepossessing,' she recorded. 'But his manners are excellent, dignified and simple. However, he gives me the impression of not being a happy man, and not being quite at his ease. He seldom smiles, and when he does, it is hardly an amiable expression. Altogether, to me, he is not fascinating and Albert agrees...'[14]

The 'wild' expression the queen noted was said to be due to mental illness inherited from his unbalanced father Emperor Paul, and which had also affected Alexander I during his final years. It made Nicholas impatient and impulsive. 'Albert thinks he is a man inclined to give way too much to impulse and feeling which makes him act wrongly often,' Victoria wrote to King Leopold.[15]

A few days later she wrote to her uncle again. 'If we can do anything to get him to do what is right by you, we shall be most happy, and Peel and Aberdeen are very anxious for it. I believe he leaves on Sunday...'[16]

* * *

On Monday morning the tsar visited the Bond Street jewellers Mortimer & Hunts, where he was later reported to have spent £5,000 on jewellery and gold plate. He then called on the Prime Minister Sir Robert Peel and various members of the aristocracy.

In the afternoon the court left for Windsor Castle. Although the emperor gave Victoria the impression that he was enchanted with the place, in a letter to the tsarevich he described it as a 'superb and rich prison'.[17] To the astonishment of the servants, he insisted on sleeping on the military camp bed which always travelled with him, and the requests of the tsar's valets for straw from the stables so that they could stuff the mattress were met with amazement by the castle's staff. (His camp bed could still be seen in the Winter Palace in 1922.)

Mourning for Prince Albert's father who died in January, combined with Victoria's advanced state of pregnancy, precluded a ball being given but that night sixty-three people attended a glittering state dinner in the Waterloo Gallery where fifty-three dishes were served on the magnificent silver-gilt Grand Service. As the queen's private band played during the meal, Nicholas remarked how good it was to see each other sometimes rather than trust everything to diplomats. He was, however, uncomfortable in civilian clothes and complained that it was the custom at the British court not to wear uniform. By now Victoria was recording that 'I am very glad that the emperor came.'[18] The banquet was later immortalised in a watercolour by Joseph Nash, which hangs in the castle.

Nicholas discovered that Victoria had not forgotten the visit of his son. 'What pleased me most,' he told the tsarevich, 'was the good impression you left after your visit. The queen especially remembered you and praised you with all her heart.' Victoria thought that the father of her 'beloved Alexander' was 'severe and gloomy. I don't think he is very intelligent; his mind is without any refinement; his education is very inadequate.'[19]

The emperor was ready for every occasion with military punctuality, sometimes even early, which the queen found embarrassing. Nevertheless, he seemed to appreciate the royal family's home life and endeared himself to Victoria by praising Albert, admiring her children and being a respectable husband and father in his own private life.

The following day Albert took the tsar to the races at Ascot where, accompanied by the King of Saxony, they rode in the royal procession down the racecourse. After watching the Queen's Cup, the royal visitors came down to examine the winning horse, 'with whose points,' *The Times* reported, 'the emperor seemed particularly pleased.' The tsar was loudly cheered as he walked among the public without fear. The Ascot Gold Cup was to be run on Thursday and before leaving the racecourse 'it was announced that he was endowing the Gold Cup with £5,000 – not in cash but in the form of a plate that would bear the Russian coat of arms.'[20]

Victoria was warming to her guest, finding that his 'sternness is less remarkable, when one gets to know him better'. At dinner that night 'he talked again of the great advantage of seeing one another occasionally, which I quite agree in, as it does great good and gives feelings of friendship and interest, which one cannot otherwise have for a complete stranger, that one could do more *"dans une conversation"* than by all sorts of messages; that one could explain one's feelings and emotions so much more easily.'[21]

On 5 June there was a grand military review in Windsor Great Park, where the tsar and the royal family received a very enthusiastic reception. The emperor, wearing a dark green uniform faced with red, rode through the ranks on Milbank, but Victoria did not think the uniform, and still more the helmet he wore, suited him. She had far more praise for Albert, who looked superb on his Arab grey horse with its splendid new accoutrements. The Princess Royal and the Prince of Wales were present with their governess Lady Lyttelton and did not mind the firing of the guns at all. Nicholas felt much more at home in uniform than in civilian clothes, saying that uniform was like a second skin. During the review he told the queen that she could rely on his troops as if they were her own.

Later at dinner the emperor wore his more becoming uniform of a Cossack general. As the band of the Life Guards played and the company dined from the silver-gilt service, he and the queen discussed political matters. Victoria decided that the emperor 'gains on being better known'.[22]

Despite occasional rain triggered by the great heat, the queen accompanied the royal party to Ascot on the Thursday. That afternoon the Gold Cup was won by Lord Albemarle's horse, which he immediately named The Emperor. (Until 1946 it was possible to name a horse *after* it had raced. 'It would be identified by its breeding.') The horse won the race again the following year, when the Gold Cup was renamed the Emperor's Plate, with a magnificent new silver trophy on which were depicted the palaces of Peterhof and Gatchina and heroic events in the life of Peter the Great.[23]

※ ※ ※

Nicholas had made no secret of the fact that the purpose of his visit was political. Face to face meetings, he thought, were essential. During his stay the tsar had discussions with Prince Albert, Sir Robert Peel, the Duke of Wellington and Lord Aberdeen. All were surprised that he expressed his views so frankly; the queen thought almost too much so: '…he talks so openly before people, which he should not do, and with difficulty restrains himself,' she told King Leopold.[24]

On the subject of Leopold, the tsar denied any unkind feelings towards him. They knew each other well, Leopold having served in the Russian army. Nicholas said he would like better relations but it was impossible to enter into direct communication while the Polish officers remained in the Belgian army.

He hoped Britain and Russia might become allies as they had a common interest against France but his main cause of concern was Turkey – the 'Sick Man of Europe' – and what would happen when the Ottoman Empire crumbled. He hoped to improve Russia's relations with Britain at the expense of France. Nicholas had a high regard for England but was uneasy about the close relationship that was being forged with France, especially between the queen and King Louis Philippe. France's current good relations with

Egypt and the Ottoman Empire would affect his own plans for the expansion of Russian territory at the expense of Turkey. 'I highly prize England; but for what the French choose to say about me, I care not at all – I spit upon it,' he said.[25] He spoke so loudly and fiercely on one occasion that Peel had to move him well away from the open window, as those outside could hear all he was saying. He would not, he said, 'claim one inch of Turkish soil, but neither will I allow that any other shall have an inch of it...,'[26] although for now he was content to maintain the status quo. Nicholas had repeated Baron de Brunov's earlier statement and one day Europe would learn that he meant it.

Nicholas wanted friendship with England but not to the exclusion of everyone else, as the queen told King Leopold on 11 June. The tsar nevertheless thought that Britain and Russia should act together to prevent an indecent scramble for territory, or even a European war, when the inevitable happened and the Turkish Empire collapsed. Aberdeen and Peel agreed this should happen when the need arose. Count Nesselrode had already warned Nicholas that the English 'never make commitments for a more or less uncertain future, but ... wait for the event in order to decide what course to adopt'.[27] It was a warning that Nicholas appears not to have heeded.

It is alleged in Lord Malmesbury's memoirs that a secret memorandum was drawn up between the tsar, Wellington, Peel and Aberdeen, although it was never signed. Whether this is true or not, Turkey was certainly to the forefront of the tsar's mind.

Nicholas loved the life of an English country gentleman but the problem was that he was unable to comprehend the parliamentary system, its debates and the constrictions under which English diplomats had to work. Most important of all, he did not understand the way English statesmen negotiated and, as an autocrat, he did not understand that the ministers were answerable to parliament. He took the statements of Peel and Aberdeen as statements of policy, and any unsigned memorandum would doubtless have been viewed as an agreement on the Eastern Question.

Victoria later had a talk with Lord Aberdeen, who said that the emperor was 'exceedingly pleased with his visit, that he was very friendly towards England and wished to be on the best terms with her.' He was, the queen thought, 'extremely pacific, only wishing the French would not meddle in his affairs as he certainly would not meddle in theirs. He was very anxious about the East...' Lord Aberdeen was of the opinion that the emperor was almost overwhelmed by his responsibilities as sovereign. He had really only come to visit the queen, who thought that a personal visit sovereign to sovereign was a good idea. 'By seeing one another, one gets to know people's characters, their faults and their good qualities; one gets to understand their feelings and consequently what are their *own* actions, and what are *not*, and takes an interest in one another, which is not likely to be effaced.'[28]

Nevertheless, the queen thought that the Emperor and Autocrat of all the Russias had developed 'that sombre *ennui* which is so often a fruit of unopposed despotism'. Even his children viewed him with fear and respect, rather than love. Although he had some love for his daughters, only the eldest son Alexander occupied his time, the other sons were of less importance and would go into the army or navy. He adhered to the protocol of the Russian court like a puppet, lacking the imagination to make any alterations. Victoria called him 'uncivilized' and his courtesy, a blatant contradiction, was 'alarming'. Unlike his son, with whom she had danced the mazurka, Nicholas was only interested in 'politics and military matters'.[29] He was totally insensible to the arts.

* * *

The royal party returned to London on 7 June. Nicholas stayed in Buckingham Palace, where he again refused a comfortable bed in favour of his own camp bed from St Petersburg and asked that his valet be permitted to collect straw from the Royal Mews to stuff the mattress.

At lunch with the King of Saxony in the small drawing room the emperor again spoke frankly and fairly about politics. That night after dinner, at which the queen recorded Nicholas looked 'magnificent and dignified', there was a reception for 239 guests.

While in London the emperor visited the United Services Club at Pall Mall, saw the Houses of Parliament (still undergoing reconstruction after the fire of 1834) and attended a grand fête at Chiswick House in West London, a frequent gathering place of the Whigs, where he got on well with Lord Melbourne. In the evening the royal party went to Her Majesty's Theatre for a performance of The Italian opera, where the queen took the tsar's hand and led him to the front of the royal box to acknowledge the enthusiastic greeting. On Sunday the tsar attended a service at the Russian Chapel in Welbeck Street.

Before he departed, the tsar left substantial charitable donations, as well as money towards Nelson's Column and the

Wellington monument. The royal families also exchanged the usual gifts. The tsar gave the queen an album of watercolours (which Elizabeth II presented to the Soviet President Kliment Voroshilov in 1956) and left the Order of St Andrew for the Prince of Wales (the queen later sketched him wearing the star and ribbon on his Russian blouse); Victoria sent a diamond and enamel bracelet containing a lock of her hair for the empress and gave the emperor a sketch of the Waterloo Gallery at Windsor Castle, which she had drawn for him. She also promised to send a cup similar to the one she had presented to the winner at Ascot, which Nicholas had much admired. The emperor was overcome as he kissed the queen's hand in parting, convinced that his charm had worked on Victoria and her ministers, not realising that friendship was not enough.

Prince Albert accompanied the tsar to Woolwich, where he boarded the *Black Eagle*. 'There is much about him that I cannot help liking,' Victoria wrote to her Uncle Leopold, 'and I think his character is one which should be understood, and looked upon for once as it is. He is stern and severe – with fixed principles of *duty* which *nothing* on earth will make him change; very *clever* I do *not* think him...'[30] The tsar had stressed again to Lord Aberdeen that he would send a minister to Brussels to open diplomatic relations as soon as the Polish officers were no longer employed in Leopold's army.

As thanks for the queen and prince's hospitality Nicholas sent them a hardstone and gilt-bronze table whose top was decorated 'with a bouquet of flowers of different stones', and a huge vase on a marble pedestal made by the Imperial Porcelain Factory in St Petersburg. On one side was a view of the Catherine Palace at Tsarskoe Selo, and on the other the Grand Palace at Peterhof. In her letter of thanks Victoria told the tsar that the table had been placed in the White Drawing Room and the vase in the bay window of the Green Drawing Room at Windsor. In return, Victoria sent a sixty-two piece Coalport dessert service decorated with the Russian orders of chivalry and a Minton dinner and dessert service for the new Imperial Yacht *Queen Victoria* (built on the Isle of Wight), which arrived in Kronstadt in 1846 with its English crew. The luxuriously appointed vessel was incorporated by the tsar into the Baltic fleet and used by the imperial family for sailing trips in the Gulf of Finland. The Minton service had a blue and gold border, the Romanov double-headed eagle in the centre, and above it 'the imperial crown in red and gold with St George and the dragon, and the sceptre and orb in gold'. Underneath, written in Cyrillic on a banner, was 'The Queen Victoria'.[31]

The British people were very flattered by the tsar's visit, which was seen as a great compliment to the country. The 1844 Room at Buckingham Palace was later named in the tsar's honour. In 2017 Queen Victoria's great-great-granddaughter Queen Elizabeth II recorded her Christmas broadcast in this room.

***

On 6 August 1844 Victoria gave birth to her fourth child Prince Alfred, whose life was later to be inextricably linked with Russia.

The queen remained in touch with the tsar and on 25 August was saddened to learn that his nineteen-year-old daughter Alexandra, who she had heard in June was already very ill, had died. The grand duchess, wife of Prince Frederick of Hesse-Cassel, died 6 hours after giving birth to a son, who also did not survive. 'Our grief is lifelong,' Nicholas wrote to his sister Queen Anna in The Hague, 'it is an open wound we shall carry to the grave...'[32] Victoria immediately sent a message of sympathy. At the end of September she received letters of thanks from the emperor and empress, the latter also sending her a pretty bracelet.

As the year ended, relations between Britain and Russia continued to be friendly. In December the queen received Konstantin Ton, the architect who had built the Grand Kremlin Palace for the emperor. He was able to show Victoria and Albert plans of a palace he was building for Nicholas in Moscow.

In June 1845 the emperor sent Albert two droshkies (Russian carriages) and four horses. 'Only 1 horse goes in each,' Victoria noted. 'The Russian coachmen (one, being one of the emperor's once) were in their dress, and they drive from one low seat, quite close to the horses, and with the reins divided, and carrying no whip. The carriages are narrow and low, one being for two people, and the other for only one. The harness is very peculiar, without any blinkers. There is one very handsome black horse, the others being grey ... the pace they go is tremendous.'[33]

It would be two more years before the queen had another Romanov visitor.

***

Between 19 August and 2 September 1845 Victoria and Albert visited Coburg and Gotha, so that the queen could see the places where her husband grew up. Among the many relatives present when they arrived was Juliane.

Victoria's half-sister Princess Feodora had seen Aunt Julie in 1841 and told the queen, 'I find [her] very much changed, she looks now an old woman, such a pity, for she was so lovely once.'[34] In 1844 the queen commissioned William Corden to copy Elizabeth Vigée Le Brun's portrait of Juliane, and Prince Albert arranged for him to travel to Coburg to reproduce this and other family portraits. The resulting picture of Victoria and Albert's Aunt Julie hung in the queen's bedroom. Now they would see each other in person.

The meeting took place at the Ehrenburg, the formal residence of the Dukes of Coburg, situated in the centre of the town. Victoria described it as 'very handsome, with a nice open Platz in front of it'. As their carriage approached, the band played and white-clad girls threw flowers. At the foot of the stairs her mother and aunt were standing alongside Albert's brother Ernest (now the Duke of Coburg), his wife Alexandrine and a large gathering of Coburg relatives. Ehrenberg was to be their base, although they did not actually stay there. That honour was reserved for Albert's birthplace, the Rosenau, which, although small, the queen pronounced 'lovely'.[35]

During the next few days there was a children's festival complete with procession, dances and a pretty dinner for the Feast of St Gregory. Victoria spent evenings in the theatre and attended services in the Moritzkirche.

One morning, accompanied by Juliane and a large party, she and Albert set out for the Festung, the fortress of Coburg (now known as Veste Coburg) situated high above the town, parts of which dated from the twelfth century. There they were joined by King Leopold and Queen Louise of Belgium. Victoria admired the armoury with its display of medieval weapons, the horn room with panelled walls and Martin Luther's room, which Albert's father had decorated lavishly to honour the Festung's most famous occupant, who stayed there while translating the Bible into German. Later they drove back through a pretty little village where the people, Victoria recorded with pleasure, looked happy and prosperous.

Albert celebrated his birthday on 26 August, the first one in twelve years that he had spent at the Rosenau. It was also the couple's last day there. All the family arrived bringing gifts, and peasants in gala dress came to greet him.

Victoria and Albert then moved on to Gotha, where again Juliane accompanied them on several excursions and was also present on 30 August at the annual festival of the Rifle Society, which for the queen's benefit this year included a large procession of local residents in national costumes. That evening there was a grand reception at the Friedenstein Palace attended by Victoria, Albert and some twenty-six of their relatives. On 2 September, to the queen's great regret, it was time to say goodbye.

The queen and Prince Albert continued to stay in touch with Juliane. On 18 December 1846 the Prince wrote to her, 'horrified to see that I still owe you an answer to your last kind letter'. Victoria had given birth to her fifth child, Princess Helena (known as Lenchen) at Buckingham Palace on 25 May 1846 and they were now looking for tutors for their elder children Vicky and Bertie. 'It is very good of you to suggest candidates for the post of tutor to our children,' Albert continued, 'but I hardly believe we would appoint someone from abroad. Today we go back to Windsor, which will be a cold sort of pleasure.' His cousin, Juliane's nephew Alexander Mensdorff (son of her sister Sophie) 'is now back in Lisbon, where he has not been made welcome, and where they would like to be rid of Colonel Wylde [Albert's equerry, who he had sent to advise the Portuguese King Consort, Ferdinand, another Coburg cousin]. A certain Herr Dietz [Ferdinand's former German tutor] of ancient memory would rather see the Rhone dry up than his influence diminish. Ferdinand is thirty years old and is not supposed to have a tutor.' The envelope is clearly marked in Juliane's handwriting *'Verbrennen'* – to be burnt. Luckily the instruction was ignored.[36]

***

The next Romanov visitor arrived in 1847. This was Grand Duke Constantine Nicolaievich, the nineteen-year-old second son of the emperor. 'Costy' was in the navy and in the process of completing his first sea voyage abroad, which took him to Constantinople, France, Spain and then England. He was already engaged to Princess Alexandra of Saxe-Altenburg (a niece of Grand Duke Michael's wife Grand Duchess Elena Pavlovna), and the wedding was to take place the following year.

On 25 May the queen received the young grand duke at Buckingham Palace. Victoria thought him not as tall as his father, 'very unaffected and lively and has nothing very Russian about him'.[37] In fact some people thought him quite ugly. He attended the queen's birthday parade with Prince Albert, before the court left for Windsor, where Constantine joined them on 31 May.

On 1 June the royal party went to Ascot racecourse, Constantine riding in the carriage procession with Victoria and the Hereditary Grand Duchess Sophie of Saxe-Weimar. This was the former Princess Sophie of the Netherlands (only daughter of King William II and Grand Duchess Anna Pavlovna of Russia), who had married her cousin Charles-Alexander of Saxe-Weimar, Victoria's one-time hopeful suitor, in 1842. Queen Victoria and her guests watched five races, including the Queen's Cup, but Victoria noted that there were few people there to cheer on the winner.

After dinner that night they danced until one in the morning in the Waterloo Gallery, which the Queen thought 'makes a splendid ballroom'. She partnered Constantine in the final dance of the evening, a Country Dance. 'All was very merry and gay.'[38] The following day was the grand duke's Name Day (his Saint's Day), more important to Russians than a birthday, and Victoria presented him with some shirt studs. There was one more ball at Windsor before the court returned to Buckingham Palace.

In London the queen took him to the opera where they saw the second and third acts of *La Sonnambula (The Sleepwalker)* with Victoria's favourite, Jenny Lind, singing exquisitely. There was a dinner and concert at Marlborough House, and a large ball at the palace for 1,750 people at which she partnered Constantine in the quadrille.

One evening Constantine spoke about Russian history, which the queen noted 'he seems to know extremely well,' talking about Catherine the Great 'whose great qualities he admired, but whose immoral conduct he abhors. I like that in him, that he has such a horror of immorality, and certainly the emperor takes great pains in having his son morally brought up.'[39]

The social whirl continued with a dinner and concert given by the Duke of Wellington at Apsley House and another ball at Stafford House. On 17 June Albert and the grand duke, the latter wearing the uniform of the Imperial Guard, rode out to a review, followed by the queen with her eldest children Vicky and Bertie and the Hereditary Grand Duchess Sophie of Saxe-Weimar. The Duke of Wellington was there with a huge staff and 'it was an extremely fine sight. Some manoeuvring followed and a great deal of firing, which Bertie hugely enjoyed, but Vicky less.' That evening 300 people assembled for a ball at Gloucester House. Grand Duke Constantine 'dances extremely well and is a very pleasant height for one so short as myself to dance with,' the diminutive Victoria recorded gratefully.[40]

In mid-July Victoria and Albert took their family to their new villa, Osborne House, near Cowes on the Isle of Wight, later described by Benjamin Disraeli as 'a Sicilian Palazzo with gardens, terraces, statues and vases shining in the sunshine'. There they were joined on 4 August by Grand Duke Constantine. Victoria and Albert had only spent their first night there the previous September, so Constantine was one of the first visitors to their new holiday home. Osborne was looking its best and among the guests was Victoria and Albert's cousin Alexander Mensdorff-Pouilly. Again the grand duke spoke about Russian history, especially the French and Russian armies and the Napoleonic wars of which he showed a considerable amount of knowledge. They went for a carriage drive round the island to Ryde and Binstead, and in the evening took up the carpet in the drawing room and had a lively dance, Victoria partnering the grand duke in a polka.

Constantine left two days later. Before Albert accompanied him down to the tender *Fairy* which would take him out to his ship, he presented Victoria with a beautifully bound album containing watercolours of the principal palaces in St Petersburg, Tsarskoe Selo and Peterhof. The grand duke told them that his frigate would come past Spithead and the queen (who was probably in the early stages of pregnancy) had rashly promised to go on board, so a few days later, despite wind and rain, they drove to the pier and embarked on the *Fairy*. 'When we got close to the frigate at Spithead, which looked very handsome, with the sailors in a sort of uniform and a fine military band on board, it was so rough that it was considered unadvisable for *me* to attempt to visit the ship; the getting in and out of the boat would have been so difficult and disagreeable. But Albert and the other gentlemen of the party went on board, remaining there nearly ½ an hour.'[41]

The emperor was once again delighted at the reception given to his son and expressed his hope that Victoria would visit Russia one day, which he said 'would be the thing of all others which could afford him the greatest and most heartfelt pleasure'. On 10 November Baron de Brunov presented a large portrait of the Emperor Nicholas to the queen at Windsor, which she thought 'an excellent likeness'.[42]

***

The queen's sixth child Princess Louise was born on 18 March 1848 at Buckingham Palace and the tsar wrote to congratulate Victoria on her safe delivery.

It was a 'year of revolutions', as angry protestors swept through Sicily, France, Germany, Italy and the Austrian Empire in an attempt to overthrow their monarchies. In Europe only Russia, Spain and the Scandinavian countries were exempt. Britain suffered a few Chartist demonstrations and there was some republican agitation in Ireland. Victoria gave sanctuary to King Leopold's father-in-law King Louis Philippe of France and his family (some of whom were Coburgs), when they fled their kingdom.

With only Britain and Russia unscathed, the tsar's letter to the queen stressed the need 'to link the bonds of friendship that we have been happy to form in better times… Would it not be natural to contend that our intimate union is perhaps called to save the world?' he concluded, signing himself her 'devoted and loyal good brother and friend'.[43] The queen's ministers disagreed and the tsar, who defined his mission as stopping all revolution (a term which to the queen's incredulity included constitutional government) was left to worry about his own empire.

* * *

The previous good relations between the British and Russian courts were not destined to last.

In 1851, Russia exhibited at the Great Exhibition at the Crystal Palace in Hyde Park, the first time such a display had been mounted in England. However, the Russian section, which contained malachite vases, plate, jewellery and even doors and chimney pieces, only opened to the public on 7 June, as shipment was delayed due to ice in the Baltic. Nevertheless the queen was impressed with the Russian exhibits when they did finally arrive. She and Albert purchased a large malachite vase on a pedestal, as well as a paperweight, and the prince commissioned John Nash to paint a watercolour of the Russian stand.

The British Minister told Lord Palmerston that the tsar had refused to grant passports for members of the Russian nobility to come to the opening of the exhibition in May, fearing contamination in the British capital. Furthermore, hearing that the diplomatic corps were scheduled to present an address to the queen, Nicholas forbade the Russian Minister Baron de Brunov to join them and the event was therefore cancelled (although a few days later, de Brunov attended a costume ball at the palace dressed as a boyar, complete with beard and wig). All this was merely a curtain-raiser for what was to follow.

There was trouble brewing between Russia and Turkey where, since 1850, the emperor had been demanding the right to protect the Orthodox citizens of the sultan's empire. The Catholics (backed by France) and the Greeks (backed by Russia) were quarrelling over who should control the Holy Places which lay within the borders of the Ottoman Empire. Sultan Abdul Mejid had previously respected the rights of the Orthodox Church but in November 1852 Turkey granted the Catholics the right to hold the key to the Church of the Nativity in Bethlehem giving them free access to the building. The French were aggressively promoting their rights, determined to be seen as a Great Power again after years of suppression after the fall of Napoleon.

The tsar, furious that Turkey had submitted to French pressure and believing that after the meetings with Peel and Aberdeen in 1844 he had the British government's support, outlined his plans for Turkey to the British Minister Sir George Hamilton Seymour early in 1853. In a series of conversations he stressed that Turkey was a very 'sick man' and it was imperative that Britain and Russia reach agreement before the Ottoman Empire collapsed. Maybe Britain and Russia should carve up the Ottomans' European possessions between them. 'Frankly, then,' the tsar continued, 'I tell you plainly that, if England thinks of establishing herself one of these days at Constantinople, I will not allow it. For my part, I am equally disposed to take the engagement not to establish myself there – as proprietor, that is to say.'[44] However, he would have no objection if Britain occupied Egypt or Crete.

Seymour was alarmed at Nicholas's statement that Russia might have to temporarily occupy Constantinople, the link between Europe and Asia which was Britain's lifeline to India, and he was suspicious of proposals that Wallachia, Moldavia, Serbia and Bulgaria should be placed under Russian protection as independent princely states to save the Orthodox Christians there. France was equally suspicious of Russia's plans to increase her territory. Seymour immediately contacted the Foreign Office, who declined to enter into any kind of secret agreement with the tsar.

Nicholas was furious. In February he despatched Prince Alexander Menshikov to Constantinople as his envoy to force the sultan to restore Russia's rights to the Holy Places and demand the nullification of the ruling in favour of the Catholics. Britain attempted to mediate and arranged with the European Powers a reasonable compromise, the Vienna Note, the terms of which Nicholas accepted. The sultan rejected the proposals and asked for amendments.

By June 1853 Queen Victoria was telling King Leopold that 'it is the Emperor of Russia who must enable *us* to help *him* out of the difficulty. I feel convinced that *war will be avoided*; but I don't see how exactly.'[45]

In the middle of all this talk of war, on 3 August Crown Prince Carl and Crown Princess Olga of Württemberg arrived at Buckingham Palace accompanied by Baron de Brunov. The crown princess was the second daughter of Tsar Nicholas I. The couple had married in 1846 but their union was not destined to be happy and to Olga's regret, there were no children. She had been renowned as a great beauty and, the queen told her Uncle Leopold, 'is *still* very handsome as to features, figure etc., but she is a wraith, which is a sad thing for one who was so beautiful and is so young.' Writing in her journal, Victoria noted the crown princess appeared pale and thin. 'She is extremely like her father – very tall, pleasing, and amiable,' and, thanks to a Scottish nurse, spoke perfect English.[46]

The couple obviously had to be entertained. With Victoria and Albert, Crown Prince Carl attended the review at the army camp at Chobham where the queen rode her horse Baghdad. Unfortunately Carl spurred his mount on, which resulted in him falling off and feeling very annoyed.

Then a few days later Olga's sister arrived. Grand Duchess Marie, who was dressed in deep mourning for her husband Maximilian, Duke of Leuchtenberg, was the favourite child of the tsar. She visited Buckingham Palace accompanied by Baron de Brunov and Lord Clarendon. Marie was the same age as the queen, even born in the same month. 'She is quite a miniature of her father, and very handsome, much more lively than her sister Olga, and I should say cleverer,' Victoria noted in her journal on 8 August. 'Her frank, easy manner is very agreeable.' Marie asked to see the queen's children, so Vicky, Bertie, Alice, Alfred, Helena, Louise and Arthur (born in 1850) were brought in. Only baby Leopold did not appear. Grand Duchess Marie 'appeared delighted with little Arthur, who was quite at his ease and did not mind being taken on her knee and kissed over and over again!'[47]

That evening there was a large dinner party for the crown princely couple at which Olga was resplendent in a blue dress and beautiful jewels, which the queen did not fail to notice. She 'pleases everybody very much, and is very attractive and graceful,' Victoria noted. The years had not been kind to Olga, who had once been 'slight and fair as a lily'. Lord Hardwicke later told Victoria that she had been 'an angel of light' in 1845, when he had seen her in

Russia. He was not alone in thinking this, as Lord Clanricarde said that Olga was 'sadly altered, but that she had certainly been the most beautiful vision one could imagine...'[48]

Although the queen commissioned miniatures of both sisters (Marie in 1853 and Olga in 1857), this would be the last meeting between the British and Russian royal families for some time.

* * *

Menshikov's mission had failed. The tsar refused to make amendments to the Vienna Note to appease Turkey and he now resorted to military means. His troops occupied Turkey's Danubian principalities of Moldavia and Wallachia, ostensibly to protect the Orthodox subjects there. Then they crossed the River Pruth. Turkish nationalism was stirred and, with diplomatic means having failed, on 23 October the Ottoman Empire declared war on Russia. 'The Emperor of Russia is a tyrant!' Prince Albert fulminated to King Leopold.

'The government should take a firm, bold line,' the queen told Lord Aberdeen. 'This delay – this uncertainty, by which, abroad, we are losing our prestige and our position, while Russia is advancing and will be before Constantinople in no time! Then the government will be fearfully blamed and the queen so humiliated that she thinks she would abdicate at once.'[49]

Nicholas's last letter to the queen was sent in November and reminded her of their past friendship, but even as the Russian court was assuring the British Minister of Russia's 'peaceful intentions' their ships were sinking the Turkish fleet off Sinope. Replying to the tsar's letter, the queen said she appreciated his high loyalty, before continuing: 'But whatever the purity of motives which direct the actions of even the highest sovereign by character, Your Majesty knows that these personal qualities are not sufficient in international transactions by which one binds to another in solemn engagements. I will not hide from Your Majesty the painful impression that the occupation of the Principalities has produced on me.'[50]

The tsar replied on 3/15 December. After justifying the actions of Russia, he continued: 'I was hoping that I had answered to Your Majesty's doubts and regrets with the utmost frankness... She [the queen] is telling me that she does not doubt that, with my help, it is still possible to restore peace, despite the bloodshed; I reply wholeheartedly, Yes, madam, if the organs of Your Majesty's wishes execute faithfully her orders and kind intentions.

Mine [my intentions] have not changed since the beginning of this sad episode. Shrinking from the danger, such as wanting now something different that I did not want by violating my parole, would be beneath me, and the noble heart of Your Majesty must understand it.'[51]

The queen and Lord Aberdeen had at first been in agreement that the Russian invasion of Moldavia and Wallachia should not be seen as a cause for Britain to go to war. 'A decided victory of the Russians by *land*, may, and I trust *will* have a pacifying effect by rendering the emperor magnanimous and the Turks amenable to reason,' she wrote in her journal on 15 December.[52]

At that stage Victoria still liked and trusted the emperor, but by the end of March 1854 she had changed her mind. The Russians had been victorious on all fronts and reports appeared in the press that Albert, distrusted as 'a foreigner and an interloper', was a Russian agent in direct contact with the tsar and had been sent to the Tower of London. 'The power and encroachment of Russia must be resisted,' the queen urged the Prime Minister.[53]

Britain and France, fearing a collapse of the Ottoman Empire (and in Britain's case, a Russian threat to shipping routes to India), sent their fleets to the Black Sea to protect the Ottoman transports. The tsar ignored their ultimatum to withdraw from the Danubian principalities and early in February he recalled his Ministers from Paris and London. On 27 March 1854, fearful of Russian penetration into the Mediterranean, France declared war on Russia; on the following day England also joined the Turks and declared war on the Russian Empire.

'Unfortunately,' Victoria wrote to her Uncle Leopold as her elder sons played with a stuffed lion which when wound up swallowed toy Russian soldiers whole, 'the emperor *does not like* being *told* what is unpleasant and *contrary* to *his wishes,* and gets very violent when he hears the *real* truth – which consequently is not told [to] him.'[54]

The war that began with disputes over sites of religious significance in the Holy Land would be fought in the Crimea. For a while there would be no more cosy meetings with Russian grand dukes and emperors, who were now England's enemies.

* * *

The queen's patriotism now knew no bounds. Watching from Buckingham Palace when the Guards departed for the war with hearty cheers, she began to see herself as a latter-day Elizabeth I. This was *her* army; the fleet which sailed from Spithead was noble; the tsar who she had once entertained was now an ogre.

This is not the place for a discussion of the Crimean war which, despite the confidence of the British troops after the successful end to the Napoleonic wars forty years earlier, was disastrous for all the countries who took part. After the allied victories at the Battle of the Alma and Inkerman, the siege of Sevastopol (Russia's principal naval base on the Black Sea) began in October; it took a year to fall to British, French and Ottoman troops. Accounts sent to Victoria were heavily sanitised to disguise the disease, illness and heavy losses suffered by the soldiers. By the end of 1854 there was dissatisfaction in England over mismanagement of the war and following a defeat in the House, Lord Aberdeen resigned and, in February 1855, Lord Palmerston became Prime Minister.

While the queen presented medals and visited the wounded in hospital, the important thing as far as we are concerned is that in the middle of hostilities the Emperor Nicholas became gravely ill with pneumonia. Heavy defeats during the autumn, as well as the carnage on all sides at Balaclava (although the Russians claimed it as a victory), had weakened his health. The serious illness of Empress Alexandra, 'the defeats of his armies ... the loneliness of standing alone against the Allies (who now included Austria), the gruelling strain of ruling Russia for nearly three decades' all placed a mental and physical burden on the tsar during the winter of 1854/55.[55]

On 2 March 1855 Queen Victoria received a telegram from Ralph Abercromby, the Minister Plenipotentiary in The Hague: 'The Emperor Nicholas died this morning at 1 a.m. of Pulmonic Apoplexy, after an attack of Influenza.'[56]

In England nothing had been known about the tsar's illness and the announcement of his death caused a sensation. There was no rejoicing; the British people sensed that the tragedy of recent Russian defeats had hastened the monarch's end. Lord Palmerston told the queen that he thought Nicholas's death would make no difference to the state of affairs and that the tsarevich would quietly succeed and not be superseded by his younger brother Michael who was born after their father became tsar in 1825.

Despite the war, Victoria received news of Nicholas's death with regret. 'Poor emperor, *he* has alas! the blood of many thousands on his conscience, but he was once a great man, and he had great qualities, as well as good ones...' Whether his son Alexander would now follow the policy of his father, or revert to the peaceful policy which it was thought he advocated, remained to be seen. 'What the consequences of [Nicholas's] death may be, no one can pretend to know,' the queen wrote thoughtfully in her journal on 2 March. *The Times* had no doubt that 'the agonising sense of humiliation and remorse at the loss of all he had reason to prize has terminated his life.'[57]

To Tsar Nicholas's niece Princess Augusta, wife of Prince William of Prussia, the queen wrote that she 'had not forgotten former and more happy times'. She asked Augusta to convey her 'heartfelt condolence' to her mother the former Grand Duchess Marie Pavlovna of Russia, Tsar Nicholas's sister; and to the Dowager Empress Alexandra Feodorovna (the former Princess Charlotte of Prussia) and her family. As Nicholas had died as Victoria's enemy and their countries were still at war, she was unable to do this *officially* but the queen knew she could rely on her good friend Augusta to pass on the message in a way that would not compromise her.[58]

The queen was among those who received a copy of the post-mortem daguerreotype picture of the tsar on his deathbed.[59]

4

Mending Fences

'Romanoffs [sic] are not to be compared to the houses of
Brunswick, Saxony and Hohenzollern.'

– Queen Victoria.

In February 1856, after two years of fighting, Russia agreed to
accept peace terms and the Crimean War came to an end. By
the Treaty of Paris, signed in March, Turkey gave a voluntary
promise to reform and Russia was forced to dismantle her Black
Sea naval bases. The Black Sea was declared neutral territory open
to all nations with neither Russia nor Turkey stationing warships
there (thus acting as a barrier against Russia). The Danubian
principalities of Wallachia and Moldavia became independent
from Russia as Romania. The Ottoman Empire was proclaimed
a European power, while Montenegro and Serbia soon became
autonomous states.

Consequently Russia no longer appeared the strongest power
on the continent and was now reduced to the same level as
Britain and the other powers. Nevertheless, the queen was
unhappy that there had been no major victory for Britain (even
Sevastopol had finally fallen to French troops) and no broader
war against Russia. 'I own that peace rather sticks in my throat,
and so it does in that of the *whole* nation,' she wrote in her
journal on 11 March. There was no victory parade or any
official ceremony of welcome for the returning troops, just a
'feeling of outrage and national shame at the blunders of the
government and military authorities'.[1]

* * *

On 3 May the Russian Minister Baron de Brunov arrived in London to formally announce the accession of Tsar Alexander II. It was the first official meeting between Victoria and the tsar's representative since the Crimean War and de Brunov was quite overcome with emotion. The queen received him at Buckingham Palace, saying kindly that she hoped they would always be on the best of terms and that past times would be forgotten.

The Russian emperor with whom Queen Victoria now had to deal was the same man who in 1839 had whirled her giddily round the room at Buckingham Palace and with whom she had fallen a little in love. He and Empress Marie Alexandrovna had five surviving children: Nicholas (Nixa), Alexander, Vladimir, Alexei and Marie. Their eldest child Alexandra, named after the tsar's dead sister, had tragically died shortly before her seventh birthday in 1849, but two more sons, Sergei and Paul, would join the imperial nursery before the empress's childbearing years were over.

The queen did not send a royal representative to the emperor's coronation on 26 August/7 September; instead George Leveson-Gower, the 2nd Earl Granville, travelled to Moscow at the head of a diplomatic mission. He was accompanied by Corporal James Mack, who had been commissioned by the queen to take photographs of the Kremlin as well as other buildings, monuments, people and anything else of interest he encountered.

Lord Granville, who was not popular in Russia, was presented to the emperor and empress at Peterhof on 14 August. He submitted a long report to Victoria in the third person regarding Alexander's character.

> He is handsome, but thinner and graver than when he was in England. When speaking with energy to Lord Granville his manner seemed to be rather an imitation of someone else than his own, and he did not look Lord Granville in the face. His usual manner is singularly gentle and pleasing. He does not give the idea of having much strength either of intellect or of character, but looks intelligent and amiable.[2]

Granville estimated that it was possible a popular revolt would take place and he feared for the result under the present organisation of the country, which offered a fair chance of success to the socialists. Yet he had no knowledge of conditions in Russia and his assessment of the country's future seems to have been based on conversations with anxious men who feared, for purely selfish reasons, that Alexander would initiate reforms.

Lady Granville also wrote to the queen, reporting on everything from the size of the imperial jewels and the behaviour of the Russian maids, to the comments of superstitious observers at the coronation when Empress Marie's crown slipped from her head. Another member of the delegation, Lieutenant Colonel Maude, told the queen that the court was barbarous and servile but he was impressed by the way the enormous St George's Hall, which had 2,300 candles in its chandeliers connected by cotton threads, was illuminated in a matter of minutes by a flame running from candle to candle.

Corporal Mack's photographs were given to the queen in November and she was evidently impressed. The following month Prince Albert arranged for them to be exhibited by the Photographic Society of Scotland in Edinburgh.

* * *

In Russia the end of the war had reinforced 'a long-felt sense of resentment against Europe', where, for the first time, an alliance had been formed with a Muslim power against another European Christian state. Nevertheless, with his hands tied in Europe, Alexander II now turned his attention towards expansion in Asia, where his eye was fixed firmly on India, Afghanistan and Persia. Then he would take back the Black Sea and realise the age-old Russian dream of capturing Constantinople. Although he was warned by his new Minister of Foreign Affairs, Prince Alexander Gorchakov, that this would hinder 'attempts to mend relations with the British and the French', the tsar was becoming convinced that only Britain stood in the way of Russia fulfilling its destiny in Asia.[3]

Britain had temporarily annexed Afghanistan in 1842, the government believing that if they did not move in that direction the Russians would threaten their interests in India. The British also now had a growing presence in Persia and Alexander was afraid that they would 'use their influence in Tehran to install themselves on the southern shore of the Caspian Sea'. This would not only harm Russia's foreign trade but also 'the political independence of the [Russian] empire'. The tsar also feared that the British might expel Russia from the Caucasus by using their Indian army to conquer Central Asia.[4]

In an atmosphere of mutual suspicion the Great Game – Russian imperial rivalry with Britain for supremacy in Asia – now began. In the wake of the Indian Mutiny of 1857 when the country rebelled against the growing influence of the British, the East India Company was abolished and Parliament took responsibility for governing the country. Alexander now began reconsidering his own plans for Central Asia.

***

Meanwhile, with peace finally concluded, it was time for the royal families of Britain and Russia to try and mend fences. After the queen gave birth to Princess Beatrice in April 1857 some feelers were put out from both sides.

That same month Victoria and Albert sent their twelve-year-old son Alfred to Geneva to improve his French. One of the people he visited was the queen's aunt Julie, who was living at a small estate near Geneva called the Châtelet de la Boissière. Victoria recorded in her diary that she and Albert had received 'excellent accounts of dear Affie, and [we] had a very pretty description of his leave taking of his young Genovese friends, who gave him a flag, making a speech, to which he replied, and being much affected. Aunt Julia [*sic*] has written most kindly about him and is quite distressed at his going.' Before moving on to Berne and Coburg, Alfred also met the tsar's aunt Grand Duchess Marie Nicolaievna, Duchess of Leuchtenberg. She and her sons, the queen heard, had been 'very civil' to Alfred.[5]

The following month the tsar's uncle Grand Duke Constantine Nicolaievich announced that he wished to spend a day with the queen and Prince Albert at Osborne. Having more or less invited himself, Victoria and Albert could hardly refuse. Constantine was now Admiral General. As such, he was head of the Russian fleet and also Minister of Marine, a full ministerial position. Since the end of the Crimean War he had been engaged in carrying out delicate diplomatic missions around Europe for the emperor, to whom he sent regular reports. It was in this capacity that he now wanted to visit England on a private visit of friendly courtesy.

The queen sent the old royal yacht *Osborne* to Cherbourg (flying the Russian flag) to bring him to the Isle of Wight, which the grand duke had last visited in 1847. A lookout man was stationed at Hurst Castle so that the queen could be informed as soon as the *Osborne* came into view. The queen's barge from the royal yacht then went out to meet the Russians and bring them to the pier, where they were received by Prince Albert, the Prince of Wales and Prince Alfred, who had recently returned from Europe. After the formal greeting, carriages took them up to Osborne House.

The grand duke and his suite were met by a guard of honour of the 93rd Highlanders on Osborne's lawn. Victoria was waiting at the hall door with her daughters, as well as the Duchess of Kent and the queen's cousin George, Duke of Cambridge. Constantine 'jumped out of the carriage, shaking hands most warmly and looks unchanged', the queen recorded. She was annoyed that the Russians had arrived in uniform as if it was a state visit, rather than dressing in civilian clothes like their hosts. Constantine, she continued, 'was astonished at all the changes here, and the growth and increase of our children'.[6] The queen had given birth to four more since his last visit. Nevertheless, due honours were paid to him and he was given the Council Room to use as a drawing room. The weather was warm and fine, so after lunch they took a walk around Osborne's beautiful grounds. The queen took him to nearby Whippingham Church, saying it was the first time she had been there since the birth of Beatrice.

Constantine seemed happy to talk about the recent war, saying that both of his *aides-de-camp* had been in the Crimea and that one was wounded. Rather less tactfully he then proceeded to give the details. He also discussed the size and calibre of the Russian guns, the navy and defences. Rather less welcome were some conversations he had with the Foreign Secretary Lord Clarendon and the Prime Minister Lord Palmerston when he tried to get one of the clauses of the peace treaty annulled.

At four o'clock the next afternoon they all went for a cruise on the re-embellished royal yacht *Victoria and Albert*. With the queen and her husband were their four eldest children Vicky, Bertie, Alice and Alfred, and the Duke of Cambridge. It was a beautiful day with the blue sky reflected in the sea but, Victoria recorded, 'how strange it seemed to me, as we steamed past Spithead! There we were, with the Grand Duke Constantine on board, flying the Russian standard on the foremast, Russian Officers there, who had served and even bled at Sevastopol...' The grand duke tactfully admired the yacht. 'As well he may,' the queen added ruefully.[7]

That evening at dinner Constantine wore the shirt studs that the queen had presented to him ten years earlier. He spoke of his wife Grand Duchess Alexandra Josifovna, who unfortunately was in poor health, and his children, seven-year-old Nicholas, five-year-old Olga, and three-year-old Vera. At eleven o'clock that evening the grand duke left Osborne after thanking the queen for her warm welcome and her friendship. If he noticed how rattled the queen had been during his visit, particularly seeing the Russian flag flying from her vessels, he had the tact not to show it.

***

In January 1858 Vicky, the Princess Royal, married Prince Frederick William of Prussia (Fritz) at the Chapel Royal, St James's Palace. It was a union that was unpopular in Russia. The bridegroom would one day inherit the Prussian throne and Albert (who had been created Prince Consort the previous June) had great hopes that the couple would eventually liberalise a united Germany. A few days later Vicky set off for her new home in Berlin. The queen's letters to and from her daughter would now provide a valuable source of comment on people and events.

It was not long before Vicky ran into difficulty with one of the Romanovs. In September 1858 the emperor's sister the Grand Duchess Olga Nicolaievna, the Crown Princess of Württemberg who had visited Queen Victoria at Buckingham Palace five years earlier, visited her relatives in Berlin. In a letter to her mother Vicky now accused Olga of being cold and almost rude towards her, keeping her standing during their interview although she herself was seated with her back turned, and asking condescendingly whether Vicky was yet sixteen. (She was seventeen.)

Queen Victoria was outraged at this treatment of *her* daughter by 'the Russian family, who have never been considered as better or as high as our family'. She was indignant that in Berlin Olga was always called the *Grand Duchess* Olga, while Vicky, the Princess Royal 'the eldest daughter of the Queen of England, with a title and rights of your own', was simply referred to as Princess Frederick William. 'Our princes never admitted the grand dukes of Russia having precedence over them; Romanoffs [*sic*] are not to be compared to the houses of Brunswick, Saxony and Hohenzollern,' the queen continued, her anger in full flow. 'Therefore there must be one rule for all, and one system.'[8]

Earlier, when the queen heard that Vicky had been awarded the Russian Order of St Catherine, she had been less than gracious. 'You can wear it with the others if you like,' she sniffed, oblivious to the fact that she herself had been awarded it in 1837 and that her permission for Vicky to wear it was not really necessary.[9]

The following year, hearing that the crown princess of Württemberg was going to Ryde on the Isle of Wight, the queen expressed the fond hope that she and Albert would have left the island by the time Olga arrived.

Vicky also complained to her mother about 'a flood of grand duchesses' who had come to Berlin in June 1859 after the death of Fritz's grandmother Marie, the Dowager Duchess of Saxe-Weimar-Eisenach, who had been born Grand Duchess Marie Pavlovna of Russia. The queen sympathised, calling the Russians 'wolves in sheep's clothing'.[10]

The Dowager Empress Alexandra Feodorovna of Russia, sister of King Frederick William IV of Prussia, had shown Vicky her jewels, but in a letter home the Princess Royal pronounced her mother's jewels 'finer'. Although the empress had a profusion of huge pearls, rubies, sapphires and emeralds Vicky thought only the diamonds were magnificent. The quality of the others she pronounced 'not very fine'.[11]

* * *

The month of August in 1859 saw more imperial visitors to England. After another brief visit to Osborne by Grand Duke Constantine, who was very chatty at dinner and praised everything, his sister arrived.

Grand Duchess Marie Nicolaievna and her daughter Princess Marie of Leuchtenberg, known as 'Maroussy', arrived on 11 August, with Baron de Brunov and members of her suite. The grand duchess's first husband was Duke Maximilian of Leuchtenberg, grandson of Napoleon's wife Empress Josephine. Marie, however, was never referred to as the Duchess of Leuchtenberg because, as with the Crown Princess of Württemberg, Tsar Nicholas I insisted that she was first and foremost Her Imperial Highness the Grand Duchess. Maximilian and Marie's home was the Maryinsky Palace in St Petersburg. It never became known as the Leuchtenberg Palace.

Earlier that summer Queen Victoria had met Marie's sons Nicholas, the young Duke of Leuchtenberg, and his brother Eugene, 'nice intelligent, lively boys of fifteen and thirteen, and good looking',[12] who had just come from Rome and were seeing the sights of London.

After Maximilian's death in 1852 the grand duchess had contracted a morganatic marriage with Count Gregory Stroganov. He had been her lover for some time and was rumoured to have fathered some of her younger children. The wedding took place in the utmost secrecy so that Marie's father would not hear of it, as he would never agree to his daughter marrying a subject. When Tsar Nicholas died in 1855 he was still unaware that the marriage had taken place. Although Marie's brother Alexander II was a little more accommodating and turned a blind eye, Count Stroganov never lived in the Maryinsky Palace with his wife, only visiting when his duties as Master of the Horse at her court (and his conjugal duties) required, and he was never accepted by society. The couple gradually spent long periods abroad.

Grand Duchess Marie was, Victoria thought, 'very handsome, with splendid features and profile', and she admired her jewellery, which consisted of 'beautiful diamonds and pearls'. She was President of the Academy of Arts in St Petersburg and consequently had a great liking for pictures and sculpture. She greatly admired the artistic treasures at Osborne and was 'very clever and agreeable'. Marie was also tactful enough to speak kindly of her aunt by marriage Grand Duchess Anna Feodorovna, the queen's Aunt Julie, telling the Duchess of Kent that 'aunt' had been very maternal towards her.

Eighteen-year-old 'Maroussy', the favourite grandchild of the Dowager Empress Alexandra Feodorovna, was cheerful, sociable and 'extremely pretty, with a lovely complexion'. The grand duchess had obviously brought her daughter along with the express intention of introducing her to seventeen-year-old Prince Alfred, whom she had met in Switzerland two years earlier, but both mother and daughter were to be disappointed. Alfred was away serving with the Royal Navy.[13]

Over the coming years, the attractive children of Grand Duchess Marie were to cause Victoria much anxiety on the matrimonial front as she sought to settle her own children's futures. The lovely Maroussy, especially, was seen as a possible rival to the queen's rather plainer daughter, Princess Alice.

Before the queen left Osborne that summer there was one more visit from Grand Duke Constantine, who dined there on 25 August and once again was very polite and friendly.

* * *

The queen was at Balmoral, her Highland retreat, in August 1860 when she heard from King Leopold that Aunt Julie had suffered a paralytic stroke on 5 August, although it was believed that the danger was now over.

Juliane had left Elfenau in 1837 after the deaths of her former lover Schiferli and her daughter Hilda, and moved to the Châtelet de la Boissière near Geneva where she lived under the pseudonym the Countess de Rono. Queen Victoria's half-sister Feodora described Juliane's 'life full of trials of all kind, her youth thrown away at that [Russian] court, and now alone, amongst strangers here is indeed a bitter cup to the last ... poor aunt, life must be a burden to her, and her feelings are so young still.' In 1848 the queen had commissioned another portrait of her aunt, this time by Winterhalter, which she and Albert gave to the Duchess of Kent on her birthday in August. Juliane is pictured with the Châtelet de la Boissière in the background and on her wrist is a bracelet with a miniature of her niece Victoria, who described the latest portrait as 'an indescribably like and beautiful picture of Aunt Julia'.[14]

At the end of July 1860, feeling unwell, Juliane had unwisely returned to Elfenau where her condition worsened. Then news arrived at Balmoral that Juliane's legs were paralysed and there was no improvement. 'It makes me very sad for dear Mama, who cannot go to her,' the queen wrote sympathetically. 'Aunt Julie will be seventy-nine this September.' During the next few days Juliane lost the power of speech and had difficulty swallowing, although she was still conscious. But by 14 August her life was in imminent danger, with all hope gone. The queen was feeling terribly low. 'We are very sad and anxious about poor dear Aunt Julie,' she told Vicky, '... for though I have only seen her twice – and not for fifteen years – she is dear Grandmama's only [surviving] sister...'[15]

Her son Eduard von Lowenfels was summoned and the last rites of the Orthodox Church were administered by her chaplain. On 15 August news arrived of Juliane's death at her beloved Elfenau. 'When I think of poor Aunt Julie, she was so alone that I cannot help to pity her even in all the objects she valued and left behind,' King Leopold wrote to Victoria the following April.[16]

After a funeral service conducted according to the Orthodox rites, Grand Duchess Anna Feodorovna was buried in the Rosengarten cemetery at Berne on 18 August. Her grave was covered by a simple marble slab containing the simple inscription:

Julia-Anna.
Christ est ma vie et la mort m'est un gain
(I. Phil. v.21)
1781–1860.[17]

Thus ended the tragic story of Queen Victoria's aunt – but it was not the end of the queen's family connection with the Romanovs.

***

In October the emperor's brother Grand Duke Michael Nicolaievich and his wife Grand Duchess Olga Feodorovna stayed the night at Windsor. Victoria was charmed by them, noting with delight that Michael conversed the whole time in German. He was, she told Vicky, not handsome but had quite pleasant looks, and was quite unlike his brother Constantine and his sisters. The Grand Duchess (born Princess Cecilie of Baden) looked very delicate, although she was clever and good humoured. The couple already had a son, Nicholas (the first of the six Michaelovich grand dukes) and the queen was sorry that she was unable to see him. That night at dinner in the Waterloo Gallery Grand Duchess Olga displayed her spectacular diamonds.

On 1 November the queen was saddened to hear of the death of Michael's mother the Dowager Empress Alexandra Feodorovna of Russia. As the sister of the King of Prussia, Alexandra had exerted quite a hold over the members of the Prussian royal family. Victoria sympathised with their sorrow, knowing they were very fond of her and treated her smallest wish as law. In fact, as she noted in a letter to Vicky, 'Russian precedents are gospel at the Prussian court.' The empress was also a respected and loved member of the Russian royal family. Victoria admired the dowager empress for being kind-hearted and a devoted wife and mother, telling Vicky that the emperor and his siblings in St Petersburg would greatly feel her loss.[18]

Another tenuous family link with the Romanovs was formed at the end of 1860 when, to the queen's relief, Princess Alice became betrothed to Prince Louis of Hesse-Darmstadt (who had also been attracted to the beautiful Maroussy of Leuchtenberg). Prince Louis was heir to his uncle Grand Duke Louis III of Hesse-Darmstadt, the ruler of the relatively minor German state but, more significantly, he was also the nephew of Empress Marie Alexandrovna of Russia. Victoria was nevertheless grateful that 'no fresh Russian blood or Russian elements' were coming into the family.[19]

The betrothal was announced in the spring of 1861 and it was decided they would marry in January 1862.

***

The year 1861 did not get off to a good start. King Frederick William IV of Prussia died in January. He was succeeded by his brother William I, elevating Fritz and Vicky to the status of crown prince and princess. The health of Prince Albert, who was overworking, declined, which the queen found very trying. Then in March the Duchess of Kent died. Although Victoria resented the control her mother exerted over her as a child and ruthlessly cut her out of her life on her accession, they had become reconciled thanks to the influence of Prince Albert. Now, as she finally realised how much the duchess had loved her, the queen felt like an abandoned orphan and went into paroxysms of self-indulgent grief. She suffered a nervous breakdown and as her unremitting anguish continued; rumours circulated that she was going mad.

In August, on the first anniversary of Aunt Julie's death Victoria wrote to King Leopold with typical melodrama: 'I thought much of poor, dear Aunt Julia on the 15th; that loss was the signal for my irreparable one!'[20] The anniversary of her aunt's death almost coincided with her mother's birthday on 17 August.

※ ※ ※

On 7 November Grand Duke Constantine Nicolaievich arrived at Windsor Castle for a two-day stay, accompanied by his wife Grand Duchess Alexandra Josifovna and their young daughter Grand Duchess Olga Constantinovna.

Constantine was once again 'very amiable' and Grand Duchess Alexandra Josifovna, known in the family as 'Sanny', was still 'very handsome', making a favourable impression on the queen and Prince Consort, who both liked her a lot. Sanny told Victoria all about the education of the Russian grand dukes, which did not meet with her approval, and she also spoke of the 'perpetual bustle' of Russian life, which she hated. She proved to be a pleasant, friendly companion for the grief-stricken Victoria. Sanny 'says she is so happy here,' the queen wrote to Vicky.[21] Prince Albert and Princess Alice took the grand duke and duchess to St George's Chapel and Victoria showed them around the State rooms.

She thought ten-year-old Grand Duchess Olga was 'a great darling, with a lovely face'[22] but was intrigued by her hair, which had been cut short so that it would grow stronger. Victoria enquired how long Olga's hair had been like this. 'Since I was a child, Your Majesty,' the little girl replied, as the adults burst into laughter.[23] Nevertheless, the queen thought her very clever and marked her out as a possible future bride for Prince Alfred. Lord Palmerston later told the queen that Grand Duke and Duchess Constantine left 'overflowing with thankfulness for the kind and gracious reception they had received at Windsor Castle'.[24]

Unknown to the queen, this visit in November 1861 was to be the last in what she would come to regard as the happy times. Even so, it had been a difficult year. Then during November and December several Coburg cousins, including the twenty-five-year-old King Pedro V, died of typhoid in Portugal, plunging the British court back into mourning.

Now death was about to place its icy hand on Windsor.

An Uneasy Courtship

'The German element is the one I wish to be cherished.'
— Queen Victoria to Vicky, 1862.

Prince Albert's death on 14 December 1861 left the queen stunned and totally devastated by another paroxysm of grief. From now on, she declared to King Leopold on Christmas Eve, '....*his* wishes, *his* plans about everything, *his* views about *every* thing are to be *my* law. And *no human power* will make me swerve from what *he* decided and wished.'[1]

In the wake of this all-consuming loss Victoria retreated to Osborne House, receiving few people. She was unable, she maintained, to see the ministers personally. For the next six months she conducted official business mainly through the medium of General Sir Charles Grey (Albert's secretary) or Princess Alice.

* * *

In July 1862, as arranged by Prince Albert, Alice married Prince Louis of Hesse-Darmstadt. The service took place in the drawing room of Osborne House in a ceremony which was more like a funeral than a wedding. Then the couple went to live in Darmstadt.

Grief had done nothing to dim Victoria's distrust of the Russians. Louis's family connection with the Romanovs through Empress Marie soon persuaded the queen that 'good Alice seems quite Russified.' Before long Victoria was complaining to Vicky that Alice wrote only about 'Aunt Marie, Uncle Sasha, Nixa, dear Sasha, Alexei, Misha, etc.', adding, 'I own I think it is a little too much.'[2]

As the queen emerged from the first shock, there was one piece of business that she had to attend to. This was the marriage of Bertie, the Prince of Wales. With a lack of suitable German princesses, Albert had been keen for him to marry the beautiful Princess Alexandra, seventeen-year-old eldest daughter of Prince and Princess Christian (from 1863 King Christian IX and Queen Louise) of Denmark – and Albert's wishes were now sacrosanct.

Early in 1862 Vicky dashed off a warning letter to her mother. Alexander II was trying to find a bride for his eldest son Tsarevich Nicholas (Nixa) and he had his eye on the two elder daughters of Prince Christian. Although Bertie and Alexandra had already met, all thoughts of his marriage had been put aside after Prince Albert's death. 'I hear that the emperor of Russia has not given up his intention of asking for Alexandra or Dagmar for his son,' Vicky wrote. 'Princess Christian feels very nervous now for fear that Bertie should not be in earnest after all, and for that case she would still wish to have the tsarevich in reserve.'[3]

Alexandra's fourteen-year-old sister Dagmar had already been rejected as a future daughter-in-law of Queen Victoria without even realising it. Vicky had suggested her as a bride for Prince Alfred. 'I should be sorry if anything were decided for Dagmar before you had seen her as it would be one chance less for Affie,' Vicky wrote, 'and it is surely to be desired he should have as large a choice as possible.' The queen vetoed this idea. 'Let the emperor have her,' she replied.[4]

Naturally Victoria wanted a German marriage for Alfred. 'The German element is the one I wish to be cherished,' she wrote a few months after the death of the Prince Consort.[5] In 1862, when touring the Scandinavian Courts, Alfred was pointedly told to avoid Copenhagen.

By November 1862 Prince Alfred's name was in the hat as a candidate for the throne of Greece after the Greeks threw out King Otto, a Bavarian prince who had reigned for thirty years. Alexander II objected to the candidacy of Prince Nicholas of Nassau; he would prefer his eldest and favourite nephew, Duke Nicholas of Leuchtenberg, who had visited Queen Victoria in London in 1859. Meanwhile, Victoria was worrying about what reply to send to the tsar. Britain did not want the Duke of Leuchtenberg, because he was the tsar's nephew; Alfred could not take the throne, as he was the queen's son; so a neutral candidate whom all three guaranteeing powers – France, Russia and Britain – would support was needed. Various candidates were proposed before seventeen-year-old Prince William of Denmark, the brother of Princesses Alexandra and Dagmar, was selected as the final choice.

William took the throne as King George I of the Hellenes in 1863 shortly after his sister Alexandra (Alix) had married Bertie in St George's Chapel, Windsor, becoming the Princess of Wales. Victoria found the whole business very trying indeed without the support of Albert.

* * *

In late 1861 Alexander II appointed his brother Constantine as his Viceroy in Poland, a country seething with unrest and under martial law. The grand duke and his family therefore moved to the Lazienki Palace in Warsaw. Shortly afterwards Constantine survived an assassination attempt when a tailor's apprentice fired at close range. The bullet glanced off his shoulderblade and lodged in the chain of his monocle. The tsar recalled him but Constantine refused to leave.

Constantine had some sympathy for the Poles. He ended martial law and began a programme of liberalisation but his attempts to introduce reforms were a failure. In 1863 he called for a conscription levy, which was the signal for young men of the underground revolutionary movement to escape into the forests and begin a mutiny.

In England and France there was open sympathy for the Poles. The tsar, infuriated by this, nevertheless declined help from William I of Prussia. Queen Victoria wrote to King Leopold at the end of February 1863, 'I shall prevent [the war] by all means in my power, but Prussia has made a mess...'[6]

A draft despatch by the Foreign Secretary Lord John Russell was declared 'too abrupt and peremptory', so it was finally decided to instruct the ambassador Lord Napier to deliver a note saying Britain 'might intervene in the dispute in accordance with the first paragraph of the Treaty of Vienna which embodied the conditions linking Poland to Russia.'[7] Britain wanted a general amnesty and national representation restored to the Poles. Alexander, buoyed up by the offer of Prussian support, rejected this.

As the bloodshed continued, Constantine was recalled to St Petersburg, where he concentrated on naval reform. Not until the spring of 1864 was the Polish revolt quelled. The tsar ordered 'measures of most thorough Russification'.[8]

***

The tsar's sister Grand Duchess Marie Nicolievna, Duchess of Leuchtenberg, visited Windsor in the summer of 1864. For the past two years the grand duchess and her (morganatic) husband Count Gregory Stroganov had been living in the Villa Quarto in Florence, which had once belonged to Jerome Bonaparte, King of Westphalia. They had been in England since early August staying at the Villa Syracusa, Torquay, which, although now losing its reputation, had once been 'a favoured place of Russian royalty and aristocracy'.[9]

Marie had a brief meeting with the queen and Princess Alice on 26 August. It would have been Prince Albert's forty-fifth birthday. 'Saw the Grand Duchess Marie of Russia for a moment, who was very anxious to see me', Victoria noted in her journal, without saying what the meeting concerned.[10]

One of the few things that made the queen happy was Balmoral, where she could ride in her pony cart round the Highland estate and visit the simple people in their cottages. Victoria, while describing herself as a 'poor broken-hearted widow' had taken a liking for the tall, handsome Scottish ghillie John Brown who led her pony. On the recommendation of Dr Jenner, and at the urging of Princess Alice, thirty-seven-year-old Brown was brought south in the summer of 1864 and soon became The Queen's Highland Servant, Victoria's constant attendant at all the royal residences. This, at least, lessened somewhat the burden on Alice's sisters, who found the queen's need for regular companionship exhausting. Brown, the Empress of Russia later said, treated the queen like a little girl.

***

In September Tsarevich Nicholas (Nixa) became engaged to Princess Dagmar of Denmark, the sister of the Princess of Wales. The situation was awkward for the queen because Denmark and Prussia had recently been involved in a war over the Duchies of Schleswig and Holstein, which resulted in the defeat of Denmark and the loss of half of King Christian IX's realm. The war divided the family, with Bertie and Alix supporting Denmark, while Vicky and Fritz supported Prussia.

That June Vicky told her mother that she was not looking forward to a visit from the Russian emperor and empress, complaining that the imperial family had become very Danish. Grand Duchess Elena (widow of the tsar's Uncle Michael) had arrived in Berlin but the tsar's brother Grand Duke Constantine had been rude. The Russian emperor, she decided, was 'not good looking now but I suppose he must have been,' (a comment with which the queen, remembering 1839, would have agreed) while the empress 'looks delicate, is not good looking but pleasing.'[11] Alexander had not been a faithful husband and Marie turned for comfort to the Orthodox religion as well as the many charities she headed. She also spent more time abroad for the sake of her health.

By April 1865 the queen was receiving very bad accounts about the health of Nixa, who was in Nice with the empress. Alexander II went to the South of France to see him. Nixa's fiancée Princess Dagmar and her mother Queen Louise of Denmark were on their way; they reached his bedside just in time.

On 24 April 1865 Nixa died from cerebrospinal meningitis. Victoria called his loss tragic and immediately sent a message of sympathy to the emperor and empress, as well as to the Queen of Denmark. A few weeks later Queen Victoria heard that the emperor's grief was still 'very great, and that it was very likely that Dagmar would marry the new tsarevich', the emperor's second son Alexander.[12] Both families urged caution but the tsar was anxious not to lose the Danish marriage and, after a suitable interval of mourning, it was arranged that Tsarevich Alexander would marry Princess Dagmar on 9 November 1866.

To Queen Victoria's surprise, the Prince of Wales wanted to go to Russia for the wedding. The government was very keen for him to attend, as was the emperor. Above all, Princess Dagmar wished it, as her parents were too poor to travel to St Petersburg and the Princess of Wales was pregnant so unable to go either. Victoria raised a whole series of objections, including that from a political point of view the government overrated the importance of the visit. Nevertheless, she grudgingly gave her approval, saying that if he really wanted to go, then 'I will not object to it.'[13]

The tsar wrote a letter of thanks, telling the queen that it was 'a real satisfaction to see the effects of sympathy added to those of the relationship which unites us'.[14] If he had heard about the queen's reluctance to let her son go to Russia he did not let it show.

* * *

In 1867 Tsar Alexander and his sons Tsarevich Alexander and Grand Duke Vladimir attended the Paris Exhibition as guests of Napoleon III of France, who had become emperor in 1852. Apart from Queen Victoria, every crowned head of Europe flocked there, including Sultan Abdul Aziz of Turkey who, after weeks of argument, the queen had finally consented to invite to Windsor.

The tsar was also expecting an invitation from Queen Victoria, but with typical selfishness she refused to break her planned seclusion at Balmoral Castle or to have it violated by the visit of a foreign dignitary. (Victoria may also have heard that the tsar's mistress was with him in Paris, conduct of which she certainly would not have approved.)

She also refused the suggestion of the Prime Minister, Lord Derby, to send the emperor the Order of the Garter in recompense, with a handwritten letter explaining that his visit would be impossible due to her absence from London. 'The queen,' she replied abruptly in the third person, 'is UTTERLY *incapable* of entertaining any royal personage as she would *wish* to do, except those who are very nearly related to her, and for whom she need not alter her mode of life.'[15]

A few days later Lord Stanley, the Foreign Secretary, reported learning from Baron de Brunov (whose post had been upgraded to Ambassador in 1860) that 'the emperor would, in his belief, be greatly flattered and pleased ... to receive the Garter from Your Majesty.' Stanley and Derby both felt that the gesture would go some way to healing the broken relations caused by the Crimean War. Victoria still refused. She had only ever given the Garter to sovereigns when they visited England, 'or in very exceptional circumstances'. Even Emperor Franz Joseph of Austria had not been given it and she saw no reason to make an exception for the Emperor of Russia.[16]

The Prince of Wales then weighed in, saying he regretted that his mother had not seen fit to invite the emperor to stay for a few days, citing the magnificent welcome he had received in St Petersburg when he attended the tsarevich's wedding the previous year. Both he and Lord Derby worried about the unflattering comparison which would be made between the tsar's treatment by England and the reception he would undoubtedly receive in Paris from Napoleon III. It was all to no avail.

The queen was at Balmoral when she heard there had been an attempt on the tsar's life in the French capital. 'The French and Russian emperors had been shot at yesterday, in returning from a review, but had not been hurt,' she recorded in her journal on 7 June. Vicky was in Paris and her account of the attempt reached the queen a few days later. A disaffected Polish man had fired two shots at the tsar's carriage as he was driving down the Bois de Boulogne with the Emperor Napoleon. Nobody was hurt but, Vicky reported, the tsar had aged much and was not looking well. Nor was she very complimentary about the tsarevich and Vladimir, who 'grumble at everything, keep talking Russian to one another and won't admire anything in Paris'.[17]

When the tsarevich and his wife visited Berlin in October, Vicky formed a very favourable impression of Dagmar (now Tsarevna Marie Feodorovna). 'She certainly is a very attractive, charming and interesting little person. I never thought she would become so pretty. She seems quite happy and contented with her fat, good-natured husband who seems far more attentive and kind to her than one would have thought. I was pleased to see that she has not become grand – and does not give herself airs as all the Russian grand duchesses do...'[18]

The following year Vicky recorded her thoughts on Sasha (as the tsarevich was called by the family). 'I like him very much – although I did not when I first saw him,' she told the queen. 'He is awkward, shy and uncouth, from being so very big, but he is simple and unpretending, not proud and capricious as most Russians are, and has something straightforward and good-natured about him which I like and I think you would also...'[19] Vicky's assessment was confirmed to the queen by the Princess of Wales, but it would be some years before Victoria would meet Sasha and find out for herself.

Despite the queen's earlier objections, she was finally persuaded that the tsar should receive the Order of the Garter after all. The investiture took place in the Throne Room at the Catherine Palace, Tsarskoe Selo, on 16/28 July 1867 by a delegation led by Queen Victoria's Envoy Extraordinary Earl Vane (later the 5th Marquess of Londonderry). Accompanied by Heralds and officials of the College of Arms, the delegates travelled to Tsarskoe Selo in state carriages with liveried groom and outriders, and proceeded to the Throne Room bearing the Garter regalia. Bertie later told his mother that he had heard (presumably through Alexandra and her sister) that the tsar was enormously pleased.

Although the insignia was returned to the queen after Alexander's death, as is the custom, and displayed at Windsor Castle, his Garter Robes are preserved in the State Hermitage Museum in St Petersburg.

The following year Princess Alice told her mother that the emperor looked much older and more careworn than when she had seen him the previous year. He had suddenly grown old. He was fifty.

* * *

Although the queen's mentor and father figure (and Russian hater) King Leopold of Belgium died in December 1865, as Victoria struggled to cope after the loss of Albert she had few personal contacts with the Russians during the 1860s. She occasionally received a kind message sent via Vicky when one of the imperial family came to Berlin; or through Alice, who remained one of the conduits between the queen and the Russians whom she frequently saw in Darmstadt.

Then on 5 August 1869 Grand Duchess Marie Nicolievna, the Duchess of Leuchtenberg, took her son Sergei to Osborne. Victoria, who had not seen Marie since her very brief visit to Windsor five years earlier, thought her still very handsome, although she had aged somewhat and bore a strong resemblance to her father the Emperor Nicholas. The purpose of the visit was probably so that twenty-year-old Sergei could meet Victoria's twenty-one-year-old daughter Louise. Sergei was tall, good looking and shared Louise's taste in painting and the fine arts. He was also a superb pianist but the queen thought he looked rather delicate.

Marie had assembled a fine collection of art and Napoleonic artefacts in her Florence villa and was anxious to have a proper look around Osborne. So after lunch Louise took her on a tour of the house and terrace. 'She went all over this dear, sweet place and was delighted with it,' the queen told Vicky, adding that she found the grand duchess charming and very easy to get on with, 'most amiable and as usual very unaffected'.[20] Marie was keen to see Victoria's own room, which the queen showed her before Louise's sister Helena and her husband Prince Christian of Schleswig-Holstein (who married in 1866) drove them round the grounds.

Nothing came of the projected match with Sergei. Having turned down advances for Louise from Denmark and The Netherlands, among others, the queen preferred her to marry a man who would make his home nearby. Sergei died unmarried, killed during the Russo-Turkish War in 1877; Louise married John Campbell, Marquis of Lorne (later 9th Duke of Argyll) in 1871.

In fact, Queen Victoria had already tried to forge a link with Grand Duchess Marie's family. After she had been disappointed in her hopes of getting the tsar's niece Grand Duchess Olga Constantinovna as a bride for Prince Alfred (Olga married King George I of Greece in 1867) Victoria came to the conclusion that, as the choice of bride was so limited, they would have to overcome any difficulties about the Orthodox religion. She therefore turned her attention to Marie's twenty-two-year-old daughter Eugenie. Although she was nowhere near as pretty as her sister Maroussy, the queen described Eugenie as good, steady, clever, honest 'and very German in her feelings', something that was always of great importance to Victoria. She was also resolute, keen on horseriding and a talented artist. A marriage between her and Alfred, the queen thought, would bring some much-needed new blood into the family. Confiding her hopes to Vicky, the queen continued: 'The mother is of course a terrible drawback, but hardly so bad – not even so dangerous – as Queen Louise [of Denmark] for mischief.'[21] Nothing came of this scheme either and in 1868 Eugenie married Prince Alexander of Oldenburg, another descendant of the Romanovs.

* * *

The Franco-Prussian War broke out in the summer of 1870. It lasted for six weeks and ended with the surrender of Emperor Napoleon III at Sedan. France became a republic and the following January, the King of Prussia was proclaimed Emperor William I of a united Germany, with Otto von Bismarck as Chancellor. The queen's daughter Vicky was now Crown Princess of Germany.

By the early 1870s diplomatic relations between Russia and England had become very strained. In October, alarmed at the overthrow of Napoleon III and the proclamation of the French Republic, Alexander II denounced the neutralisation of the Black Sea which had been stipulated by the Treaty of Paris after the Crimean War. He wanted the Powers to recognise Russia's right to keep warships there. Queen Victoria, although 'concerned and alarmed', did not want matters to escalate so that armed force would be necessary. She was especially concerned about inflammatory content in the newspapers. The Prime Minister William Gladstone sought the backing of Bismarck in his wish to assert that 'treaties could be changed only by international agreement.' Russia backed down and withdrew the declaration. A conference met in London the following year, at which Russia was permitted 'to resume her sovereign rights in the Black Sea' but conceded that 'international treaties could not be changed by unilateral action.'[22]

The result delighted the tsar and in the summer of 1871 he sent his second surviving son Vladimir to England. On 22 June the queen gave a state concert at Buckingham Palace, where the grand duke, who was staying at Claridge's Hotel, was among the many guests.

Vladimir, born in 1847, was completely unlike his older brother. More cultured, intelligent and articulate, Vladimir possessed the social graces that Sasha sadly lacked. At the Paris Exhibition in 1867, he had made a far more favourable impression and many, including Vladimir himself, thought that he [Vladimir] should have been proclaimed tsarevich after Nixa's death. Consequently there would always be rivalry between the brothers.

The day after the concert the grand duke had an audience with the queen. She described him as 'tall and stout for his age', with a 'handsome face'.[23] That afternoon there was a garden party at the palace. The queen, the grand duke, the Prince and Princess of Wales and other members of the royal family went down onto the lawn, where the American and Danish Ambassadors (the latter described by the queen as vulgar, with ugly daughters) were presented. Before taking tea with the princesses in the royal tent, Victoria went to the dancing tent where she watched one or two dances, but then it started to rain and the people began to scatter. What Grand Duke Vladimir made of it all is unfortunately not recorded.

In the midst of all this, and the alarm caused by Russia's intentions over Asia, there was serious talk of a Russian marriage.

* * *

In August 1868 during a visit to his sister Alice at Schloss Heiligenberg near the small German village of Jugenheim, the handsome twenty-five-year-old Prince Alfred, Duke of Edinburgh, met the tsar's daughter, sixteen-year-old Grand Duchess Marie Alexandrovna, the most eligible girl in Europe. The young grand duchess was accompanying her mother Empress Marie Alexandrovna on a visit to their relatives in Darmstadt.

Alfred had been the first member of the British royal family to visit Russia, travelling there in 1862 while serving with the Royal Navy on HMS *St George*. He was received very kindly by the imperial family at Oranienbaum, their palace on the Gulf of Finland, where he dined with Alexander II and his family on 10 August. The queen was pleased at the success of her son's visit but Grand Duchess Marie, then ten years old, would have made no impression on the then eighteen-year-old prince.

As the only surviving girl among six brothers Marie was her father's favourite, idolised by her parents and members of the Russian court. At sixteen she was described by the American Consul in Moscow as 'rather pretty, though her nose and mouth are not good' and she looked older than her years.[24] Although she had grown up in the magnificent imperial residences of Peterhof, Tsarskoe Selo and the Winter Palace, she was unsophisticated and something of a tomboy with a rather abrupt manner. Nevertheless, Alfred was very taken with her and he was encouraged by Alice, who had met the grand duchess often in Darmstadt and thought her 'dear and nice, with such a kind fresh face, so simple and girlish'.[25] Shortly after this meeting Alfred left for his second cruise on board the *Galatea*. On his return home in 1871 he told Queen Victoria that he was determined to make Marie his wife.

Victoria took up the matter with the government. Although Marie was said to be affectionate towards her parents and not terribly clever (both characteristics which found favour with the queen) she was also Russian Orthodox, which would not be ideal. The queen had visions of a 'constant procession of priests'[26] coming and going from Alfred's London home, Clarence House. Worse still, if any disaster wiped out the Prince of Wales and his entire family, the country would have an Orthodox Queen Consort. There was also the question of the constant tension between England and Russia over India and Afghanistan, which could cause problems if the queen had a Russian daughter-in-law. But Victoria also knew that the choice of bride for Alfred was very narrow, so, with her son's mind made up, she spoke to the Foreign Secretary, Lord Granville. His opinion was that despite the fact that there were still great suspicions about Russian intentions in the Black Sea and Asia, Marie would be more suitable than a Catholic princess, an English subject, or one of the daughters of the queen's cousin King

George of Hanover, who had been dispossessed of his kingdom by Prussia in 1866 and had no money.

Alfred broached the subject with Alexander II during a visit to Germany in July. The tsar, however, said his daughter was only seventeen, too young to think of marriage (which was nonsense, as her mother had married at an even younger age) and that anyway Marie did not want to leave her home. Alexander told the ardent suitor that he would have to wait for a year before he could see, or even be mentioned to, Marie. The British Ambassador, Andrew Buchanan, reported that Alfred had made no particular impression on the tsar's daughter who, although she was of an age at which many princesses were already married, was still very childish. She dreaded marrying because she would then be separated from her parents.

Alfred begged his mother to write to the tsar to inform him that he did nothing without her approval. The queen did so. The answer she received was civil but cold: 'Your praises for our daughter flattered us a great deal, but [Alfred] has surely told you, madam, that while not in any way opposing a union between our two families, we have made it a principle never to impose our will upon our children as regards their marriages. Although speaking to him of a term of one year before taking any definite decision, we expressly declared that neither he nor we would consider ourselves bound in any way, neither before nor after, and he seemed to understand this perfectly.'[27]

With feelings still running high after the Crimean War, the emperor objected to a son-in-law from England. The empress said that she could not understand the English and their peculiar ways, while admitting that the English nurses she employed to look after her children were indeed excellent. Apart from the possible political objections they may have had to the marriage, the sovereigns expressed the wish that Alfred should live a great deal in St Petersburg, which the queen told Lord Granville she 'could *never* consent to'. She would not take the responsibility of urging the tsar and tsarina to agree to the marriage.[28]

Alfred also wrote to the empress and sent a present to Marie. After a long interval the empress scolded him for doing this and accused him of lack of openness. Alfred asked her in what way should he be more open, but no answer was forthcoming.

The queen was annoyed that Alfred had been rebuffed by the Russians. 'For my son to be a humble suitor of a young Russian grand duchess and to be left dangling, till she condescended to say whether she meant to have him or not – was a thing which I am sure your pride would have arisen against as much as mine,' she wrote to Vicky.[29] From Germany, Princess Alice reported that Marie was much too fond of her home and family to think about marriage.

In May 1872 Lord Granville reopened the marriage question with Baron de Brunov but he had no information on the subject. It was decided that Alfred should write to the empress. He asked the queen to draft a letter for him, which she did. The reply when it came was devastating:

'How could we invite you to come to us whilst we are unable to hold out to you any distinct promise beforehand – and our daughter who is to be left perfectly free in her choice, has up to this time shown a marked dislike to binding herself in any way for the future,' the empress wrote on 13 June. '... How should we venture to form hastily a resolution which will bind her for all her lifetime and must naturally separate her from us! ... This is the plain truth, as I am bound to tell you, my dear Alfred; you may believe me, when I say, that I am very sorry to be obliged to send you this reply.'[30]

The queen blamed Princess Alice for encouraging Alfred in the whole affair, 'without the *slightest real ground* for hoping that he would succeed. It is truly very annoying to the queen to have been deceived and misled,' she told Lord Granville.[31] She had also heard through the Russian Ambassador and from other relatives that Marie was spoilt and indulged. Although the proposed match was also being championed by the Princess of Wales and her sister Tsarevna Marie Feodorovna, Queen Victoria reflected that perhaps it was best if the whole matter was brought to an end at once. And there, for the moment, the matter rested.

* * *

In January 1873 Grand Duchess Marie suddenly asked for the negotiations to be reopened. There was little choice. She realised that the court of Queen Victoria would surely be preferable to a life at a small German court and, with prospects limited by her rank, there was a dearth of suitable prospective husbands. Also her home life was not as happy as before.

The tsar was now quite openly acknowledging his mistress Princess Catherine Dolgoruky (who was nearly thirty years his junior), by whom he already had a son and would go on to have three more children before 1878. His other children were shocked at this behaviour, as was the empress, who had advanced tuberculosis and now spent more and more time in the Crimea for her failing health. She was concerned for her daughter's future and would have much preferred a son-in-law who would be prepared to live in Russia, but realistically this was never likely to happen. Grand Duchess Marie would soon have to think seriously about her future and it seemed that it lay with Alfred.

He was still very keen on the marriage but by now both Tsar Alexander and Queen Victoria were against the match, partly because of the tensions in Central Asia. This anxiety over Asia was ostensibly the reason for the visit to London of Count Peter Shuvalov (the tsar's confidant and head of the Russian police) in January 1873. Russian troops were moving towards the Khanate of Khiva, over which they eventually gained control later that year. Count Shuvalov had been authorised to tell Lord Granville that even a temporary occupation of Khiva (which the Russians captured in June) would be avoided by Russia, and the Foreign Secretary was able to assure parliament that Russia's intentions were peaceful.

It quickly became apparent that Khiva was not the main reason for Count Shuvalov's visit and he was soon discussing the Russian marriage question with Prince Alfred and other members of the royal family. The tsar's main objection was the distance that Marie would be living from her parents, who clearly doted on her and were genuinely upset at the prospect of her leaving home. However, this could be alleviated if Alfred and his bride would be willing to visit the emperor and empress in either Russia or Germany during their first few years of marriage, a stipulation to which Prince Alfred would undoubtedly agree, as Lord Granville told the queen. These words would prove important later.

Granville told Shuvalov that the queen regarded the matter as closed and naturally would want to know why the empress had written to Prince Alfred last June saying they could not give him any promise if the question was now to be reopened. The empress, replied Shuvalov, was 'in general a procrastinator when it came to making decisions'.[32] This explanation did nothing to clarify matters for Victoria, who still could not understand why the negotiations had been reopened. She remained suspicious.

At Alfred's request, the Prince of Wales spoke to the Russian Ambassador. In the interests of his brother's happiness he also tried to persuade the queen to accept the conditions laid down by the tsar, especially as she was so anxious for him to marry.

After consultations with the Foreign Secretary the queen laid down some conditions of her own. Alfred and Marie had only met twice, so they should be allowed to spend some time together to make sure there was a mutual attachment. After this a final decision on whether the marriage would take place could be made before August. Neither the queen nor the government was pleased but, as Prince Alfred had rejected all the possible Protestant princesses, Gladstone, like Victoria, felt that a Russian Orthodox grand duchess was preferable to a Roman Catholic princess. Victoria was doubtful about the political desirability of the union, but was prepared to bend to Alfred's strong desire. In the strictest confidence the queen wrote to Vicky (she no longer trusted the pro-Russian Princess Alice, who was *not* to be informed), that 'I can't, of course, after what has passed, entirely refuse these (to me somewhat suspicious) *avances*.'[33]

Several months later, after the engagement had been announced, Queen Victoria wrote privately to Vicky's mother-in-law, Empress Augusta of Germany, telling her, 'you know that I did not desire this alliance on various quite serious grounds.'[34]

***

The queen's doubts were brought into focus on 1 February, when the reasons for Count Shuvalov's urgent visit to London became clear. After over two weeks' of silence from the count, who had promised to write sending Alfred some new photos of Marie within ten days of his return to Russia, a telegram arrived from the British Ambassador Lord Loftus. Excitedly he reported that 'extraordinary rumours' were circulating in St Petersburg about Marie. A secret letter with an explanation was on the way and in the meantime he asked that all negotiations for the marriage be suspended. The letter Lord Granville finally received concerned persistent rumours of Marie's 'love affair with one officer and a secret correspondence with another'. The ambassador felt there must be some truth in these unpleasant and embarrassing reports.[35]

The queen agreed, saying that 'the *worst* stories are *untrue*' but that the Russians had such loose morals and 'this emperor's sons, sisters and brothers are no exception to this rule.' The tsar obviously had good reason to want the marriage to go ahead as soon as possible, before any more harm was done to Marie's reputation.[36]

Alfred refused to believe that Marie's affections might be engaged elsewhere, even when he received a warning letter to this effect written by the queen on 12 February. As her Private Secretary General (later Sir Henry) Ponsonby remarked, Prince Alfred's valentine message that year was not a pleasant one.

Then, when Count Shuvalov finally wrote his long-awaited letter, he said nothing about Marie's feelings. Alfred's reaction was to go to St Petersburg and find out, but he was persuaded that he would be putting himself at the risk of a personal rejection. He remained in England.

Another letter then arrived from Lord Loftus reporting rumours that Marie had become so infatuated with her father's *aide-de-camp* Prince Galitzine that she was willing to give up her royal title and privileges to marry him. The tsar, thinking of his daughter's happiness, was willing to let her do this but the empress refused to hear of it and Prince Galitzine was sent abroad on indefinite leave. Loftus reported that the rumours had now died down and seemed to have no further substance; they were more likely little more than Marie's 'romantic fancy'.[37] The queen was now considering preventing the marriage altogether and anxious to know why Shuvalov had been so anxious to press Marie's claims if her attachment to Galitzine had been no more than a brief fancy. Yet with Prince Galitzine ruled out by her parents, Marie knew she could do a lot worse than become the wife of Alfred.

In March the empress invited Alfred to meet her and Marie in Sorrento the following month. The prince seized his chance, writing to the empress that he 'hoped his presence would be agreeable to the grand duchess'.[38]

Queen Victoria was angry and wanted assurances that Alfred would not be going on a wild goose chase. 'The son of the Queen of England would *not* be ready to run to the other end of the world, for the chance of being graciously looked at by the grand duchess, daughter of the Empress of Russia, and for the equal chance of being refused.'[39]

Lord Granville pointed out that the marriage had been agreed in principle when Count Shuvalov visited England and there was no way out now. The queen then laid down two stipulations, as she told Vicky: 'That there must be mutual attachment and if there is – then they must be married within this year or else it must finally be put an end to.'[40] Prince Alfred took no notice whatsoever.

He had received an encouraging letter from the empress, written on 31 March: 'Your visit will be very welcome to me – or I had better say, to us – for I should, of course, not have made this proposal, had not my daughter fully agreed with me as regards a renewed meeting.'[41]

* * *

At Osborne the queen anxiously awaited news from Sorrento but the next thing she heard was a message in cipher from Alfred saying that Marie was ill and that he 'was obliged to wait until she's well enough to receive him!!!' The exclamation marks in the queen's letter to Vicky say it all. Princess Alice, who had arrived in Sorrento on 18 April, told the queen that Marie had been suffering from bad headaches and homesickness but that Alfred 'remained very patient and hopeful'.[42]

With Alfred prepared to wait, the queen became annoyed at the 'insolent' conduct of the imperial family, which her son appeared not to notice. In the event he was only permitted a short time with Marie before being asked to leave.

Despite Vicky hearing through diplomatic channels that in St Petersburg the wedding was considered as settled, the empress had still not agreed to the marriage. Queen Victoria put this down to what she considered signs of an anti-English movement in St Petersburg.

The queen once more went on the attack. If Marie married Alfred, Victoria told her private secretary, she would have 'to accept very altered circumstances according to Russian which are *half Oriental* notions... She has been very much spoilt and *indulged*, in every whim and fancy and accustomed to every possible luxury ... and this with the falseness of the Russians, this want of principle and a different religion...' The queen could see great difficulties and objections ahead: 'Those Russian princesses *never* are contented when they marry out of Russia.' It would be better if Alfred went to live in St Petersburg rather than 'bring a discontented spoilt wife to England...'[43]

But Marie had now made up her mind and she asked her mother's brother Prince Alexander of Hesse for support. Reluctantly, with Prince Alexander's persuasion, the tsar gave in and agreed to the marriage. In June the tsar, tsarina and their daughter would be travelling to Ems and they invited Prince Alfred to join them at Jugenheim during the summer. Marie was ecstatic. 'How happy I am to belong to him,' she wrote. 'I feel that my love for him is growing daily. I have a feeling of peace and inexpressible happiness and a boundless impatience to be altogether his own.'[44]

In England the queen was less pleased. She drafted a letter detailing all the personal and political problems Marie would face as Alfred's wife in England, intending to send it to Princess Alice to show to the tsar and tsarina. It was *not* to be shown to Alfred. For some unexplained reason the letter was never sent.

Before Alfred could leave for Jugenheim Grand Duchess Marie's brother arrived in England.

A Russian Marriage

'I hope and pray it will turn out for Affie's happiness.'
– Queen Victoria.

Tsarevich Alexander (Sasha), his wife Marie Feodorovna (the former Princess Dagmar of Denmark) and their children, five-year-old Nicholas and two-year-old George, arrived at Woolwich on board the imperial yacht *Standart* on 16 June 1873 for a family visit with the Prince and Princess of Wales. Although the visit was officially said to be incognito, they were met by a guard of honour, a 21-gun salute and the Band of the Royal Artillery who played the national anthem of both countries on the quayside.

The Russian visitors stayed with Bertie and Alexandra at their London home, Marlborough House, just along The Mall from Buckingham Palace, where Nicholas and George joined their cousins the Wales children – Albert Victor (Eddy), George (later King George V), Louise, Victoria (Toria) and Maud – in the nursery.

Marie Feodorovna, who the queen called 'Minny', had met Queen Victoria when she came to England as a fifteen-year-old girl in 1863 for her sister's wedding but this was Sasha's first meeting with the monarch.

The Shah of Persia, Naser al-Din, was visiting England at the same time and staying at Buckingham Palace. This was rather unfortunate because he disliked Russia. Not only that, the queen refused to budge from Windsor, leaving the Prince and Princess of Wales to entertain all the visitors in London. With Queen Victoria fuming against Russia, and society there retaliating by calling her a 'she-devil', Princess Alexandra and her sister were determined to do their best to improve Anglo-Russian relations.

They hit on the novel idea of dressing identically throughout the visit. Such a sight had never been seen before on a royal occasion and it caused a sensation when they attended the opera and went to Madame Tussaud's in identical gowns. Every morning crowds gathered to watch them driving in Hyde Park and in the evening ballrooms became battlefields as society ladies strained to catch a glimpse of them.

The queen invited the tsarevich and tsarevna to lunch at Windsor on 21 June. She thought Sasha 'very good natured and kind', while Minny was pronounced 'very simple and unaffected'[1] and in manner very like the Princess of Wales.

On 25 June there was a great military review at Windsor, which to the queen's annoyance was late in starting because the trains bringing the principal guests, including the shah, were delayed. It was on this occasion that the tsarevich and his wife had to give way publicly for the first time to the shah, who looked impressive on his huge horse with its trappings studded with sparkling precious stones. The Russians could hardly disguise their annoyance that the eastern potentate was getting all the attention, and Victoria thought it rather unfortunate that they should be in England at the same time and thus were practically ignored.

To add to their humiliation *The Times* picked 25 June to reply to a scathing attack in the St Petersburg *Mir*, which accused England of fêting the shah in order to show 'her spite against Russia rather than her friendship for Persia'. *The Times* took issue with this: 'Such acrimonious rant as the comments of *The Mir* ... has seldom been our lot to read,' the newspaper thundered. 'Their Imperial Highnesses ... have borne a chief part in all these ceremonials. Is it to be supposed that they, too, have been aiding the moral conquest of the British tiger?'

The tsarevich felt his role as the guardian of Russian honour deeply. He soon grew edgy and impatient at what he felt to be slights inflicted on Russia. Nevertheless, during his visit he attended a naval review at Spithead, military reviews at Woolwich and Aldershot, visited the Tower of London and sat in on a trial at the court of the Lord Chief Justice. He and the tsarevna went to art galleries, visited hospitals and attended racecourses. Alfred invited him to dine with the Elder Brethren of Trinity House, during which he thanked the assembly in French for his reception and expressed the hope that relations between England and Russia would always remain as cordial and affectionate.

Victoria came to London ('a great effort and fatigue' she told Vicky) on 28 June for the garden party given by the Prince of Wales at Chiswick House. The shah was pleased with everything in England, unlike his recent visit to St Petersburg, and as the queen told Vicky, the Russians 'are not judicious enough to conceal their anger and jealousy'.[2] It was very hot and a lot of people were present, among them 'Alix's dear little girls (the boys had chickenpox) and Minny's two dear little boys'. Once again, 'Alix and her sister were dressed alike.'[3]

On 1 July the queen invited the Russians to dine and sleep at Windsor. Sasha and Minny arrived with the Prince and Princess of Wales. Victoria was delighted to see that, now she was married into the Russian imperial family, the former Princess Dagmar had not put on any airs and graces. 'Dear Minny is so nice and simple, just as she used to be,' the queen recorded in her journal that evening. The queen and Princess Beatrice took Alix and Minny to Frogmore, where they had tea. Afterwards there was the inevitable pilgrimage to the mausoleum, then a drive around Windsor Park and a tour of the Castle. At dinner the queen was led in by Sasha, just as thirty-six years earlier 'his grandfather, the Emperor Nicholas had done'. She thought Sasha 'very good-natured', and sat between him and Minny while a military band played in the quadrangle and pipers came round the table during dessert.[4]

The dinner in their honour may have gone some way to easing the tsarevich's bruised feelings, although what he thought of the bagpipes is not recorded.

***

On 11 July, as the queen was taking tea with Beatrice on the lawn of Osborne House, a telegram arrived from Alfred announcing his engagement to Grand Duchess Marie. It had taken place at Schloss Heiligenberg near Jugenheim. 'The murder is out!' the queen told Vicky.[5]

Victoria was left bewildered at how rapidly things had been settled and all the difficulties overcome, especially since talks and negotiations had been going on for some while. She voiced these rather mixed feelings in her response to Alfred. The prince was embarrassed at the lack of congratulations, telling Lord Granville how disappointed he was that the only telegram he could not show his fiancée and her parents was the one from his own mother.

Shortly afterwards, a telegram arrived from the tsar and tsarina, which the queen translated from German into her diary: 'We implore with you God's blessing on our dear children and recommend to you our daughter, who kisses your hand.' As Victoria sent out telegrams to relations and friends, she added in her journal: 'I hope and pray it may turn out for Affie's happiness.'[6]

Nevertheless, she was worried. Firstly, she had never even seen Marie. Secondly, the morals of the Russian imperial family were hardly above reproach, as she complained to Vicky. Marie's brother Alexei was unable to return to Russia for a while as he had 'got into a scrape with a maid of honour'. If it happened here, Victoria continued, 'I think it would upset the throne and I fear this.' Marie's other brother Vladimir she pronounced 'very bad and so is Sanny's son [Nicholas]', and the son of Marie of Leuchtenberg she thought 'dreadful, and his mama not exemplary'.[7]

The queen was naturally concerned about the religious question and foresaw many problems ahead. General Ponsonby reported concern about the bride's Orthodox religion and the possibility of rivalry between the Prince of Wales's establishment and that of the Duke of Edinburgh. It was, the queen told Vicky, the first time that a princess from another church had entered the family since the Jacobite revolution of 1688. If the family were not firm they would have 'to pack up – and call back the descendants of the Stuarts'. It was pointed out to her by Dean Stanley (who had studied in Russia) that although the Orthodox Church 'held many of the superstitions and erroneous views of the Roman Catholics, they did not as the Roman Catholics did, refuse to acknowledge any other church but their own.'[8]

The couple seemed to be very happy and Victoria thought Marie seemed 'a very sweet girl, who married him entirely for his sake (!!) – I wonder – but never mind that'. It had been a great wrench for the imperial couple to agree to part with their only daughter but the queen thought that they wanted this marriage because they were so afraid of the alternative with Prince Galitzine.[9]

The tsar later admitted in a letter from Germany that he gave his blessing to Marie's marriage 'with a heavy heart' after a meeting with Alfred. 'The fate of my daughter has been decided,' he wrote sadly.[10]

* * *

The emperor and empress now hoped Alfred would come to the Crimea for a few days in the autumn. Meanwhile, the prince forwarded a letter from Marie, written to the queen from Heiligenberg on 12 July. Victoria appended a copy to her journal:

> My dear Mama, Excuse my at once addressing you so, as I hope that the time is drawing near when I shall have the right to call you by the name of mother.
>
> It shall be my constant endeavour by affection and confidence to became a true daughter to you and merit your love and trust.
>
> After the events of yesterday, which caused me such great happiness, I have felt the desire to write to you to express the joy I feel at the prospect of becoming a member of your family, in which after the many proofs of interest you have already shown me, I cannot doubt, but I shall be welcome! My love to Alfred is a true warrant of our future happiness and in the various steps I am going to take in leaving my own parents and country it will make it easy for me to settle with him in my new home! Looking forward to the day when I kiss your hands.

She signed the letter, 'I remain, Your dutiful and affectionate daughter.'[11]

On 17 July the queen declared the marriage in Council and in the evening went up to the tower to watch the firework display held in honour of the occasion.

The proposed marriage brought questions in the House of Commons about whether a union with a Russian Orthodox bride would infringe the Royal Marriages Act of 1772. At the queen's request, Mr Gladstone made it clear that 'a marriage with a princess of the Greek [Russian Orthodox] faith is strictly within the law and will in no way affect the succession to the crown.'[12] The only ban was on Catholic princesses.

The tsar was to make Alfred honorary Chief of a Guards' Regiment and he offered a similar honour to the Prince of Wales. To Bertie's annoyance the queen would not allow him to accept. Alfred would be living a good deal in Russia as the emperor's son-in-law; if the Prince of Wales accepted a like honour 'it would mean a departure from precedent and be highly unpopular in England,' she told him. It was not just Bertie who was upset. Grand Duke Vladimir was particularly angry and his strong Anglophobia was accentuated. Others in the family also felt it was a slight against Grand Duchess Marie.[13]

The queen was now very anxious to see her future daughter-in-law before the wedding but of course there was no question of her travelling to the Continent on such an errand. As the emperor and empress were at Jugenheim, Victoria thought it would be a good idea if Alexander and his daughter paid a private visit to her in England, as Princess Alexandra had done before she married the Prince of Wales. She immediately wrote to Princess Alice to this effect. The tsarevich, who was going to Germany to see his parents, also offered to suggest the idea to his father. The emperor stood on his dignity and was having none of it, privately calling Victoria a 'silly old fool'.[14]

A few days later a telegram from Princess Alice informed her mother that it was impossible, as the tsar had to return to Russia the next day. The queen remarked that it was 'very provoking and disappointing'.[15]

The tsarina, whose poor health did not permit a trip to England, then offered to meet the queen at Cologne. Victoria considered this 'impertinent', saying that she could not just pack up and leave the country in a few days. When Princess Alice took the side of the Russians and tried to persuade her mother to go, the queen's anger knew no bounds:

> I do not think, dear child, that *you* should tell *me,* who have been nearly twenty years *longer* on the throne than the Emperor of Russia and am the Doyenne of Sovereigns and who am a *reigning* sovereign which the empress is not, – what I *ought to do...*[16]

Her own daughters had been required to visit their future in-laws and she dismissed the empress's proposal as 'just what is to be expected from people who have *Asiatic ideas* of *their rank.*'[17]

The next battle was over the date of the wedding. Victoria wanted the end of October or the beginning of November. The empress vetoed that, saying that marrying in the winter would be unlucky; she suggested the spring. The emperor would not permit that and proposed it should be in January, which, as the queen pointed out to Vicky, was still in the winter. By this time queen and emperor were not even corresponding with each other, so she decided to hand over the negotiations to her ministers.

The tsarevich complained to his mother that he was tired of the queen's imperious ways, while his brother-in-law the Prince of Wales was in despair over it all and did not know what to do. 'Every day there is a new telegram from the queen,' Sasha told his mother, 'and there are new suggestions as to the meeting with Marie... I am just afraid to come into her [Victoria's] sight, she will bite my head off after everything!!'[18]

Matters had reached an impasse. The tsar refused to write to the queen, who now could not write until she received a letter from him. Everyone now distrusted Princess Alice, who the queen blamed for encouraging the marriage in the first place. The tsarevich was refusing to take a message, while the Prince of Wales refused to ask him anything about it. Lord Granville's telegrams to de Brunov (who he now accused of being silly) went unanswered. So, Ponsonby wrote to Granville, 'unless this letter at Darmstadt unlocks the difficulty we are in a fix.'[19]

* * *

On the Isle of Wight the queen was expecting the Russian visitors. On 28 July the children of the Prince of Wales and the two sons of the tsarevich left for Osborne to stay at Albert Cottage on the estate.

The following morning little Grand Duke Nicholas joined the queen and the Prince of Wales's children in Victoria's elaborate tent, pitched on the lawn, where they all ate breakfast surrounded by dogs, ladies-in-waiting and liveried attendants. The children were excited. 'They were in tremendous high spirits,' Victoria wrote in her journal.[20] A couple of days later the tsarevich and tsarevna arrived at Osborne Cottage, which was linked to Albert Cottage by a covered corridor.

At the end of July Prince Alfred returned from Darmstadt with a letter from the emperor for Queen Victoria, after which no more was heard of Marie visiting Britain before her wedding. He also gave the queen a locket of gold and blue enamel with his and Marie's ciphers. Victoria noted that he seemed agitated, although happy, as they discussed his forthcoming marriage. He showed her the plans for enlarging his London home, Clarence House, which had been built for the queen's uncle the future King William IV between 1825 and 1827 when he was Duke of Clarence. As Marie's money and property were all in Russia, Alfred also told the queen that she would require a Russian secretary.

The queen and Princess Beatrice walked to Albert Cottage the next morning to visit Sasha and Minny. They saw all the children apart from Grand Duke George, who still had chicken pox. The following day the queen stopped at Osborne Cottage to speak to Alix and Minny as she returned from her customary drive.

On 3 August Victoria again called at Osborne Cottage, where she sat in the garden with the Princess of Wales and her sister.

Alix had brought her sons to play with their Russian cousins and Sasha was also there. By the Russian calendar it was 22 July, the name day of the empress, her daughter-in-law the tsarevna, and her daughter Grand Duchess Marie. At dinner that night the health of all three Maries was drunk.

Prince Alfred celebrated his twenty-ninth birthday at Osborne on 6 August and that night the queen gave a large family dinner. Among the guests were the Prince and Princess of Wales, the tsarevich and tsarevna, the queen's children Leopold and Beatrice, and the tsarevich's cousin Princess Eugenie (now married to Prince Alexander of Oldenburg), 'a nice agreeable natural person who is staying at Ventnor and has come for the night', as the queen recorded. Eugenie had once been considered as a bride for Prince Alfred; her mother Grand Duchess Marie, the Duchess of Leuchtenberg, had already visited Victoria several times. It was a lovely warm, moonlit night, and after dinner they all sat out on the terrace.[21]

On 8 August the Russian children Nicholas and George were present at the Cowes Regatta, along with Princess Beatrice and the children of the Prince of Wales, and the next morning the 'two little Russian boys' and Princess Maud of Wales had breakfast with the queen. Victoria was anxious to learn more about the tsar's daughter. That afternoon Fanny Baillie, whose sister Augusta was married to the Dean of Westminster, spoke to the queen about the young grand duchess, 'whom she has seen and much likes. She thinks her very pleasing and says she is much beloved by all her own people, high and low.'[22]

***

The tsarevich and tsarevna left England on 13 August after a stay of two months. The queen departed for Balmoral, where on 26 August she received letters from Grand Duchess Marie and her mother. She sent her future daughter-in-law some white heather for good luck.

One of the questions that exercised everyone was where the wedding would take place. The queen assumed it would be in England, as had been the case with the Princess Royal's marriage in 1858. But the tsar and tsarina proved as obstinate as Victoria had done on this earlier occasion and declared that there was no question of Marie leaving Russia before she was married. The ceremony would take place in January 1874 at the Winter Palace.

Beaten on this point, Victoria asked Arthur Stanley, the Dean of Westminster, to go to St Petersburg to perform the English marriage ceremony, which she insisted would follow the Orthodox wedding. His wife Lady Augusta would report proceedings in the fullest detail to the queen. There was then some discussion about whether a ceremony abroad would be legally valid under the Royal Marriages Act, with the Dean suggesting that to ensure this point the setting for the Anglican ceremony should be temporarily declared British sovereign territory. This idea was rejected, the Lord Chancellor saying that a legal marriage under foreign law was equally legal in Britain. There was also the problem of Queen Victoria's wedding gifts. In September the Princess of Wales reported to her sister that the queen had decided to give Marie some emeralds.

Then there was the little matter of the marriage treaty, which would deal with such things as the full and free unrestricted practice of Marie's religion, inheritance and financial support. Gladstone told the queen he thought it 'most objectionable and imperiously worded'. The queen commented that it would be necessary for 'the whole thing to be completely rewritten'. They were having difficulty making out the marriage portion, which seemed to amount to an incredible £30,000 a year. In fact the dowry was one million roubles (about £100,000 then) and Marie would receive 5 per cent interest on this capital per year, paid half-yearly. This was on top of various special marriage portions allotted to his daughter by the tsar (an annual 75,000 roubles for life, plus another 1 million roubles, plus she retained possession of her private capital amounting to some £90,000), all which made Marie an extremely wealthy young woman.[23]

Concerns were raised regarding various unnecessary stipulations about religion. Gladstone promised to write to Lord Granville the Foreign Secretary and get things sorted out via personal communication either in England or St Petersburg.

The cards were very much all in the tsar's hands as, one by one, Victoria was forced to abandon one irrevocable point after another. After months of disagreeable wrangling the marriage treaty was finally agreed four days before the wedding.

Reports appeared in *The Graphic* about Marie's elaborate trousseau, which was displayed in the White Hall of the Winter Palace. Comprising 'fifty magnificent dresses, not including ball dresses, to say nothing of splendid furs and lace at 1,000 roubles a yard', it was estimated to have cost £40,000.[24] There was also 'a set of straw-work veneered furniture', a tea service by Pavel

Ovchinnikov whose design was based on ancient Russian ware, 'a gold toilette set of over a hundred pieces which was a family heirloom', and a magnificent set of liturgical silver made by Nicholls & Plincke (the official suppliers to the imperial family) for Marie's private chapel.[25]

Alfred left for Russia on 30 December. This would be the only one of her children's weddings that Queen Victoria did not attend. She admitted feeling it dreadfully, even though she now thought weddings were 'sad and painful'. She was afraid that Alfred would become 'quite a humble servant of Russia', as she told the Princess Royal.[26]

With mutual suspicion simmering over the Eastern Question these were certainly 'interesting times for an Anglo-Russian alliance'.[27]

Daughter of Imperial Russia

'Who comes first, a louse or a flea?'
— Dr Johnson

Alfred and Marie's wedding was to take place in St Petersburg on 11/23 January 1874 which was, Victoria noted poignantly, the anniversary of her own father's death. The queen, who was at Osborne, sent with Lady Augusta a sprig of myrtle from the Princess Royal's wedding bouquet, which was to be placed in Marie's bouquet before the English service. She also sent two prayer books, one each for Alfred and Marie. Inside Marie's white-bound volume was an appropriate illuminated verse.

There was one final incident before the marriage took place. Alexander II objected to the inclusion in Alfred's retinue of Thomas Michell, who had been interpreter during the Prince of Wales's visit in 1866. Without giving any reason, he now wanted him removed. The queen told Lord Granville that the Russian government, taking advantage of the marriage, were being 'more than usually haughty and *exigent,* and mean to *try* and order us about as they *formerly* did *other Courts* related to them!' She accused the tsar of acting like an eastern potentate 'who expects to have all his wishes yielded to. The empress is much the same…' In fact, after speaking to Michell, Lord Granville finally agreed that the Russians had been right in insisting on his removal.[1]

On 18 January Gustav Richter's portrait of Marie arrived at Osborne as a gift to the queen from the tsar. Victoria described it as 'a lovely picture ½ length, and beautifully painted. She is standing on a balcony in a light blue evening dress, with a fan in her hand. The face is very pleasing and very like the photographs, so that

I should think it must be a good likeness.'[2] It was later hung in the Oak Room at Windsor.

'I am so glad you like the picture and am sure you will love her dear face. As the time is rapidly approaching, I feel the more your absence at this the most important and the happiest moment of [my] life,' Alfred wrote to her from St Petersburg.[3]

On 23 January Marie's portrait was surrounded by a wreath of evergreens and orange flowers, with bows of the Russian colours tied to it. The wedding was to be at one o'clock Russian time but, as Victoria realised, St Petersburg was 2 hours ahead of England. This was the first and only time a Romanov married into the British royal family.

***

The Orthodox ceremony in the Great Cathedral Church of the Winter Palace was impressive. Sixty chamberlains led the way to the church walking in pairs, followed by the tsar (who displayed his Garter insignia) and tsarina, Alfred wearing Russian naval uniform, and Marie wearing a cloth of silver gown with a long train and an ermine-trimmed mantle, which took six men to carry. Across her breast was the red sash of the Order of St Catherine. Queen Victoria heard later that Marie seemed overwhelmed with the weight of her heavy mantle and gown, plus the weight of the crown of diamonds sparkling on her head, while both parents seemed emotional.

The Metropolitans of Moscow, Novgorod and Kiev conducted the service wearing their magnificent robes. Three of Marie's brothers and Alfred's brother Arthur, the Duke of Connaught, took turns in holding golden crowns over the couples' heads during the ceremony. The Prince of Wales represented Queen Victoria; Vicky, the Crown Princess of Germany, was also present.

To the tsar's displeasure and at the insistence of Queen Victoria, this was followed by a Church of England ceremony in the Alexander Hall of the Winter Palace, where they were married by Arthur Stanley, Dean of Westminster in front of an improvised altar covered with crimson velvet. Ten thousand candles lit the impressive room, while the weak light of the January sun added to the glittering effect.

Afterwards there was a banquet for 800 people in the Nicholas Hall, during which the sopranos Adelina Patti and Emma Albani sang as guns thundered out from the SS Peter and Paul Fortress.

The banquet was followed by a ball for 3,000 people in St George's Hall, which began with the Polonaise. The tsar led the bride and the tsarina followed with the bridegroom, with the Prince of Wales and his sister next, and then Crown Prince Frederick of Germany and the Princess of Wales.

The emperor told Lord Sydney that he and the empress placed their daughter entirely in the hands of the queen and he hoped she would let him come to England for a day or two in May to see his daughter. Only at eleven that night could the newlyweds escape by train to Tsarskoe Selo.

At six o'clock that evening a telegram arrived at Osborne from the tsar: 'We hasten to announce to Your Majesty that the double wedding ceremony of our dear children has just taken place. May the Divine Blessing watch over them; we recommend our darling daughter to your maternal solicitude.' The queen received the news with 'much emotion, replying that she was looking forward to the moment 'when I will be able to kiss my dear daughter who will be the object of my most lively solicitude and tender affection.'[4]

That evening at dinner the queen wore the star and Order of St Catherine as the health of the Duke and Duchess of Edinburgh was drunk. The meal was followed by a servants' ball as fireworks filled the sky. It was one thirty in the morning before Victoria went to bed.

As a token of the new friendship several English towns returned the guns captured in the Crimean War. Not to be outdone, the Russians promptly rechristened their newest frigate, so that the *Alexander Nevsky* now became *Herzog Edinbourgsky*.

The wedding celebrations continued in Moscow, a city which the queen, on reading the various reports, said sounded wonderful. To ensure that his mother did not completely miss out, Alfred commissioned Nicholas Chevalier, whom he had met in 1867, to execute a series of watercolour sketches of both wedding ceremonies and the banquet, which the queen received early in February. One was so cleverly contrived that by moving the flaps Victoria could follow the different parts of the unfamiliar Orthodox ceremony. The following year the queen commissioned Chevalier to do an oil painting of the ceremony in the Winter Palace Cathedral, which was hung in the Grand Corridor at Windsor.

The emperor and empress wanted their daughter to stay in Russia until the end of February, which the queen thought disrespectful as she had not even been given the chance to meet her before the wedding. 'The Russians expect to have everything their own way,' she complained to Vicky.[5]

* * *

After a honeymoon at Tsarskoe Selo and a distressing parting with Marie's parents ('I do indeed feel and think much of them,' the queen wrote sympathetically)[6] the newlyweds arrived in England on 7 March.

Windsor town had pulled out all the stops to welcome the grand duchess. The streets were lined with troops from the Guards and the Berkshire Volunteers, flags and bunting were everywhere and a triumphal arch had been erected. Some of the inscriptions were in Russian the queen noticed, as she drove to the South Western Railway Station with Bertie, Alexandra and Louise. A guard of honour and a band were on the platform when the Duke of Edinburgh and his bride stepped out of the train. Victoria, who even had her black jacket trimmed with miniver and her cloak lined with ermine for the occasion, was nervous. 'Marie, who is very like her photographs, wore a light blue dress with a long train and a white tulle bonnet with white roses and white heather, which I had purposely sent to Antwerp in the yacht,' she recorded.[7] The queen embraced and kissed Marie before presenting the rest of the family and the suite. Then they drove to the castle through streets lined with cheering crowds. Schoolboys from Eton lined the Long Walk and there was a guard of honour in the quadrangle.

To Vicky, the queen later wrote that Marie was not graceful at all, walked badly, held herself badly and was not as pretty as she expected. In fact Marie was plain, with none of the fine-boned elegance of her mother, while her frame could only be described as stocky. 'Dear Marie has a very friendly manner, a pleasant face, beautiful skin and fine bright eyes, and there is something very fresh and attractive about her,' Victoria noted. Although in looks Marie could not compare with the lovely Princess of Wales, who had arrived from Denmark this very week eleven years earlier, she did speak excellent English.

The Tapestry Rooms had been refurbished for the Duke and Duchess of Edinburgh's arrival and their cipher was put on the doors. After lunch the queen invited Marie to her own room, where she showed her the Russian album containing watercolours of the principal St Petersburg palaces presented by her uncle Grand Duke Constantine Nicolaievich in 1847, and gave her some Scottish tartan items with which Marie was probably bewildered but professed to be pleased. 'She was very nice and natural and not at all shy.'[8] The young couple gave the queen an enamel, sapphire and diamond brooch with their cipher and the date; later Marie showed the queen the Russian alphabet.

At dinner that night the queen noted her daughter-in-law's lovely pearl necklace. The duchess was probably less impressed when a few days later Victoria showed her some of the palace's many rooms, including the 1855 room where scenes from the Crimean War decorated the walls.

Things seemed to have got off to a good start but they were destined not to stay that way. Queen Sophie of the Netherlands was doubtless not the only person who wondered how the spoilt Marie, only daughter of the tsar, would 'accept her secondary position' at the British court.[9]

***

Two days later the queen gave a large dinner in St George's Hall, the first state dinner since 1855 and the first time she had used the hall since 1860. Marie was dressed in white silk with a wonderful ruby parure, and the princes wore their Russian Orders.

Before leaving for Buckingham Palace, Marie was obliged to accompany the queen on the inevitable visit to the mausoleum at Frogmore, something with which she would become all too familiar.

They arrived at Paddington on 12 March in bad weather and set off to the palace in an open carriage procession through the streets of London. In spite of the snow great crowds had turned out, ladies threw flowers into the carriage and at Trafalgar Square there was a great crush of people wanting to catch a glimpse of the new Duchess of Edinburgh. 'The decorations were very pretty with numbers of kind, and some funny, inscriptions. One was "Welcome fair Russ",' the queen noted that night, although she thought it a shame that the troops lining the route had to wear greatcoats because of the weather. It spoilt the whole effect.[10] Luckily it had stopped snowing by the time they arrived at Buckingham Palace so the royal family went out onto the balcony to greet the crowds.

There was a special court on 13 March at which Marie was the only princess present. She was dressed in pale pink satin, a diamond diadem sparkling on her head and wearing her splendid parure of sapphires and diamonds.

Marie's magnificent jewels (many of them by Bolin and other leading suppliers to the Russian court) which the queen had earlier viewed in the audience room at Windsor, included sapphires which had belonged to the tsar's mother and a set of jewellery bequeathed by Catherine the Great. They were soon to be the cause of much jealousy at Victoria's court.

***

The queen moved to Osborne, where Alfred and Marie paid their first visit on 13 April. Marie was shown the farm and the Swiss Cottage erected by Prince Albert for his children, and she visited the local school. However, she did not find Osborne a relaxing place and particularly hated the rather bracing windy conditions. As a girl she had never been taught how to put a hat pin in with her left hand and 'did not propose to begin trying now'.[11] Consequently her hats, anchored with one pin instead of two, blew off all too easily.

On 18 April, the couple took a carriage drive to West Cowes with the queen and Princess Beatrice. The town had requested their visit and the narrow streets had been specially decorated with flags and evergreens in honour of the duke and duchess. Near the post office was a triumphal arch, bands played on the green, crowds of people were everywhere and a little girl presented a posy to Marie. '… certainly it was most successfully done,' the queen wrote later. 'We came back by Newport. Affie and Marie were very cheery and she is such a charming companion.'[12]

Everybody at first agreed that Marie was charming, but it soon became apparent that she was finding it difficult to forget that she was by birth an Imperial Highness, a higher rank than that of Royal Highness, which she now held after her marriage. In England, Marie discovered, she ranked below all the queen's daughters and the Danish-born Princess of Wales. To her this was unacceptable.

Shortly after Marie's arrival in England Queen Victoria received a letter from the tsar insisting that his daughter's rank of Imperial Highness should come before Royal Highness, 'as in all civilised countries'.[13] The queen's rather sharp rejoinder was that she did not care whether Marie used imperial or not, but royal must come first. Then there was the question of whether the title 'grand duchess' should come before 'Duchess of Edinburgh,' which prompted more comments from Victoria about the Russians and their Asiatic ideas of rank. This led Ponsonby to quote Dr Johnson to his wife: 'Who comes first, a louse or a flea?'

The matter was complicated by the queen's recognition that she was not an empress herself, a question made all the more painful after King William of Prussia became emperor of a united Germany in 1871.

Worse still was the question of precedence. Although the tsar was willing to concede that the Princess of Wales as wife of the heir should rank before Marie, even though Alexandra came from humble Denmark, he insisted that the queen's daughters and other future daughters-in-law should come *after* his daughter. The queen pointedly refused. Marie felt affronted and exacted her revenge by wearing her spectacular jewellery at all court functions as befitted a Russian imperial grand duchess. The queen's daughters could not hide their jealousy, while the queen, whose feathers were visibly ruffled, pronounced it 'too good' for a young princess.[14]

As one by one the stipulations of the marriage contract began to unravel, Baron de Brunov (who had appreciated the queen's kindness when his wife died just as Marie arrived in England) wrote to Tsarevich Alexander, explaining that the queen made up for the fact that she had to submit to the limits imposed by constitutional monarchy by exercising absolute power over her family.

Marie maintained the strict etiquette and trappings of her Russian upbringing and insisted on being treated as a grand duchess. She was haughty and asked questions abruptly as if they had been 'fired from a pistol'.[15] At Clarence House nobody was allowed to turn her back on the Duchess of Edinburgh; she expected the staff to back out of her presence. This was no mean feat in rooms cluttered with icons and Russian *objets d'art* carved from semi-precious stones, and with barely an inch of clear floor space. This rule even extended to other people's homes. Once, while visiting the gardens at a country estate, Marie summoned the gardener to pass on her compliments. The poor man then 'discovered that there were no gates within reasonable distance for him to make the required backwards retreat' and Marie stood watching as he was forced to walk backwards for a considerable distance until he was out of her sight.[16] Her childhood memories included driving in a carriage escorted by liveried attendants. 'When she visited her neighbours at Stafford House (now Lancaster House) thirty yards from her front door, she drove there in state in her carriage complete with footmen.'[17]

To accommodate his wife's religious observances Prince Alfred built an Orthodox Chapel on the first floor of Clarence House. Designed by C. B. Waller, it contained an ornate iconostasis with icons painted by Carl von Neff and 'glittering jewelled icons and mysterious shrines' with icons lamps burning day and night. A Russian priest and two chanters officiated daily and accompanied Marie on all her travels. The Orthodox Chapel was dismantled when Clarence House was altered for the Duke of Connaught in 1900 but two of the panels survive on the wall.[18]

Marie wore soft leather boots made especially in St Petersburg to fit either foot. She refused to abide by the normal rule that royal ladies refrained from smoking in public. Although her English was perfect, she 'preferred to speak French as being the only elegant language in Europe' and the only language in which 'really beautiful letters could be written', even though she disliked 'immoral republican France'.[19] The queen of course preferred Germany and the German language.

Sometimes, when Marie had left the queen, she 'would stamp her feet and wave her fists in rebellion against the aura of omnipotence' which Victoria exuded.[20] Nevertheless, she persisted in her opinion that the queen was a silly, obstinate old fool and refused to be overawed. 'You only have to give [the queen] a good fight to make her draw in her horns,' she told her mother,[21] aware that Victoria respected people who stood up to her. The queen and her daughter-in-law were in fact more alike than either would care to admit.

In short, Marie remained Russian to the core and her likes, and aversions, remained as inflexible as those of Victoria. Arrogant, autocratic and with a sharp wit, she was unable to forget that she was a Romanov and found that being an emperor's daughter in England did not make her feel as special as she had expected. Nor did the British warm to her and she was sometimes called 'the most unpopular princess in Europe'.[22]

* * *

On 13 May Windsor was in state of excitement awaiting the imminent arrival of Tsar Alexander II of Russia who was coming to visit his daughter. It had been almost thirty-five years since the young Queen Victoria had welcomed the then Tsarevich Alexander and danced the Mazurka with him.

Earlier that year the queen heard reports from Vicky about the great contrast between the fantastic riches accumulated by the Romanovs and the extreme poverty of the poorer people. Vicky was deeply shocked, concluding that 'Russian foreign policy derived entirely from the personal ambitions of an unfettered ruler and a callous and selfish oligarchy.' She warned the queen to be on her guard, as 'the Russians cannot be trusted.'[23]

Alexander's gift to the queen, an enormous porphyry vase and pedestal, arrived on 9 May and was presented to her at Buckingham Palace in the presence of the Duchess of Edinburgh. It was later placed in the Crimson Drawing Room at Windsor.

The tsar's visit nearly did not happen at all due to the queen's refusal to change the schedule of her planned visit to Balmoral. Relations between Britain and Russia were fragile and Benjamin Disraeli, appointed Prime Minister in February that year, had to use all his considerable powers of persuasion and 'stake his personal relationship' with Victoria to get her to change her plans. Even then, it was only grudgingly done, 'for Mr Disraeli's sake and as a return for his great kindness'.[24]

On 6 May the satirical magazine *Punch* published a list of 'Things the tsar won't do.' These included 'burst into tears at the sight of the Crimean War Memorial in Waterloo Place, and renew the Treaty of Paris on the spot, out of consideration for the feeling of the neighbourhood'. Passions still ran high after the Crimean War.

* * *

The tsar's yacht *Derjava* was scheduled to land at Gravesend where the Mayor, Corporation and the townspeople were waiting to greet him. Meanwhile, at Windsor Castle, the Grand Staircase was lined with Yeomen of the Guard and decorated with flowers but as time ticked on there was still no sign of the tsar. Then came news that the yacht had run aground off Flushing during the night and Prince Alfred telegraphed that they were waiting for the tide. Everyone had to be put off until the evening.

The Prince of Wales, the Duchess of Edinburgh, Prince Arthur and the Duke of Cambridge had gone to join Prince Alfred at Dover, where the tsar arrived that evening accompanied by Grand Duke Alexei. It was past ten o'clock that night before the queen and assembled members of the royal family heard the sound of the escort approaching the castle. She stepped out to greet the emperor as he alighted from his carriage followed by Marie, Bertie and Arthur. 'We embraced, and he gave me his arm. I presented my three daughters and then we walked upstairs, and went into the Rubens Room (the emperor's drawing room) where, soon after, Affie and the Grand Duke Alexis [*sic*] joined us.' Victoria noticed how the handsome young man she remembered from 1839 had changed. He 'was very kind but is terribly altered, so thin, and his face looks so old, sad, and careworn.'[25] His son Alexei was very handsome but an enormous man. They finally sat down to supper at quarter to eleven and the emperor went to bed, exhausted, at midnight.

The following day the queen took Alexei for a walk round the grounds, including of course a visit to the Mausoleum, and later the emperor planted a tree. Then they all took a drive to Virginia Water, where the Russians went out on the water in an old barge built for Queen Anne.

At dinner in St George's Hall that night Victoria wore diamonds on her black dress and a diamond coronet with her veil. The Order of St Catherine was also worn by the queen and many of the royal ladies that evening. The tsar wore the Garter insignia on the scarlet uniform of the Chevalier Guards and Marie displayed her beautiful parure of sapphires.

Alexander spoke much about his previous visit and also recalled his father's stay in 1844, saying how attached Nicholas had been to England but that ten years later everything had unfortunately changed and the two countries were at war. 'You have been poorly served,' Alexander told the queen, referring to Lord Palmerston, 'but that is no longer the case.' Victoria replied that she regretted the misunderstandings and still retained affection for the late Tsar Nicholas. Alexander then said that he 'did not see any reason why our countries should not be on the best terms,' and that if he saw any difficulties, 'if you will permit, I will write to you directly,' to which Victoria was happy to agree. Then, with tears in his eyes he thanked her again for her kindness to his daughter, at which the queen reached out across the emperor and took Marie's hand, 'she herself being nearly upset', as Victoria recorded. The healths of emperor and queen were then drunk and the pipers walked around the table.[26]

Alexander was 'most kind and amiable' at breakfast with the queen the next morning. For both of them the visit brought mixed emotions and memories of an earlier time when they were young and carefree. Perhaps less tactfully, the queen showed him a painting of a roll call in the Crimea after the Battle of Inkerman in 1854, which showed in equal measure the suffering and friendship between ordinary soldiers after combat. It had been brought from the Royal Academy especially for the queen to display. Later that day Alexander left for Marlborough House where he dined with Bertie and Alix.

'There is no reason why Russians and Englishmen should quarrel,' *The Times* wrote on 14 May. 'Each nation has its mission in that quarter of the globe where they are neighbours; and it is perfectly possible that each of these missions might be fulfilled without harm to the other.' Yet Alexander found (as had his father before him) that public opinion was not as welcoming and he did not command the respect that was given to him in the small German states he was used to frequenting.

He returned to Windsor briefly for a private visit, this time wearing civilian clothes. The queen showed him Prince Albert's rooms where he admired the prince's favourite picture, an intimate Winterhalter portrait of the young Victoria with her hair alluringly on one shoulder, painted as a surprise for Albert in 1843.

Upon leaving, he expressed the hope that it would not be the last time they would meet. 'Poor man,' Victoria wrote in her diary that night. 'I hope he may be spared, he looks so sad and worn; he is very kind hearted and has done a great deal for his people.'[27]

***

Although he would never see the queen again, Alexander remained in England. He attended Sunday service at the Russian Chapel in Welbeck Street and an alfresco concert of popular music (which also included the Preobrazhensky march) followed by a dinner at the Crystal Palace on 16 May with the Prince and Princess of Wales and the Duke and Duchess of Edinburgh. Among the many courses on the menu were Russian caviar, *d'Agneau en Baron, Ortolans* and *Filets d'Anchois à la Grande Duchesse.*

Two days later he attended a reception given by the Lord Mayor and the Corporation of the City of London at the Guildhall, at which the emperor was presented with a very ornate golden casket with enamelled side panels made by the goldsmith George Benson. During his speech Alexander's voice faltered when he mentioned his 'beloved daughter', words that an onlooker noted were enough to melt even the hardest of hearts. An elaborate menu was produced, with the imperial crown and double-headed eagle at the top and the crest of the City of London at the bottom, a gesture of Anglo-Russian friendship.

He met Disraeli and Gladstone (who noticed the tsar's rather sad countenance), telling the latter that he hoped Anglo-Russian relations would always be good, and attended a military review at Aldershot on 19 May. Alexander travelled down by train accompanied by Grand Duke Alexei, the Prince and Princess of Wales, the Duke and Duchess of Edinburgh and other members of the royal family. The official programme listed rank upon rank of cavalry, artillery and infantry who marched past as the emperor took the salute on horseback. The tsar, a soldier to his fingertips, was very impressed by the 15,000 troops, who had recently returned from the Ashanti war.

A dinner was given at the Foreign Office, with the menu designed in the shape of an oval dish with the Russian imperial arms at its head and those of the Foreign Secretary Lord Derby at the foot. The six-course meal included 'turtle or pea soup, several joints and roast duckling'.[28]

There was a state concert at the Albert Hall organised by the Duke of Edinburgh, who had tried to guess his father-in-law's taste in music. The tsar took Marie's advice to attend only the second half of the performance, which was mostly Russian Orthodox Church polyphony, the lovely choral music which employed multiple harmonies. Although Marie enjoyed music she found that concerts in England always seemed to last for several hours, but told him that it was worth seeing the Albert Hall, a venue she had visited many times.

Alexander went to the Royal Arsenal at Woolwich and had lunch in the Mess, and attended a state ball at Buckingham Palace hosted by the Prince and Princess of Wales. He also found time for a courtesy call on the recently widowed Empress Eugenie of France, now living in exile at Chislehurst, who had been so kind to him after the attempt on his life in Paris in 1867.

Throughout his stay, which was relatively free of anti-Russian demonstrations, Marie hardly left his side. There were no attempts on his life and the crowds, marshalled by the police, were largely friendly.

In contrast to his previous visit, this time Queen Victoria at first refused to prolong Alexander's stay beyond the date originally fixed by her, and she only changed her mind when Disraeli interceded.

Before leaving Windsor she wrote to the tsar, saying how much pleasure it had given her to see him after so many years and how she admired his emancipation of the serfs. 'You have given me personally great pleasure by the assurance of your wish that our two countries will remain not only on friendly but on cordial terms,' she continued. 'You cannot desire this more earnestly that I do both on account of the great national interests involved and for the sake of the daughter whom I have learnt to consider as my own.' In return, the emperor telegraphed to thank her for the kind reception and the proof of her friendship, saying how enchanted he had been with his visit, confident that in her Marie would find a second mother. 'I thank you again from the bottom of my heart for all the proofs of friendship with which you have not ceased to overwhelm me.'[29]

But by the time Alexander left on 21 May, Victoria was already at Balmoral.

* * *

By mid-July it was confirmed that the Duchess of Edinburgh was pregnant. Empress Marie Alexandrovna was anxious to be at her daughter's side for the birth and Prince Alfred travelled to Balmoral to discuss the arrangements with the queen. He hoped to be able to lease Eastwell Park, near Ashford in Kent, as a country residence while keeping Clarence House as their London home.

On 29 August Victoria welcomed the Duke and Duchess of Edinburgh to Balmoral. It was Marie's first trip to Scotland. The queen was at Ballater station when their train drew in. In her journal, the queen recorded that in their honour a triumphal arch had been erected with the English and Russian standards above it, saying 'Welcome to Balmoral' on one sign and on the other the traditional Gaelic salutation '*Cead milleambh Failte*' – 'A hundred thousand welcomes'. The rain having stopped, they set off in open carriages for the castle. 'When we reached the bridge, we went slow and from there to the arch, stood all our people, as well as the Ballater Company of Volunteers and my Highlanders, all their families and the tenants with theirs, as well as the ladies and gentlemen. The piper walked in front, playing, and all the people followed the carriage. In this way we proceeded, through the arch, to Balmoral...'[30]

The turreted white granite castle had been completed in 1855. The tsar's daughter, used to the gold and the glitter of the Russian imperial palaces, was now faced with interiors in which carpets, curtains and even the upholstery were tartan. Prince Albert had even designed his own red, black and grey Balmoral tartan. The woodwork was covered in dark, marmalade-coloured paint, much of the furniture was made from antlers, while the walls were decked with hunting trophies. Even the candelabra, again designed by Albert, were made of stag horn. Few visitors shared the queen's enthusiasm for the seventy-roomed castle and what the court called 'tartanitis'. Lord Rosebery was probably not alone in thinking that the ugliest drawing room in the world was the one at Osborne, until he saw the drawing room at Balmoral with its blue thistle-patterned wallpaper and tartan furnishings.

For the next three weeks Marie was subjected to the usual Balmoral routine, which consisted of walks or drives with the queen in all weather conditions, excursions, visits to tenants and to neighbours. She found it difficult to adjust. Accustomed to the over-heated atmosphere of the Russian palaces, Marie liked a roaring fire in her rooms; the queen, however, could not stand warm temperatures. When she found a fire in her daughter-in-law's room she ordered it to be extinguished and the windows opened. Marie's maid had to try and convince her mistress that the queen forbade fires to be lit in the bedrooms.

The duke and duchess left on 21 September, with little regret on Marie's part. She had at least managed to fool the queen, who recorded in her diary: 'I have learnt to love and esteem her and she is so pleasant, even tempered, and easily pleased with everything, not at all spoilt and very unselfish. Everyone likes her.'[31]

Unfortunately, not everyone did. Nor was Marie's opinion of her adopted country favourable. She hated the fog in London and the rain in Scotland. She disliked England and found it impossible to adapt to the more relaxed etiquette and the differences between the sparkling court of St Petersburg and the gloomy English court. 'Between you and me,' the empress wrote to a relative, 'Marie thinks London hideous, the air there appalling, the English food abominable, the late hours very tiring, the visits to Windsor and Osborne boring beyond belief.' She also disliked the English idea of visiting, when the men went out shooting and the women idled around gossiping the whole day. (It was a dislike she shared with Queen Victoria.) Alfred, a keen sportsman, organised regular shooting parties at Eastwell Park but Marie, with her 'almost masculine intelligence', preferred stimulating conversation, complaining that when the men returned from a day out shooting they were too tired for such intellectual persuits.[32]

Marie summed up her feelings many years later in a letter to King Carol of Romania, the father-in-law of her daughter Missy. '...for years I suffered from a sickness of country of the highest degree, not only a simple longing for my own country, but a longing more than anything else for the environment in which I was born and bred. This homesickness sometimes became a true illness, in spite of my always very calm and reasonable character. The only thing that sustained me on this painful journey was the frequent visits I was able to make to Russia…'[33]

* * *

On 13 October Alfred telegraphed to the queen that 'symptoms had shown' and it would be impossible for him and Marie to move to Eastwell Park before the birth as they had planned. They would have to remain at Buckingham Palace. Rooms now had to be hurriedly arranged there for Empress Marie Alexandrovna who, Victoria said, 'dreaded coming to London'.[34]

The baby was born on 15 October. 'On getting up found many telegrams and the welcome news that Marie had been safely delivered of a son and that both were going on well! All greatly pleased,' Victoria recorded. The Empress of Russia arrived at the palace shortly after breakfast accompanied by Tsarevich Alexander. They had travelled almost non-stop since leaving the Crimea on 11 October, hoping to reach London in time for the birth. Unfortunately, Marie's mother had not reached her bedside in time. 'It was sad the empress coming just too late so that she could not be with her daughter, when she so much needed her. Doctor Farre had been most indefatigable and very clever,' Victoria wrote.[35]

The following day more reassuring news arrived. Mother and son were both well, although poor Marie had suffered a very trying time, during which she had showed much courage. Marie's twenty-first birthday was on 17 October, although she was obliged to spend the day resting in bed, but she recovered quickly from the birth which, the queen noted, showed she had a strong constitution. The baby was also strong but on 4 November news arrived that the empress, whose health was always delicate, had a cold and a fever.

Prince Vladimir Bariatinsky reported: 'A few days after our arrival in England, Her Majesty caught a loud catarrh together with fever and a violent side pain. Her health condition was so concerning that Doctor Hartmann requested the help of Professor Botkin [Sergei Botkin, the empress's own physician] who was asked to travel from Saint Petersburg and we expect his arrival next Saturday.'[36]

The following day the empress consulted Sir William Jenner, who advised her to leave town as soon as the fever had gone but the Russians preferred to wait for Doctor Botkin. He arrived on 15 November and also advised the empress to leave London as soon as possible.

The queen was by now very worried and suggested that the christening should take place privately at Buckingham Palace on 12 November, a suggestion that the empress gladly accepted as no house in the South of France could be prepared for her until the following week.

The queen returned to Windsor on 21 November, where she heard that the empress was slightly better. It had been agreed before the marriage that the children would be raised in the Anglican Church and there was much to do to sort out arrangements for the christening. Getting everything ready would be 'rather a scramble', Victoria lamented.[37]

At Buckingham Palace on 23 November the queen found the Duchess of Edinburgh looking pale. Her baby was lying in the cot given by the queen with the knitted quilt Victoria had made placed over him. The queen met the empress as she walked through the Bow Room. As they walked together towards the empress's room Victoria thought her guest 'most kind and amiable, but looks terribly delicate and coughs.... [She is] very tall and thin, very distinguished looking and *"très-grande dame"*.'[38] She was wearing dark blue satin while Victoria, of course, was in her usual black. The queen and empress spoke in German (the empress's native tongue) but she spoke French to her daughter.

The ceremony took place at one o'clock in the Bow Room, where the Archbishop of Canterbury christened the baby Alfred Alexander William Ernest Albert. Among the guests were the tsarevich (representing the tsar) and his brother Grand Duke Alexei; the Prince and Princess of Wales; Prince Christian and Princess Helena (representing her sister Vicky, the Crown Princess of Germany); Prince Arthur (representing the German Emperor); Princess Beatrice; and Prince Albert's brother Duke Ernest of Saxe-Coburg.

The Princess of Wales was amused to see the queen and the empress together. 'The queen always so polite and submissive and terribly agitated.... And the empress quite calm, but a bit agitated before [the ceremony], but pale, she told her sister the tsarevna.[39]

At lunch in the 1844 Room the queen sat between the empress and the tsarevich. A large christening cake was cut and the health of little Prince Alfred of Edinburgh was drunk. 'Afterwards we went into the Carnarvon Room and the baby, who promises to look like his large uncles, was brought in.' What the queen did not record in her journal (although she did complain about it to Vicky) was her disgust when Marie breastfed her baby in front of everyone. As the Princess of Wales reported, when he threw up over her dress she was completely unfazed. 'She stood up, the empress took the little one, and Marie ran about with her big breast hanging down in front of everyone and wiped the dress clean with a ha ha ha!'[40] Many of the English ladies were scandalised by Marie's behaviour.

Before returning to Windsor later in the afternoon Victoria sat with the empress, who 'looked very sad and was coughing a good deal. She spoke very sensibly of her daughter'[41] and said also that she was sorry not to be able to see Windsor. Before Empress Marie left for Paris the following day, Victoria gave her a copy of the painting of her daughter by Richter.

Alfred and Marie's second child Marie (known as Missy) was born at Eastwell Park in October 1875. The following year Alfred was appointed to the command of HMS *Sultan* and transferred to the Mediterranean Fleet. Marie was delighted to join him in Malta, far from her overpowering mother-in-law who was already complaining to Vicky that Affie 'is quite Russian and I have had to warn him strongly'.[42]

The duke, duchess and their children took up residence in San Antonio Palace, a small 17th-century stone building with beautiful gardens full of sub-tropical plants, where Marie could be the centre of island society for the few months of their stay.

It was at San Antonio Palace on 25 November 1876 that the duchess's second daughter was born. A royal salute announced the event and the Chief Secretary of the Council of Government declared delightedly that from now onwards the island would be able to boast ownership of its own Maltese princess. At her christening on New Year's Day 1877 she was given the names Victoria Melita, the old Roman name for Mdina, Malta's former capital. In the family she was called 'Ducky' but to the Maltese people she was always 'Principessa Melita'.

Marriage had not mellowed Alfred, despite the queen's hopes that Marie would be a steadying influence on him. 'Gruff, obstinate and boorish' he had developed a taste for drink. Marie blamed his 'thoroughly English education'.[43] Many years later Marie poured out her feelings about marrying a second son. 'Having been born at the biggest of courts, in my young years I was pleased to marry into a second-rate position but for an emperor's daughter it has been a sad experience and I felt it only as I was growing older. The world is terribly snobbish on the whole and I was only "someone" because I was rich...'[44]

* * *

In 1876 it was brought to Alexander II's attention that the headstone erected over the grave of Finnish prisoners of war in St John-sub-Castro churchyard in Lewes, Sussex, had become very worn. The men had been captured during the Crimean War and billeted in the town's Naval Prison, where they made wooden toys and carvings, which were sold in the prison courtyard and were highly sought after by the population. Twenty-eight of the soldiers died during their captivity, mainly from tuberculosis, and before they returned home after the war their comrades erected the headstone in their memory. Although the churchwardens restored the worn headstone in 1871 Alexander decided to replace it with a more robust monument. General Alex de Gorloff, *attaché* to the Russian Embassy, and the Reverend Arthur Pearson decided on an obelisk, which was designed by Philip Currey, a local architect, and built by John Strong. It bore the names of the men as well as that of the tsar. On 30 April 1877 General de Gorloff travelled to Lewes by train to inspect the monument and hand over a cheque for approximately £100 on behalf of the tsar.[45]

By this time Russia was again at war.

Princess Juliane of Saxe-Coburg (Grand Duchess Anna Feodorovna of Russia) as a young woman. Stories about her treatment in Russia greatly influenced her niece Queen Victoria. (Private collection)

Juliane (Grand Duchess Anna Feodorovna) in later life. Victoria said Aunt Julie was 'the cause of Russia's unfriendliness towards our family'. (Private collection)

Grand Duke Constantine
Pavlovich of Russia. He treated
his young wife badly.
(Private collection)

The Queen's uncle King
Leopold I of Belgium, whose
anti-Russian feeling influenced
the young Victoria. (The
Eurohistory Photo Archive)

Queen Victoria and Prince Albert at Windsor. To the annoyance of the tsar, Victoria married her Coburg cousin in 1840. (Private collection)

Tsarevich Alexander (later Alexander II) who completely bowled over the young Queen Victoria when he visited England in 1839. (Private collection)

Tsar Nicholas I. Despite an initial good rapport with Victoria, he became England's enemy during the Crimean War. (Private collection)

Above: *The Grand Review in Windsor Park on 6 June 1844* by William Spooner. Nicholas I sits at the front, with Prince Albert on the Arab Grey behind him; also present are King Frederick Augustus of Saxony and the Duke of Wellington. (By kind permission of Innes Israelsohn)

Right: Nicholas I's daughter Grand Duchess Marie Nicolaievna, Duchess of Leuchtenberg, with her daughter Hélène Stroganov. Shunned by the imperial family, Hélène was pleased to be received by Queen Victoria. (Collection of Ian Shapiro)

Queen Olga of Württemberg, daughter of Tsar Nicholas I. Queen Victoria was outraged by Olga's treatment of her daughter Vicky, the Princess Royal, when they met in Berlin. (Private collection)

Grand Duke Constantine Nicolaievich and his wife Grand Duchess Alexandra Josifovna (Sanny). They visited Windsor in 1861 shortly before the death of Prince Albert. (Private collection)

Above left: Constantine's daughter Grand Duchess Olga. The Queen hoped to secure her as a bride for Prince Alfred but in 1867 she married King George I of Greece. (Collection of Ian Shapiro)

Above right: Alexander II and Empress Marie Alexandrovna, the former Princess Marie of Hesse-Darmstadt. They married in 1841 but her health was never good. (Private collection)

Princess Alice's marriage to the Empress's nephew Prince Louis of Hesse-Darmstadt in 1862 forged another link between Queen Victoria's family and Russia. (The Eurohistory Photo Archive)

Alexander II (seated, right) with his sons Alexander (later Alexander III), Alexei and Vladimir. Victoria would meet most of Alexander's sons. (Eurohistory Photo Archive)

Right: The wedding of Prince Alfred and Grand Duchess Marie at the Winter Palace in 1874 was the only marriage of the Queen's children that she did not attend. (Courtesy of John van der Kiste)

Below: Alexander II with his son Alexei, daughter Marie and Prince Alfred, Duke of Edinburgh, at the time of the Tsar's visit to London in 1874. (Private collection)

Menu:

HORS D'ŒUVRES.

Caviare à la Russe.   Thon à l'Anglaise.

POTAGES.

Tortue Claire.   A la Victoria.

POISSONS.

Turbot au Naturel, sauce Homard.
Truite de Rivière à la Spitzbergen.
BLANCHAILLE.

ENTRÉES.

Les petites Couronnes de Foie Gras.
Filets de Volaille à la Princesse.

RELEVÉS.

D'Agneau en Baron.
Des Asperges en Branches.

RÔTS.

Ortolans.   Canetons.
Haricots Verts.   Petits Pois.

ENTREMETS.

Filets d'Anchois à la Grande Duchesse.
Les Olives farcies à l'Ecossais.

Gelée à la Grand Monarque.
Crême à la Diplomatique.
Dames d'Honneur.   Patisserie Française.

GLACES.

A l'Ananas.   Au Citron.

DESSERT.

FREDERICK SAWYER,
Purveyor.

The elaborate menu for Alexander II's visit to the Crystal Palace with the Prince and Princess of Wales and the Duke and Duchess of Edinburgh, 16 May 1874. (Collection of Ian Shapiro)

The children of the Duke and Duchess of Edinburgh were grandchildren of Queen Victoria *and* Alexander II. Left to right: Marie (Missy); Victoria Melita (Ducky); Beatrice, Alexandra and young Alfred. (The Eurohistory Photo Archive)

Queen Victoria's official proclamation as Empress of India in 1877 put her on the same level as the Emperor of Russia. (The Eurohistory Photo Archive)

Queen Victoria and the Hesse family, 1879. The Queen took a maternal interest in her grandchildren after Princess Alice's death. Surrounding the Queen are Princess Victoria, Ernest Louis, Grand Duke Louis IV, Irene, Elisabeth (Ella) and Alix. (Private collection)

Alexander III, Empress Marie Feodorovna, the Princess of Wales and Grand Duchess Olga Alexandrovna at Peterhof, 1894. Alexander was the only Tsar who did not visit Queen Victoria during his reign. (The Eurohistory Photo Archive)

Above: Despite the bad weather Nicholas II and Alexandra Feodorovna drove to Balmoral in an open landau escorted by the Scots Greys and Highlanders carrying flaming torches. (Collection of Ian Shapiro)

Right: Nicholas II and the Duke of Connaught wearing the uniform of the Scots Greys of which the Tsar was colonel-in-chief. Balmoral, 1896. (Collection of Ian Shapiro)

Above: Family group at Balmoral, 1896. Beside the two attendants are Tsar Nicholas II; Princess Patricia of Connaught; Queen Victoria; Princess Helena Victoria (Thora) of Schleswig-Holstein; Tsarina Alexandra Feodorovna; Louise Margaret, Duchess of Connaught; and Princess Margaret of Connaught. (Courtesy of Innes Israelsohn)

Left: Tatiana, Maria and Olga Nicolaievna. Although three of Nicholas and Alexandra's children were born during the Queen's lifetime, Victoria only met Olga. (The Eurohistory Photo Archive)

To the Brink of War

'Oh, if the queen were a man, she would like to go and give those horrid Russians.... such a beating!'
— Queen Victoria to Disraeli, 1878.

After the christening of Alfred and Marie's son relations between England and Russia were, for the time being, better. The previous year Victoria spoke of her confidence that the marriage of her son and the tsar's daughter would serve 'to reaffirm the ties of friendship between two great Christian nations'.[1] Friendly letters were exchanged between the queen and the emperor and in June 1875 he sent her a present of two dark bay horses accompanied by two grooms wearing the Imperial livery. Then the Eastern Question raised its head once more.

In June 1876, prompted by Turkish atrocities against the Serbs living in Bosnia and Herzegovina and in Turkish-ruled Bulgaria, Prince Milan of Serbia declared war on Turkey.

After the proclamation of the German Empire in 1871 many Russians had embraced Pan-Slavism – liberation of the Slav races from foreign rule – with the aim of enlarging the Russian Empire to include the Slavs in European Turkey and the Balkans, forming a Slav Federation. The British now feared that Russia would occupy Constantinople.

The tsar made it clear that Serbia could not expect any Russian support, but he had not anticipated public opinion. Soon the Russian Pan-Slavists, who included the empress and some members of the imperial family, began agitating for war. The tsar, who in the event of Serbia's defeat would have to stop Turkey from re-establishing her hold on the Balkans, was against a conflict and tried to organise a peace conference. During a visit to Darmstadt in June he asked Princess Alice to tell her mother, 'how happy I am, that she wants peace. We can not, we do not want to quarrel with England. It would be mad to think of Constantinople or the Indies.'[2] At his mother's request, Prince Alfred asked the tsar (via Marie) to write a letter to her. Queen Victoria received the missive on 7 July but said that 'beyond expressions of thanks for my help in maintaining peace and anxiety to act together, it contained nothing.'[3]

Yet ever since Ivan the Great married the Byzantine princess Sophie Paleologus in 1472 it had been Russia's dream to march on Constantinople in a holy mission to restore Haga Sophia to the Orthodox faith. The former cathedral had been converted into a mosque in 1453 – but if Russia vanquished the Turks this could be reversed. England wanted Turkey as a barrier against Russian expansion in the Mediterranean, so could not allow a Russian occupation of Constantinople which would threaten the route to India, but there was talk of it becoming an international zone 'with a Christian, European figure at its head, to keep the peace and ensure fair play between the Orthodox Christians and the Muslims'. The candidate most suitable, thought Victoria's cousin King Leopold II of Belgium (who succeeded his father in 1865), would be Prince Alfred, whose wife was a grand duchess of Russia.[4] Alfred was appalled and immediately turned down the idea, saying he would rather end his days in China.

The tsarevich, inspired by the thought of the Dardanelles being open to Russian ships, called for active intervention and encouraged the élite Guards regiments to volunteer. The empress became president of the Red Cross. Nearly 8,000 officers and 5,000 men joined the Serbian army and the tsar was powerless to stop them.

In London, the Russian Ambassador Count Peter Shuvalov, who had replaced de Brunov, found excuses not to meet the queen's ministers; in Russia Ivan Turgenev wrote a poem called 'Croquet at Windsor' in which, while watching a croquet match, Queen Victoria has a vision where the balls become the severed heads of Bulgarian women and children. The bottom of her dress is bloodsoaked and she asks England's rivers to wash it off, but a voice says that the innocent blood can never be cleansed. The poem was only circulated in hand-written copies, as the Russian press feared publishing it in case they offended the queen.

In England Mr Gladstone, Leader of the Opposition, published an inflammatory pamphlet calling for the expulsion of the Turks from Bulgaria. The British royal family were divided, as was the country. Prince Alfred and the Princess of Wales, both of whom had Russian connections, championed Russia. Queen Victoria and the Prince of Wales came down on the side of Turkey, who they and many others felt had been driven by Russia to take such desperate measures. The queen blamed Gladstone for encouraging the Russians and also suspected Russia of having instigated the Balkan rising in the first place.

Disraeli, now ennobled as Lord Beaconsfield, ordered the British fleet to Besika Bay, meanwhile making a secret attempt at a peace accord with Russia of which the queen seems to have been unaware. From Balmoral she asked Prince Alfred to tell the tsar 'how hated' the Russian Ambassador at Constantinople [Count Nicholas Ignatiev] was, while Alexander II asked Alice's husband Prince Louis of Hesse to tell the queen 'how he rejoiced to know that she clung to peace'.[5]

In fact although Russia was not *officially* at war with Turkey, there was a grave danger that the Russian and British fleets could be involved in hostilities. Victoria now found Prince Alfred's marriage awkward in the extreme. 'I cannot say *how* very unfortunate I think it that Affie should have married *a Russian*,' she wrote to the Prince of Wales.[6]

Victoria was making no secret of her anti-Russian feelings. Alfred showed the queen's letters to Marie, who then passed on the contents to her father. The emperor was furious and called Victoria that 'old madwoman queen, that tramp!' while the empress remarked that 'the insulting things the queen says ... were worthy of a fish-wife.'[7] She told her brother that the tsar was very anxious about England's hostile attitude, 'on Marie's account too'. The tsar asked Alfred to write to the queen and ask her to 'tone down her anti-Russian utterances'. Alfred duly obliged on 31 July, writing to his mother from HMS *Sultan* moored off the Greek coast that the emperor, a sensitive man, was 'deeply hurt by all the unpleasant (to say the least of them) and untrue things said of him in the British press'.[8] The queen thought the only solution was to free the various principalities at present under Turkish rule and establish them as an independent neutral state under a prince, thus removing Russia's excuse for constantly reviving the Eastern Question to disturb the peace of Europe.

The Serbians were routed by Turkey in November and blamed Russia for their defeat. On 3 November an armistice was signed between Serbia and Turkey and in December a conference of the Great Powers began in Constantinople. Although Alexander II ordered partial mobilisation, Queen Victoria received a cipher message from her ambassador in Russia, Lord Loftus, saying that the tsar was anxious for good relations with England (whose sympathies remained pro-Turkish although Britain was officially neutral). He had no intention of conquering Constantinople but wanted guarantees from the Turks about the position of the Christian people in the Balkans. In his *Diplomatic Reminiscences* Loftus quoted the tsar as saying 'Is it likely that I should entertain views hostile to my daughter's adopted country...'[9]

* * *

As Russia continued with her policy of expansion overland, Queen Victoria became Empress of India, encouraged by a successful tour of the subcontinent by the Prince of Wales. Victoria was declared Queen-Empress on 1 May 1876; the official proclamation was made at a Durbar in Delhi under the auspices of Lord Lytton on 1 January 1877. 'My thoughts much taken up with the great event at Delhi today, and in India generally, where I am being proclaimed Empress of India.' Victoria recorded in her journal. For many years she had been fascinated by this mysterious country, an interest which increasingly grew throughout the final years of her life. 'I have for the first time today signed myself as V.R. and I.,' she wrote proudly.[10]

Although she was only empress as far as India was concerned, it now put her on the same footing as the Emperor of Russia. This not only gave England more prestige but, it was hoped, would make the Russians hesitate before making any further moves into Asia, where they had come to within 20 miles of the border with India.

* * *

In January the tsar was still telling England that he wanted to maintain peace. A decision on agreed political reforms was handed to Turkey, who raised objections. Turkish alternative proposals were rejected by the Great Powers and the tsar refused to meet an Ambassador from Turkey at Kescheneff. The conference broke up.

By April, when Turkey rejected the London Protocol of the six Great Powers demanding autonomy for Bosnia, Herzgovina and Bulgaria, Alexander's patience was exhausted and he would not hear of mediation. On 12/24 April 1877 he declared war on Turkey.

Alexander II left for the front with the tsarevich, Grand Duke Vladimir and Duke Sergei of Leuchtenberg (the tsar's nephew). Before Alfred's wedding it was stipulated that Marie (and Alfred if necessary) must visit the emperor and empress during their first few years of marriage. The tsar was now annoyed with Queen Victoria, who refused to allow Marie to go and keep her mother company in St Petersburg while he was away.

The queen was outraged at Alexander's declaration of war. 'The Russian circular has been sent down to me and is most offensive, saying that as all attempts to settle the Eastern Question have failed, the emperor was obliged to act alone and to effect by force, for the benefit of Europe, what could not be achieved otherwise,' she recorded, adding, 'This is too bad. On the other hand, it is very provoking that the Turks refused everything.'[11]

On 8 May Count Shuvalov dined with the queen before returning to Russia with dispatches. He told Victoria that the emperor was now fifty-nine and feared he would never reach sixty, as none of his family had done so. The queen remarked that the tsar was now the same age as his father Emperor Nicholas had been when he died and Count Shuvalov pointed out that the circumstances were also similar, with Russia being in the middle of a war.

The following month the Count returned with an important document in which, among its many conditions, Russia gave an undertaking not to touch the Suez Canal (in which Britain had a large share) or Egypt (an autonomous tributary state of the Ottoman Empire), and not to occupy Constantinople permanently.

The Russian army had crossed the Danube and was now heading towards Constantinople. The queen was alarmed and urged Lord Beaconsfield to inform Russia that if their troops reached Constantinople and refused to leave, Britain would declare war. A secret courier was sent to Russia by the queen and Disraeli to inform the tsar of this fact. It made not the slightest difference. In London, Count Shuvalov described it as a plot between a half-mad woman and a political clown.

As the Russians advanced, the queen was anxious that they be shown that they could not have their own way. Britain, she told Vicky, would never 'eat humble pie to these horrible, deceitful, cruel Russians!' Victoria 'was most anxious *not* to fight Russia', but she thought that England 'could not submit to Russia preponderating in the East'.[12]

* * *

As things began to go wrong the early enthusiasm of the Russian people turned sour and they blamed the imperial family. First Grand Duke Michael Nicholaievich was forced to retreat and regroup after his supplies were cut off from the rear by mountain tribesmen; then at the sleepy little town of Plevna the Russian army was bogged down in a siege that lasted four months. The casualty lists were long, especially among the Guards. What should have been an easy victory over a relatively unimportant stronghold turned into a thorn in the emperor's side.

Duke Sergei of Leuchtenberg, once a potential suitor of Queen Victoria's daughter Louise, was killed near Tirnovo, Bulgaria, on 24 August. He was the first member of the family to die in a war. Reports of defeats and heavy Russian losses had reached the queen but it was evident that the superior might of Russia was bound to win in the end.

Although the queen told Vicky she 'rejoiced at every Russian defeat', Britain now had to consider whether 'in the interests of humanity, justice and of the British Empire, this is to be allowed to go on to the bitter end,' or whether to avoid interference by remaining neutral. Writing a memorandum in her customary third person, Victoria set out her views: 'The queen is most decidedly of opinion that this should not be. When it is clear that Russia is not inclined to make even an offer for peace ... the queen thinks we ought to declare that, having taken part in all the negotiations previous to the war, we feel determined to put an end to so horrible a slaughter...' Certain terms should then be proposed she said which, if rejected by Russia, should lead to Britain saying she would support Turkey in defence of Constantinople and in preventing the annihilation of Turkey. The Russians, she told Lord Beaconsfield, were 'more barbarous and cruel than the Turks', using imprisonment and exile to Siberia as their means and ill usage which she considered 'as bad if not worse'.[13]

Finally, on 10 December, Plevna surrendered and the Russian army advanced to the Shipka Pass where they defeated the Turks in a surprise attack. The tide had turned.

The tsar made a triumphal return to St Petersburg on 23 December. The Turkish army had evaporated; the fortress of Kars had surrendered; Sofia, Philippopolis and Adrianople had been taken and at the turn of the year the age-old dream seemed about to be realised – Constantinople seemed within reach of the Russian army.

As the Russians swarmed across the Balkans, Turkey appealed to the Great Powers for help and Queen Victoria telegraphed immediately to the tsar asking him to stop. England, anxious to prevent the growth of Russian influence, could not remain neutral if Constantinople was occupied by Russia. England sent six warships into the Sea of Marmora to 'protect' the British subjects and the country erupted in a wave of patriotism against Russian expansion, with the queen declaring firmly to Lord Beaconsfield that 'England will never stand (not to speak of her Sovereign) to become [sic] subservient to Russia.'[14]

By the end of the year the Turkish army was in a state of collapse and the Russian army was little better. Turkey sued for peace and the tsar offered an armistice, which was signed in January. Then rumours reached England that the Russians were not observing the terms. Their army had crossed the demarcation line, giving a slap in the face to the Great Powers. It seemed that nothing could prevent the Russians from entering Constantinople and the queen was indignant at this 'monstrous treachery'. Once again, anxious about Russian influence in the east, she urged Lord Beaconsfield to be firm and show that Britain 'will not be trampled upon' by what the queen referred to in her journal as 'Russia – our worst enemy in her policy of ambitious aggression and duplicity'.[15]

The reserves were called up and arrangements were hastily made to move troops from India to the Mediterranean. In the Dardanelles, Prince Alfred (who also had an honorary appointment in the Russian navy) waited anxiously to hear whether his ship HMS *Sultan* would have to fire on the vessels of his father-in-law the tsar.

The arrival of the British fleet stopped the tsar in his tracks and on 3 March the hastily concluded Peace of San Stefano was imposed upon the retreating Turks, whereby Russia gained a considerable increase in territory. Romania, Serbia and Montenegro were recognised as independent and a large Bulgarian state was created under Russian protection.

Relations between Britain and Russia were tense. In a letter to her father King Christian IX, Tsarevna Marie Feodorovna reported that the Prince of Wales had hated the Russians ever since his recent visit to India. Bertie, she said, was fanning the flames and had refused to speak to Count Shuvalov at a ball. As for the queen, the tsarevna had always thought her 'somewhat strange', but 'now she is completely mad, the poor woman.' Queen Victoria, Marie Feodorovna further reported, had called Prince Alfred a traitor because he had invited Prince Alexander (Sandro) of Battenberg, who the queen 'probably considers a Russian spy', on board HMS *Sultan* to visit his brother Prince Louis of Battenberg.[16] Afterwards Louis and Sandro went to visit the Russian army headquarters, where the tsar's brother Grand Duke Nicholas showed them some captured armaments and squired them around the Turkish prisoner-of-war camp.

When this news reached Queen Victoria she was, as Marie Feodorovna had said, furious. Although Sandro had appeared in German, rather than Russian, uniform on board the British ship, he was still a foreign officer and could be party to confidential information. The queen considered Alfred unworthy to command a frigate any longer, telling him that now he was married to a Russian wife any possibility of him being appointed an Admiral was out of the question. Eventually she calmed down, having been persuaded that no harm had been done. The empress dismissed Victoria as 'a crazy old hag'. Although the queen was soon mollified the empress's anger was slower to cool and some time later she was still telling Sandro that he had been 'victimised by the old fool'.[17]

* * *

At the hastily concluded Peace of San Stefano in March Russia gained a considerable increase in territory. A large Bulgarian state was created under Russian protection but England objected and started moving troops. Austria, seeing a threat to the balance of power, supported England. Faced with the threat of European war, Alexander backed down and agreed to a congress in Berlin, with Bismarck as 'honest broker' to divide the spoils again.

At the peace negotiations in July 1878 the tsar regained most of the territory lost in 1856 but lost most of the territory recently gained. Russia acquired Ardaka, Kars, Batum and Southern Bessarabia; Greater Bulgaria was reduced to a small Bulgarian state; and Serbia, Montenegro and Romania were confirmed as independent sovereign states free from the Turkish yoke. Greece was given Thessaly and a small piece of Epirus; Bosnia and Herzegovina were occupied by Austria and left to store up future trouble, while Britain (who had taken no part in the fighting) obtained Cyprus. As one disgruntled Russian wrote to the tsar: 'Trust the Englishwoman to land a fish from the troubled waters.'[18]

One consequence of the Peace Conference was that in this redistribution of territory Russia was denied access to the Mediterranean, which she was hoping to reach through Bulgaria; another was that passports were now only required for travel to Russia and Turkey.

Anti-British feeling in Russia was high. Shortly before Count Shuvalov was recalled to St Petersburg in 1879, Lord Salisbury suggested that perhaps he could try and clear the air between their countries. The response was a shake of the head. Shuvalov was unpopular at the tsar's court because he was supposedly friendly towards England.

There was a delay of three months before Prince Lobanov-Rostovsky was formally accredited to Queen Victoria's court, the delay said to be because he was detained in Russia by an infection. The queen was advised to ignore what Disraeli called the tsar's caprices.

* * *

In 1879 the tsar set up his nephew Prince Alexander of Battenberg (Sandro) as Sovereign Prince of Northern Bulgaria, while Southern Bulgaria remained under Turkish rule. When Prince Alexander came to London the queen was friendly, teasing him about being 'too Russian'. To Lord Salisbury, she wrote that she was 'convinced that Prince Alexander has no Russian proclivities and only asks to be left alone. But if he is worried from Constantinople, he will seek refuge in the support of St Petersburg.' Meanwhile, Empress Marie Alexandrovna had heard that the queen's devoted servant John Brown had 'deigned to approve' of the new Bulgarian state, whose rocky landscape he believed had a spiritual affinity with his native Aberdeenshire. Learning that Prince Alexander and his brother Louis had seen the queen, she wrote, 'I should have liked to see the two boys while they were in her toils.'[19]

Turkey, 'the Sick Man of Europe', had been preserved but the royal families of Britain and Russia continued their policy of mutual distrust.

* * *

In November 1878 an outbreak of diphtheria affected the family of Princess Alice in Darmstadt; only her daughter Elisabeth (Ella) escaped the disease. Alice nursed her family devotedly but, tragically, on 16 November, her youngest daughter four-year-old Princess May died. Struggling with her grief and trying to keep news of May's death from the other children, at the beginning of December Alice finally had to tell her son Ernest Louis. As tears ran down his cheeks she clasped him in her arms to console him.

On 7 December, with her children on the road to recovery, Alice went to the station to meet the Duchess of Edinburgh, who had been May's godmother. The duchess was passing through on her way to England and Alice no doubt wanted to send a message to her mother.

That evening Alice also began feeling unwell. The next morning diphtheria was confirmed. In her weakened state Alice was unable to combat it, and on 14 December, the seventeenth anniversary of her father's death, she died.

Queen Victoria was shattered. She now watched over Alice's surviving children, fifteen-year-old Victoria, fourteen-year-old Ella, twelve-year-old Irene, ten-year-old Ernest Louis and six-year-old Alix, receiving regular reports from Darmstadt on their health and progress and inviting them frequently to England with their father.

The influence of the Russian imperial family, who still often visited their Hesse relatives in Jugenheim, worried the queen, who told her eldest Hesse granddaughter Victoria that 'I *hope* you will not get at all Russian...' Princess Alice, she said, had loved the Russian language but had '*such* a horror of Russia and Russians'.[20]

The queen was relieved to hear that Russian ways were indeed not to Princess Victoria's taste – but the same could not be said for other members of the Hesse family.

***

There had been several attempts on Alexander II's life during his reign. In April 1866 a shot was fired as he returned to his carriage after a walk in St Petersburg's Summer Gardens. The shot was deflected by a passer-by who managed to hit the assassin's pistol upwards as the man fired. As previously mentioned, during a visit to Paris for the 1867 *Exposition Universelle* a Polish student fired at the tsar as his carriage travelled along the Bois de Boulogne.

Alexander still refused to take precautions, and in 1879 he dodged another assassin, who fired at him as he walked along St Petersburg's quay. The man was quickly overpowered.

Later that year as the tsar returned from the Crimea, three mines were laid on the railway by revolutionaries – but at the last moment his route was changed. Although the bomb exploded, it only succeeded in blowing up the identical train carrying the imperial luggage. 'A most awful attempt to blow up the Emperor Alexander's train, while going to Moscow, took place yesterday. The luggage train was blown up, but no one injured. No people have been taken,' Victoria recorded on 3 December.[21]

Then early the following year an attempt was made to blow up the tsar inside the Winter Palace itself.

Queen Victoria had already received reports from her Ambassador Lord Dufferin that the empress was very poorly. In fact she was dying and had returned to Russia from Cannes at the tsar's insistence. On 5/17 February 1880 her brother Prince Alexander of Hesse arrived to visit her but his train was delayed and consequently the tsar and his family were late going into dinner at the Winter Palace. As the emperor and his guests walked down the long corridor to the dining room there was a loud explosion. Prince Alexander described how 'the flooring was forced upwards, the gaslights extinguished' and they were plunged into darkness.[22] Dust filled the air and, in the confusion, someone shouted that the huge chandelier had crashed down onto the table. The walls were crumbling in and through a hole in the floor the wrecked guardroom was visible. There were no casualties among the imperial family but ten of the Finnish guards had been killed and another forty-five were injured, many with severe burns.

Lord Dufferin, who had rushed to the Winter Palace on hearing the news, was able to assure the queen that the Duchess of Edinburgh had shown great courage and was uninjured, even though her apartment was close to the scene of the blast.

Victoria was shocked at the audacity of the attack. 'All his windows were broken and shattered to powder. The confusion in the corridors [was] fearful,' she wrote in her journal on 24 February. More worrying still, Prince Alfred was due to leave for Russia to congratulate the tsar on the 25th anniversary of his accession. The queen immediately wrote to Alexander expressing her sympathy at this attack in his own palace, while also congratulating him on the approaching jubilee. He responded with a letter of thanks for her concern.[23]

While Alfred was away the queen worried the whole time until he was safely home. He brought a message from the tsar, who asked him to tell Victoria 'how much he wished there should be a good understanding between the countries; how hurt he was, at the constant suspicions of him; that he never meant to attack India, had never intended to go to Constantinople, or if he had, to remain there...' The queen, who still distrusted Russia, replied that she was 'sure [he] meant all this; but that he was not obeyed'.[24]

The empress died in her sleep during the night of 22 May/3 June. The maid discovered her body the following morning. Later the tsar said she died completely alone, without even a nurse in the room. Alexander was at Tsarskoe Selo with his mistress. At the empress's funeral, which was conducted with almost indecent haste, there was a ferocious storm during the procession to the SS Peter & Paul Cathedral and lightning lit up the sky. Many saw it as a bad omen.

The queen was at Balmoral when news of the empress's death arrived and she asked Lord Torrington to convey her sympathy to Alexander II. 'It will be a dreadful break up for the children and court, for the emperor has unfortunately other discreditable attachments!' she wrote in her journal. 'The sons were quite devoted to their mother.'[25]

The other attachments Victoria referred to were Alexander's mistress and their children.

Several years earlier Alexander II had begun an affair with the strikingly beautiful Princess Catherine Dolgoruky. Although Catherine lived very discreetly, the relationship drove a wedge between the tsar and his family; the more so when, after the attempts on his life, Alexander moved his mistress and their three surviving children into the Winter Palace for greater security. The Duchess of Edinburgh, returning to St Petersburg to see her dying mother (and eager for any excuse to leave England), soon discovered that Catherine and her family were installed just above her mother's rooms. It sparked a furious row between Marie and her father.

Victoria was scandalised when she heard that the tsar's mistress was openly living at the Winter Palace but his brothers Grand Dukes Nicholas and Constantine (whose own private lives were far from blameless) would hear no criticism of him. It was now being said in St Petersburg that the empress died from a broken heart, although she had long since accepted Alexander's extra-marital relationship and even asked to meet the children.

It was customary in the Orthodox Church for a widow or widower to wait a year before remarrying but forty-six days after the empress's death the emperor secretly married Catherine, saying that 'he could never be sure on any day that that day would not be his last on earth.'[26] The marriage was kept a close secret.

On 9 July Grand Duke Alexei lunched with the queen at Windsor. He had come to Britain for the launch of the emperor's new yacht *Livadia* which was being built at a Glasgow shipyard. He brought a malachite paperweight, 'which his mother used always to have on her table', Victoria recorded. She thought he had aged since she has last seen him.[27]

In Russia, the Duchess of Edinburgh had fallen ill. An urgent telegram was sent by the duke to Dr Clayton at Cavendish Square, London, on 20 July. 'Please start at once for Tsarskoe Selo near Petersburg, the duchess has measles. I wish you to attend her. Passports are necessary. Ask Colville.'[28]

In September the queen was still talking of the emperor 'and this dreadful lady, whom he has not yet married!' unaware that the wedding had already taken place. Not until November did she learn from Vicky that they were married on 6/18 July and that the tsar had given the name of Prince/Princess Yourievsky to his wife and children. She thought the marriage was 'a great misfortune'[29] and that he should have kept it secret.

News of the marriage caused a scandal and the imperial family now feared that Alexander would have Catherine crowned empress.

***

On 1/13 March 1881 the tsar was driving back to the Winter Palace along the Catherine Canal when a bomb exploded under the back axle of his carriage, wounding some of the Cossack escort and killing a baker's boy in the crowd. Shaken and unhurt, Alexander alighted from the vehicle but, instead of using another one to hurry back to the palace, he insisted on seeing his potential assassin and enquiring after the casualties.

While the tsar stood talking there was a second explosion as another terrorist, standing unnoticed by the canal railing, calmly hurled his missile at Alexander's feet. When the smoke cleared the badly mangled body of the emperor was seen lying among the other casualties in the bloodstained snow. 'To the palace, to die there', he muttered to his brother Grand Duke Michael.[30]

The shocking news arrived at Windsor in the form of a telegram to Prince Alfred from the tsarevich. 'New attempt. Papa seriously wounded. Come as soon as possible.'[31] Before Alfred and Marie could leave for St Petersburg another telegram arrived announcing the emperor's death. Their eldest daughter Marie (Missy) later recalled the shock of being taken to her mother's room and finding her in unaccustomed floods of tears.

The queen, who had survived several attempts on her own life, was horrified and admitted to feeling 'quite shaken and stunned by this awful news.' She told Vicky that she thought it 'too grievous' that someone who she considered 'the mildest and best sovereign Russia had' should have met death at the hands of such fiends.[32] Her thoughts went out to Marie, who had given birth to another son the previous year who died at once, and now had lost both parents in less than twelve months. Alfred and Marie immediately left for Russia, leaving their children in the care of the queen.

Later, Victoria heard all the terrible details of the tsar's death which she recorded with horror in her journal. 'Nothing but a few rays of flesh and bone, were left! Affie feels sure he must have been dead at once. They carried him up in a carpet and the marks of blood were all over the staircase. The mattress, on the small camp bed, on which, he drew his last breath, was absolutely saturated with blood! Those who suddenly entered, and saw the emperor in this state, with his clothes all torn off, and his military cloak ripped up till above the elbow, were nearly struck down by the horror of the spectacle.'[33]

From St Petersburg Alfred told the queen about the stark contrast between the Winter Palace Church where the emperor was lying-in-state surrounded by sobbing people, and the joyous day he and Marie were married there. Later, in the emperor's rooms, the valets showed him the meagre remains of the uniform Alexander had worn on that fateful day.

To Victoria's surprise, the Prince of Wales wanted to attend the funeral and the government were keen for him to go, as they hoped the visit would help to bring about a closer understanding between the countries. Bertie thought it would be the right thing to do and Alexandra also wanted to give moral support to her sister, now the Empress Marie Feodorovna. The queen was reluctant, warning Lord Dufferin that she would hold him responsible if anything befell them, but she reluctantly gave her consent. 'Alix is very low about her sister Minny; it seems the one thing she dreaded, was to become empress. Alix remained talking with me for a little while. They are to start tomorrow night.'[34]

The final funeral service took place two weeks after the tsar's death. The queen, who survived eight assassination attempts during her reign, sent a wreath of bay leaves and white immortelles with a white satin ribbon on which was an inscription in gold letters. She was outraged at the attack on a fellow monarch, calling for a ban on the sale of dynamite and an extradition treaty to include the assassins of 'poor maligned sovereigns ... placed on a pinnacle to be aimed at.'[35]

* * *

The Times was quite charitable to Alexander II, writing on 4 March that 'He might not have had the genius or energy of Peter the Great or the intelligence and far-sighted political wisdom of Catherine II, but he perhaps did as much as either of those sovereigns towards raising his country to the level of west-European civilisation.'

Immediately after the funeral the new tsar and tsarina moved back to their home, the Anichkov Palace where, in a gesture of support from the queen, the Prince of Wales invested the new tsar with the Order of the Garter at a private ceremony attended by British Embassy officials.

'We all marched into the ... Throne Room,' wrote Lord Frederick Hamilton, 'the Prince of Wales leading the way, with five members of his staff carrying the insignia on ... narrow velvet cushions. We made, I thought, a very dignified and effective entrance. As we entered ... a perfectly audible feminine voice called out in English "Oh! My Dear! Do look at them. They look exactly like a row of wet-nurses carrying babies!" ... The empress and Princess of Wales looked at one another for a moment and then exploded into laughter'. By this time the tsar was trying hard to control himself as well. 'Never, I imagine ... has the ... Garter been conferred amid such general hilarity,' Lord Frederick concluded.[36] Queen Victoria was, of course, not told.

Addressing the queen in French as his 'dear sister', the new tsar thanked Victoria for investing him with the Garter and for allowing the Prince and Princess of Wales to travel to Russia, which he said had been a great consolation to him and to his wife. He ended the letter by saying how happy his father would have been by the renewal of friendly relations between their countries.[37]

First-hand accounts of events in Russia reached Queen Victoria when Sir John Cowell, the Master of the Household, arrived from St Petersburg. He told her that the state of affairs there was dreadful, with suspicion and mistrust everywhere. The emperor was almost a prisoner in his palace and was not allowed to go to the final evening service (the one held shortly before his father's funeral) at the SS Peter and Paul Cathedral. He was not safe anywhere because nobody could be certain where mines might be laid or if there were terrorists among the servants. On the day of the funeral there was great alarm, as the police feared someone would get into the cathedral and throw a bomb. Sir John brought photographs for the queen and also reported that he and the Duke of Edinburgh had arranged for her to receive the head and shoulders portraits of the late emperor and empress which she had requested.

Sir John was even more outspoken about Russia in a private letter, in which he wrote of 'the first phase of the terrible drama what must sooner or later be enacted there'. Continuing his missive (written from Windsor Castle to 'my dear Granny' in Bedale, Yorkshire) he made an eerie prophesy: 'That the terror now reigning will be followed by two revolutions is clear to me. The first in the class which is more or less educated or imbued with Western ideas of progress and liberty, and the 2nd that in which these classes (numbering perhaps about twenty millions) will find themselves faced by sixty millions of ruined peasantry, who at the present do not know or care anything about anything outside their own hills and fields. They are just as they were in the 13th century, but instead of being serfs with no burdens to bear, they are now by the "humane" Alexander II, [who freed the serfs in 1861] freed to being peasants, with a crushing taxation that will render life intolerable, and emancipation from the oppression the one object of their existence... The emperor [Alexander III] is I believe, very well intentioned but he is a cipher, a prisoner, and I fear doomed to die. I do not see how he can live in Petersburg or indeed in Moscow, or *any* other town in his crumbling empire. A camp is his only refuge, but even in his own tent he cannot feel safe. However he is a brave man, and I hope will learn not to care for all this.'[38] Sir John died in 1894 before much of the dramatic content of his letter could come true.

The Princess of Wales remained in Russia supporting her sister until 26 March/7 April. When she returned home, a letter from Queen Victoria was waiting to greet her. Addressing her as

'Darling Alix,' the queen said: 'I purposely did not write to you, knowing how much you would be occupied with your poor dear sister, whose position is indeed most terrible! Her poor husband a prisoner in his own palace and her children guarded day and night. I feel so very much for them both and for you as I know what you must all suffer. Thank God you are all safe and far from the Lion's Den, though you must have felt the parting very much...'[39]

That autumn, the queen invited the Duke and Duchess of Edinburgh to Balmoral. The invitation was at Alfred's request and as the only parent Marie now had left, Victoria felt she could not refuse.

With the death of Alexander II the queen had a new emperor to deal with. She was soon to find that Alexander III was very different from his father.

Orthodoxy, Autocracy and Nationality

'Russia I could not wish for any of you.'
– Queen Victoria.

On 1 April 1881 Queen Victoria received a letter from Lord Dufferin in St Petersburg, who 'hoped the present emperor would be able to make improvements and changes' but, he added, the new monarch would have very great difficulties. Dufferin called him 'honest, moral, and very domestic, not caring much for military affairs, or for sport'.[1] This was a very accurate assessment of the new tsar's character.

Alexander III was the first Russian monarch since the seventeenth-century to have a beard and, at 6 feet 3 inches, was the tallest Romanov since Peter the Great. Yet with this height went a heavy build and a complete lack of grace – he shambled along like a great Russian bear. His physical strength was amazing. He could straighten horseshoes with his bare hands, bend iron bars and smash through doors with his massive shoulders. His health was excellent and his appetite enormous.

Yet behind his somewhat gruff exterior and rather formidable appearance there was a placid, even-tempered, generous man who was devoted to his family, loved animals and children and was almost transparently honest. At a ball he responded to the formal thank you of a German princess by saying, 'Why can't you be honest? It was just a duty neither of us could have relished. I have ruined your slippers and you have made me nearly sick with the scent you use.'[2]

Not by any means clever, his slow, ponderous brain was nevertheless equipped with sound common sense and a rigid code of morality. Unlike many other tsars, he never had a mistress. Although he spoke French, English and German he remained a bad linguist and his spelling, even in Russian, was poor. He had a deep horror of war which stayed with him all his life and he never possessed the love of military manoeuvres and parades so evident in the other Romanov men.

Count Sergei Witte, the tsar's Minister of Finance from 1893, recorded his impressions of the monarch: 'In many respects Emperor Alexander III did not look like an emperor. A tall but flabby man, not handsome, an unaffected, slovenly, bearlike man, one could imagine him a Russian peasant from the central provinces by seeing him in one's mind's eye in a sheepskin coat and bast [peasant] shoes. In many respects he was not majestic. But his fine heart, his strong character, his calmness, his sense of fairness were all reflected in his face, giving him the look of true majesty...'[3]

Majesty he may have had but he was an autocrat to his fingertips. Alexander III was opposed to any parliamentary government, which he called 'the great lie of our time'. Juries, he said, should be abolished 'in order to restore the significance of the court in Russia'; and one of his proclamations contained the words 'The voice of God orders us to stand boldly by the task of governing.'[4]

It was well known that the tsar (some say influenced by his Danish wife and her family) was anti-German, tending towards Pan-Slavism and Russian nationalism. His former tutor Constantine Pobedonostsev now spent half of every year at Gatchina in the dual role of adviser to the emperor and tutor to the new tsarevich, Nicholas. A reactionary to his fingertips, Pobedonostsev had for many years encouraged Alexander III to believe that his father's reforms were a threat to the autocracy, a view in which he needed very little prompting anyway. Under Pobedonostsev's influence one of Alexander's first acts was to tear up his father's unsigned manifesto for reform of the Council of State, which would have paved the way for full franchise in the future. 'Thank God this over-hasty, criminal proposal was never realised and the whole crazy project has been rejected,' he scribbled. The reactionary new tsar's watchwords were Orthodoxy, Autocracy and Nationality.

* * *

Prince Semyon Vorontzov arrived at Windsor on 8 April to officially announce Alexander II's death and the accession of Alexander III. Semyon, an undistinguished man, owned the estate of Alupka in the Crimea; his aunt Catherine was the wife of the 11th Earl of Pembroke and very well known to Victoria. From Prince Vorontzov the queen learnt that there was apathy in Russia regarding Alexander II's murder. His second marriage 'had done him great harm in the eyes of the public and lessened the sympathy felt for him' over the terrible circumstances of his death.[5]

One of the assassins was a woman, Sophia Perovskaya, and there was some debate as to whether she should be executed, as it was illegal to hang a woman in Russia. It was feared it would cause trouble and perhaps encourage the Nihilists, as the terrorists were known, to target the empress and the grand duchesses in retaliation. The court officials were anxious that the new emperor leave St Petersburg before the trials of the assassins were over and in the meantime a trench was being dug round the Anichkov Palace, where the imperial family were currently living, to protect them.

Alexander III refused all pleas for clemency and on 3/15 April the terrorists, including Sophia Perovskaya, were publicly hanged. The other woman Jessica Helfmann was reprieved because she was pregnant. Queen Victoria told Vicky that she thought the executions, although absolutely necessary, should have been carried out in private.

The accounts from St Petersburg continued to be dreadful. The queen had some sympathy for 'poor Sasha', who soon after the funeral moved his family to Gatchina, an isolated palace 30 miles from St Petersburg which was easier to guard. Alexander II's Minister of the Interior General Count Michael Loris-Melikoff resigned (which Victoria considered 'a great misfortune') and now popular opinion was so against Grand Duke Constantine Nicolaievich that there were fears for his safety. As a stunned Queen Victoria recorded, it appeared that there was positive proof of Constantine 'being implicated and connected with the Nihilists, even with plans for the assassination of the present emperor, which is too dreadful!' The object was apparently 'to put himself on the throne, and then to destroy the Nihilists!'[6] A revolution was greatly feared.

In the wake of Alexander II's assassination terrorists were hunted down and imprisoned; newspapers, books and magazines were heavily censored; university studies curtailed, student organisations suppressed and civil liberties suspended at will. Those who did not share the tsar's belief in autocracy began the long trek to Siberia.

The tsar was his own Prime Minister. There was no parliament and no elections. The State Council was purely an advisory body and ministers reported directly to him. He was not obliged to take their advice and could dismiss any of them at his pleasure. They were not permitted to resign. 'Shut up!' he bellowed at one unfortunate minister, shaking him by the collar. 'When I choose to kick you out you will hear of it in no uncertain terms!'[7] He worked through mountains of state papers, scrawling blunt comments, not always polite, in the margins. The country became a police state and corruption was rife. The Okhrana (the tsar's secret police) intercepted letters, infiltrated organisations and collected evidence against those suspected of subversion. Cut off from any liberal thought, Alexander became increasingly unenlightened, suspicious, distrustful and obstinate.

The emperor would not stand for any insubordination in the family, telegraphing his brother Sergei to 'stop playing the tsar!' when he overstepped the mark.[8] He dismissed Grand Duke Constantine Nicolaievich as Chairman of the Council of Ministers, a post he had held for sixteen years, and replaced him with Grand Duke Michael Nicolaievich, another uncle. Constantine's post as Grand Admiral of the Russian Navy was given to the tsar's handsome brother Alexei who was, his niece Missy recalled, 'a Viking type ... fair hair, blue eyes, enormous, a superb specimen of humanity', of whom it was famously said he liked 'fast women and slow ships'.[9] Society was diverted for years by the grand duke's passion for Zina, the beautiful wife of the Duke of Leuchtenberg, with whom he conducted an open affair under the roof of her husband. Grand Duke Alexander Mikhailovich called them the '*ménage royal à trois*'.[10]

The tsar appointed Count Arthur von Mohrenheim as his new Ambassador to London although, unlike his father, Alexander III had little respect for Queen Victoria. Having heard the experiences of his sister the Duchess of Edinburgh and his sister-in-law the Princess of Wales, he dismissed the queen as 'a pampered, selfish, sentimental old woman'.[11]

* * *

In the autumn of 1882 King George I and Queen Olga of Greece arrived at Balmoral, where the King's sister the Princess of Wales joined them for dinner. The Greek queen was Alexander III's cousin, the former Grand Duchess Olga Constantinovna of Russia whose remarks had so amused Victoria when as a child she visited Windsor with her parents in 1861. Queen Victoria thought the Greek queen 'pleasant and kind, and so handsome. She has the fine regular profile of the Emperor Nicholas.' To Vicky she wrote that Olga had 'none of the *brusqerie* [brusque nature] of the rest of the Russian family, even including our dear, excellent Marie.'[12]

Vicky continued to warn her mother that Russia's age old dream of possessing Constantinople had not been abandoned, even though Alexander III was not pursuing it at the moment. His army and navy were 'no match for Britain in the Baltic' and smaller than the sultan's fleet in the Black Sea.[13] The Russians also intended to keep a firm hold on Bulgaria, and there was still a danger to India even though the tsar would not invade.

In September 1883 more disturbing reports came from Russia. Sir Edward Thornton arrived at Balmoral and gave terrible accounts of the state of things, the corruption 'from the highest to the lowest', the immorality of society and the unreliability of everyone. He described Alexander III 'as a very good man, but not clever or energetic, and certainly not likely to do anything in the way of reform'. He stressed again that the emperor, having inherited an autocracy from his father, intended to govern as an autocrat. 'The climate, the state of St. Petersburg – the water in the cellars, where the poor *Mujiks* [peasants] sleep, and the bad drainage' were described by Sir Edward as dreadful, the queen noted.[14]

Given all these disturbing reports, it comes as no surprise to learn that Queen Victoria was appalled when she heard that her eighteen-year-old granddaughter Princess Elisabeth of Hesse (Ella) was considering a tentative marriage proposal from the tsar's brother Grand Duke Sergei Alexandrovich.

* * *

Ella, born on 1 November 1864, was the second daughter of the late Princess Alice and her husband Louis, who had succeeded as Grand Duke Louis IV of Hesse-Darmstadt in 1877. Kind, gentle and trusting, Ella was considered to be the most beautiful princess in Europe. At the age of sixteen Vicky's eldest son William, the future Kaiser, had fallen in love with her, calling Ella 'the most beautiful girl I ever saw', even though at the time she was only eleven. He wrote to his mother, 'if God grants that I may live till then I shall make her my bride if you allow it.'[15] Although Vicky already had another princess in mind for her son it made no difference. Throughout his years at Bonn University, when he regularly spent

Sundays with the Hesse family at Darmstadt, William still dreamt of making Ella his wife.

Then in 1878 he suddenly forgot about Ella and declared he loved Princess Augusta Victoria of Schleswig-Holstein-Sonderburg-Augustenburg – the princess his mother always hoped he would marry. The couple tied the knot in 1881.

Although William's father Crown Prince Frederick felt uncomfortable about his son's sudden change of heart it was known that Vicky was opposed to him marrying Ella. It is possible that Vicky, whose brother Leopold suffered from haemophilia and whose sister Alice had been a carrier, realised the risks to the Hohenzollern linc if Ella married William and passed on the disease to a future German Emperor.

Ella had shown no interest in William but she had known her Romanov cousins for as long as she could remember. Empress Marie Alexandrovna had often escaped to the peace of her childhood home in Darmstadt with Sergei and Paul. Here, Princess Alice's children got to know their Russian relatives and Sergei formed an attachment to Alice's family. By the time Ella was fifteen in 1879 she had begun to look more favourably on Sergei.

Sergei, seven years Ella's senior, has remained something of an enigma. Described as 'tall, fair, with light green eyes, and strikingly handsome in a saturnine way', with a neat beard, he was extremely pious, cultured and artistic.[16] Religion played a large part in his education and he visited both Rome and Jerusalem. Yet many people described him as hard and he often appeared proud and cold on the outside. He had grown up in the atmosphere of extreme tension which surrounded the Russian court after so many assassination attempts on his father's life and it is perhaps notable that Queen Victoria, always a severe critic of the Russian grand dukes' morals, never included Sergei in her criticisms.

In November 1882 Sergei and his brother Paul paid a two-day visit to Darmstadt. They had recently returned from Italy, which Ella and her sisters had also visited that year. As she told Queen Victoria, they and their Russian cousins had visited the same Italian towns and they found a mutual point of conversation in their experiences. Ella certainly did not share her elder sister's view that the two Romanovs talked 'very little and don't know what to say'.[17] Sergei had learned Italian and was fond of the country's art and culture, but it is clear that during this visit the couple spoke of other things and the idea of a marriage was being seriously considered.

The thought of another Hesse-Russian union was not new. Alexander II had once thought that Ella should marry his fourth son, Alexei, while Sergei should marry Ella's elder sister Victoria of whom he had once seemed fond. For the moment, though, nothing was formally arranged and Sergei wrote to one of his Romanov cousins: 'Everybody here has already married me off. Please don't believe it.'[18]

Queen Victoria now became alarmed and fired off warnings to Ella's sister Victoria about Russian marriages. Despite the fact that she already had a Russian daughter-in-law (who was, of course, Sergei's sister) the queen made her feelings plain. 'Russia I could not wish for any of you,' she wrote adamantly. Princess Alice had always been against such a marriage for her daughters, she continued, determined to stress their mother's horror of Russia and the Russians, whether real or imaginary.[19]

Both the queen and Ella's father hoped that she would marry Prince Frederick, the son of the Grand Duke of Baden but in March 1883 Ella turned him down. The queen was deeply distressed. 'Oh dear!' she wrote. It was so 'very unfortunate' that Ella had refused Fritz of Baden, 'so good and steady, with such a safe, happy position, and *for a Russian*'.[20] She feared that like the Hesse children's aunt Empress Marie Alexandrovna, Ella's health would never stand the Russian climate. 'A Russian marriage would be very painful to me,' she told Vicky the following week.[21]

The queen seemed to be obsessed by the fear that her Hesse granddaughters would marry Russians. Did she see the spectre of her Aunt Julie and the terrible time she experienced with Grand Duke Constantine? Russia was an autocracy, where the threat of terrorism could not be ignored. The previous tsar had been assassinated after several unsuccessful attempts on his life. Even Ella had seen the danger when her father attended Alexander II's funeral, writing to Queen Victoria that she would be glad to have him safely home from 'dreadful Petersburg'.[22]

In 1883 the queen, still reeling from shock after the death of her devoted Highlander John Brown, invited Ella to stay during the summer. After being assured by Princess Victoria of Hesse back in January that 'I do not think she [Ella] cares for one of the Russian cousins,'[23] it was clear that the idea of a Russian marriage was now very much on the cards. Ella had accepted Sergei's proposal and the queen was faced with a *fait accompli*. Now she had to persuade Ella to change her mind.

Ella arrived in June and remained until mid-August, travelling with the queen from Windsor to Balmoral and then to Osborne. While they had breakfast under the trees at Frogmore, or during their daily drives around Balmoral, Queen Victoria took every opportunity to impress her strong views on Ella. Determined to destroy any chance of this marriage, the queen told her to reflect very carefully and consider the Russian climate and the unstable state of the country, which was no place for a young princess. Ella maintained she was not in any hurry to marry and that some provision ought to be made for her to live outside of Russia.

The queen's words nevertheless had the desired effect. Shortly after her return to Germany, Ella broke her engagement. The queen was delighted, saying jubilantly that '*Anything* is better than making an unhappy marriage.'[24] Yet Ella's father Grand Duke Louis was talking of the marriage as if it was an established fact.

One person who was furious at the queen's interference was the Duchess of Edinburgh. She was already annoyed because Victoria had commissioned a painting of Alfred's family and Marie disliked what she described as her 'pug-like face' being painted. Now she claimed that Ella had insulted her brother. Ella, having been told that the duchess was coming to Darmstadt with Sergei, 'boldly declared she would have nothing to do with him.' Marie did not blame Ella, but she knew where the fault lay. 'I have no words strong enough to blame the queen,' she wrote to a friend. 'I knew from the very first that she set her heart against it saying that she had only heard his praise, but he had the greatest of all misfortunes, he was Russian and she had enough of *one Russian* in the family (meaning me of course).'[25] This was probably true because when the search was on for a bride for Prince Arthur, the queen stated quite clearly that, 'God knows, we *don't* want a *second Russian* Element' in the family.[26] He married Princess Louise Margaret of Prussia in 1879.

The queen protested that there was never any serious question of Ella marrying Sergei and that she had merely asked Ella to think carefully about it and had not tried to set her against him. 'The Russian family think it such an honour to marry any one of them – that a refusal appears to them so impossible as to be *insulting*,' she told Princess Victoria.[27] She now saw new hope in a possible match with Prince Charles of Sweden, who Ella was said to be considering.

This idea came to nothing because in September Grand Duke Sergei arrived at the Hesse country property of Wolfsgarten to see Ella. The queen was once more alarmed, firing off missive after missive to Princess Victoria about the state of the country, Russian society and how Princess Alice (although she had personally liked Sergei) dreaded a Russian marriage for any of her daughters. The queen could not see anything worse than Ella going to live in Russia and feared her granddaughter would be taken in. '...*in fact*, it will be *her ruin*,' the queen warned the following week, adding that the Russians would do anything to get hold of her.[28]

Her fears were justified. In the presence of the tall, handsome grand duke, Ella began to waver and the couple found that they had a genuine respect and affection for each other. Grand Duke Constantine Constantinovich said that his cousin Sergei was 'enraptured by her, full of her praises'.[29]

Another missive was fired off from Balmoral to poor Princess Victoria in Darmstadt, warning again about the loose morals of Russian society, who from the grand dukes downwards were totally unprincipled, which might lead to situations which would cause 'painful consequences' for lovely, innocent Ella.[30] Despite the princess's insistence that Ella would insist on spending a good deal of every year outside Russia, the queen was adamant that her granddaughter would not be able to stay with her in England. It would be impossible, she maintained, for a grand duke of Russia to stay with her frequently or for long periods. Ella must be made to consider all the difficulties before committing herself to a union she might later regret. Russians, the queen said, are 'so unscrupulous' and '*totally* antagonistic' to England.[31] Her warnings about Russia continued.

On 13 October Ella told her grandmother that she had decided to accept Sergei's proposal. 'Those few days I saw him last month have convinced me that I shall be happy with him,' she wrote. 'We have the same tastes for things and although he may have opinions you do not like, do you not think, dear Grandmama that I might do him good? ... I think I know what I am doing, and if I am unhappy, which I am sure I will never be, it will be all my doing.'[32]

Queen Victoria put the letter aside, feeling totally unable to answer it for a while. She accused Ella of being 'changeable'. Having told her grandmother how much she hated the Russians and refused Sergei's proposal three weeks earlier, 'now she takes him and forgets *all!*' the queen wrote in exasperation.[33]

Worse still Ella would be lost to her, 'as a Russian grand duke is a person belonging to Russia, and Russia is *our real enemy*'. She hoped that her son-in-law Grand Duke Louis would stipulate that an exception to the normal rule should be made for Ella to enable her to live part of the year outside of Russia.[34] Also, Ella should not be married before her twentieth birthday. Yet on 25 October the queen recorded in her journal that, according to Prince Louis of Battenberg, who had recently become engaged to Ella's elder sister Victoria, a marriage between Ella and Sergei had not been arranged.

Ella's engagement was announced privately to the family on 6 November. Although no formal announcement was made, news of the betrothal did leak. 'It is a real sorrow to me and the less I say about it the better,' was the queen's comment to Vicky. Despite Vicky's reassurance that 'Sergei will captivate you when you know him I am sure',[35] the queen was not convinced. The grand duke's new palace, which he had bought that spring, was just across the Fontanka Canal from the Anichkov Palace where the tsar still lived when he was in St Petersburg, having refused to move into the Winter Palace. Ella shrugged off her grandmother's warnings about terrorism, but the queen shuddered at the danger to which her granddaughter would be exposed.

The queen's family tried to mollify her. Even as late as December, Princess Victoria was assuring her grandmother that 'nothing is settled decidedly,'[36] even though the queen had written in November that the engagement was now a fact.

Grand Duke Louis had no hesitation in consenting to his daughter's wedding, writing to Alexander III that 'he had known Sergei since he was a child. I see his nice, pleasant manners and I am sure that he will make my daughter happy.'[37]

The formal announcement was made on 26 February 1884. 'Sergei *is* nice and seems so devoted to her,' the queen wrote resignedly to Princess Victoria.[38] Sergei arrived at the Neues Palais in Darmstadt with a staggering amount of jewels for his bride. These included an aquamarine and diamond parure, a traditional Russian *kakoshnik* headdress studded with massive emeralds; ropes of pearls; the bracelet Alexander II had given his bride Marie upon their engagement and other jewels studded with rubies, diamonds and emeralds. Sergei insisted that she try them all on at once, until she was decorated and sparkling like a Christmas tree.

Now faced with the union she dreaded, the queen sent 'a courteous letter' to Sergei while he was at Darmstadt. Ella was delighted by this gesture and quickly thanked her grandmother, saying Sergei 'was very much pleased by your kind message.'[39]

Enormous sums of money were settled on Ella in the marriage contract. The tsar placed 100,000 roubles on deposit for her; Sergei promised 50,000 roubles on which she could draw interest at 5 per cent; and for her personal expenses she could draw on an annuity of 40,000 roubles. The marriage contract also stipulated that she could continue practicing her Lutheran religion, as by this time only the wife of the sovereign and the tsarevich were required to convert to Orthodoxy.

The Romanovs' considerable wealth was despised by the queen and she could only hope that Ella would not be spoilt by it all.

***

The queen's concern seems to have been about more than just the fact that Ella was going to live in Russia. Towards the beginning of 1884 disturbing stories about Sergei began to reach her. Rumours were current in St Petersburg that the grand duke was homosexual and these accusations were made, and believed, by all classes of Russian society. The queen was worried. If these allegations proved to be correct, marriage to such a man for a young innocent girl like Ella would be barely tolerable. Greatly concerned for Ella's happiness, Queen Victoria wrote privately to the British Ambassador Sir Edward Thornton telling him her concerns and asking him to make some enquiries.

Sir Edward approached John F. Baddeley, the Russian correspondent of *The Standard* newspaper. Baddeley pointed out that there was 'no more scandal-loving society in the world than that in which we live and moved' in Russia and said that he 'would not take the responsibility of adding one straw's weight to the adverse side of the balance in Her Majesty's mind.'[40]

There was, and remains, no proof of the allegations of homosexuality against Sergei, which in those days was a criminal offence in England. Ella's most recent biographer Christopher Warwick tried to trace Sir Edward Thornton's report to Queen Victoria, but was informed by the Royal Archives that they could find 'no reference at all to any potential problem regarding Ella's marrying the Grand Duke Sergei, or any investigation requested by Queen Victoria'. They added, 'of course, this lack of evidence here does not mean the story is untrue, as it may be that papers have not survived.'[41] As Warwick points out, no witnesses to Sergei's sexuality have ever come forward and his private papers (including his letters to Ella) have not survived.

Charlotte Zeepvat points out that the most serious allegations surfaced after Sergei's marriage and seem to have emanated from Berlin, where the Kaiser 'hated Sergei for having the prize he had missed'.[42] According to John Röhl, William spread the story that Sergei 'was buggering his handsome young domestic chaplain'.[43] Another severe critic was Sergei's cousin Grand Duke Alexander Michaelovich, who had also been one of Ella's admirers. 'It was Ella's very beauty that drove her many admirers to find fault with Sergei,' Ms Zeepvat wrote.[44]

* * *

On 17 April 1884 Queen Victoria arrived in Darmstadt for the wedding of Ella's sister Victoria and Prince Louis of Battenberg. The wedding caused raised eyebrows in St Petersburg, Vienna and Berlin because Louis and his siblings were the children of Prince Alexander of Hesse (brother of Empress Marie Alexandrovna) who had eloped with a mere Polish countess, Julie von Hauke. The marriage was morganatic and Julie was given the title countess, and later princess, of Battenberg. The couple's children were Serene Highness rather than Royal Highness and also took the Battenberg name. Morganatic blood was not something that worried Queen Victoria and she was happy to welcome Louis into her family.

Earlier, Louis and Victoria's wedding had been postponed due to the death in Cannes on 28 March of Prince Leopold, Duke of Albany, the queen's haemophiliac youngest son. Telegrams of condolence flooded into Windsor, including one from Sergei's brother Grand Duke Alexei, for which the queen thanked him 'most sincerely for the deep sympathy you have shown us in our cruel misfortune'.[45]

This wedding was the queen's first chance to meet Sergei, despite her earlier protests that seeing him there 'would spoil everything for me'.[46] Ella had already sent her a photograph, hoping that her grandmother would be favourably impressed when she saw him in person. The queen heard from Vicky that the grand duke spoke 'nicely' of her and, she told her daughter, 'I think we shall get on very well, though he is a Russian and carries off my grandchild.' The meeting took place on 17 April after breakfast. In her journal the queen described him as 'tall and gentlemanlike, but very thin, pale, and delicate looking', which passed for some sort of approval.[47]

Three days later news arrived that the Duchess of Edinburgh had given birth to another daughter, who was to be called Beatrice.

She asked Queen Victoria's daughter Princess Beatrice to be godmother, which pleased the queen enormously.

The following day the queen spoke to Sergei about her concerns for Ella and before he returned to Russia she gave him the gift of some shirt studs.

On 30 April, Victoria and Louis were married. 'Ella was in great beauty,' the queen recorded in her journal that evening, 'wearing some of Sergei's beautiful presents, including an enormous cabochon sapphire drop, set in diamonds.'[48]

Unbeknown to the queen, her granddaughter's wedding was not the only marriage ceremony taking place. Victoria's father Grand Duke Louis, lonely since the death of Princess Alice, wanted to marry thirty-year-old Alexandrine de Kolemine, the divorced wife of a former Russian *chargé d'affaires* who had been his mistress for some time. Everyone else seemed to know what was afoot except the queen. Later that day in a private ceremony, Grand Duke Louis and Alexandrine were married. The queen was stunned and appalled when she heard the news. Alexandrine was not only divorced but she was Russian. In her customary style when upset, the queen immediately wrote to her granddaughter Princess Victoria saying that it would be a terrible mistake, the rest of the family would be shocked and immense harm would be done to the Hesse family in Germany. The queen was correct in her assessment and the rest of the family let her handle the matter. She summoned the Prince of Wales and ordered him to tell the grand duke that the morganatic marriage would be annulled. Furthermore, she instructed the British Ambassador to ensure that the German authorities speeded up the process of annulment. Alexandrine left Darmstadt, was living in Paris in the 1930s and is thought to have died in 1941. That, at least, was the end of one Russian marriage in the family.

* * *

In May the tsar's twenty-three-year-old youngest brother Grand Duke Paul visited Windsor before returning to St Petersburg with his sister Marie. Victoria had not met him before and pronounced him 'very pleasing, still taller than Sergei, and also very thin'. She decided that in fact she preferred him to Sergei.[49]

Ella and her father were also staying at the castle. This would be the queen's last meeting with her granddaughter before she went to Russia for her marriage. Ella had been delighted to visit 'dear England' again, knowing her wedding would probably be in the middle of June. 'I hope that when you see me again you won't find any change in my character for the worse,' she wrote to the queen.[50]

The time of parting came all too soon, as Louis and Ella had to leave soon after lunch. All three were very upset when they parted, but for the queen it was doubly poignant. 'I shall not see dear Ella again, for God knows when, and certainly never again in the happy way as has been the case now for five years! May God bless and protect her in that far off and unsafe country to which she is going!'[51]

***

On 8 June Queen Victoria heard from her son-in-law Grand Duke Louis that Ella had been very kindly received by the emperor, empress and the whole imperial family when she arrived in Russia. The queen may have been less pleased to hear from Ella's sister Victoria that as she travelled through the vast Russian plains she had admired the birch trees and the forests of firs which reminded her of the scenery in Scotland.

The court was based at Peterhof on the Gulf of Finland. Although the wedding was a week away, the social round began almost immediately as more and more relatives arrived, including the Duke and Duchess of Edinburgh. Marie was in her element, showing Ella and the other guests around her childhood homes.

Ella described to her grandmother how she had made her official entry into St Petersburg through cheering crowds, riding in Catherine the Great's coach drawn by six white horses with postilions dressed in gold livery. All the imperial family, she said reassuringly, had been very kind to her.

There was a reception on 2 June in the Grand Hall of the Winter Palace for which specific instructions were issued. Ladies and gentlemen of the court would be greeted at the palace's Saltykov entrance, members of the government and Ministers of State at the Neva entrance, and Generals, members of the cabinet, senior officers and members of commerce at the Commandant's entrance.[52] Similar instructions were issued for those invited by the grand duke and his bride to view some of the wedding gifts. 'Officers who have received the Order of the Apostle of St Andrew are required to wear their orders,' the notice read. Among the presents was a china service from Queen Victoria, for which Ella later expressed the couple's 'deepest thanks'.[53]

Ella and Sergei were married on 3/15 June. Ella's dress of silver brocade, worn with a long court train of silver tissue, had clusters of diamonds along the edges and an ermine lining and was made according to a style dictated by Catherine the Great. The formal ceremony of dressing the bride began in front of a dressing table with a large silver-framed mirror which had belonged to Peter the Great's niece, the Empress Anna Ivanovna. The hairdresser arranged Ella's hair so that long side curls rested on her shoulders. Then came the jewels bequeathed by Catherine the Great to all Romanov brides. First the empress placed on her head a diadem with a beautiful pink diamond in the centre, behind which was placed the Bride's Crown, six diamond arches rising from a diamond circlet, surmounted by a diamond cross and lined with crimson velvet. Attached to it was the bridal veil. Next came a diamond necklace, a triple-row bracelet and a pair of enormous drop earrings like cherries, which were so heavy they were attached to gold hoops and hung over the ears. Finally, after almost 3 hours, Ella stood up and the empress's ladies draped a long, ermine-lined crimson mantle, with a deep border of ermine, round her shoulders. A short ermine-lined cape was placed over this and fastened with a large diamond clasp. The weight of these robes was tremendous and it was difficult for her to move unaided. To add to this, for good luck one of the groomsmen placed a ten rouble piece in Ella's shoe. Unfortunately, it dug into her toes. Nevertheless, everyone agreed that Ella looked beautiful.

The marriage took place in the Cathedral Church of the Winter Palace. Generals, high-ranking military officers, and Russian and foreign ministers of commerce were asked to assemble at the palace's Jordan entrance; they would attend the wedding only. Members of the government and the diplomatic corps assembled at the Neva entrance and would attend the wedding and the subsequent ball.[54]

Although Ella had not converted to the Orthodox Faith she adopted the Russian patronymic of 'Feodorovna', a traditional name for foreign brides marrying into the Imperial family. Henceforth, Ella would be known as Grand Duchess Elisabeth Feodorovna.

The Orthodox ceremony was followed by a Lutheran service in the Alexander Hall and then a wedding banquet in the Nicholas Hall. It was on this occasion that an incident occurred which would have upset Queen Victoria greatly had she known about it. Ella's brother-in-law Prince Louis of Battenberg was seated not with his wife and the other royals, but alongside officers of the royal yacht HMS *Osborne* and below the yacht's captain. In Russian eyes this befitted his status as a mere Serene Highness, the offspring of a morganatic marriage. As Louis was the tsar's cousin this was a definite snub. Ella's father later spoke to the tsar about it but he said that Berlin had wanted it that way because they did not recognise the Battenbergs as pure-bred royals. In her letters to the queen, Princess Victoria said nothing about this insult to her husband. Queen Victoria had been careful to warn her granddaughters that they should write nothing *confidential* from Russia unless it was sent by the English messenger (the Duchess of Edinburgh had said that any other method was unsafe). Queen Victoria only learnt about the incident later. But the following year when the queen's daughter Princess Beatrice wanted to marry Louis's brother Prince Henry, the queen was pleased to be able to upset her arch enemies Chancellor Bismarck of Germany and Tsar Alexander by saying, 'If the Queen of England thinks a person good enough for her daughter what have other people got to say?' Her championship of this family was dubbed 'Court Battenbergism.'[55]

Meanwhile at Balmoral on Ella's wedding day the queen's thoughts were turned towards 'darling Ella' and her wish that she should be happy. Later that day telegrams began to arrive from Russia. One of the first was from Sergei. 'We kiss your hands with gratitude, respect, and affection. Thank you from the heart for your good telegram. My joy and my happiness will be to devote myself to the happiness of our beloved Ella.'[56]

By December Vicky was reporting 'tiresome rumours' that Ella and Sergei had divorced. The queen protested it was absurd. 'She is quite happy.'[57]

The Great Game

'Russia "was never to be trusted".'
– Queen Victoria.

The marriage of Alfred and Marie, which had been expected to ease the relationship between their two countries, had not removed that tension. Russia and Britain were now engaged in The Great Game – competing for influence in Central Asia. Russia, the queen had complained in February 1882, was trying to frustrate Britain in every direction.

In early 1885 the two countries were close to war over Afghanistan, where the Russian advance to the south of the Sea of Aral aroused English fears for the safety of India. This fear had been increasing since Russian influence in Persia (which had long been the target of Anglo-Russian rivalry) had grown over the previous decades.

A commission entrusted with the job of marking out the frontier between Russia and Afghanistan was suspended at Russia's request. Queen Victoria, at the request of her government, personally appealed to Alexander III to prevent any conflict with the Afghans. Then in March 1885, forty Afghans were killed when the Russians advanced and defeated them at Pendjeh, after the tsar had ordered his forces to 'drive them back and give them a sound thrashing.'[1] Britain was outraged and alarmed. The British Ambassador in St Petersburg was instructed to ask for an explanation. In England the reserves were called up and it seemed as if war was inevitable.

The situation was made all the more difficult because Ella and Sergei were expected in Darmstadt for the christening of Victoria and Louis's eldest child Princess Alice of Battenberg. Queen

Victoria would also be present. The queen now told Victoria that she was hoping an excuse would be found to call Sergei back to Russia before she arrived. Although the queen hoped war could be averted, in the current threatening atmosphere she felt 'it would be *very awkward* for me to meet a grand duke.'[2]

By April Queen Victoria was in Darmstadt and Sergei and Ella ('just the same sweet gentle creature as ever' as the queen noted) were also there. Sergei sat near the queen several times at luncheon and she discovered that they got along very well. Ella, however, was looking 'thin and pale', but the queen was assured this was caused by the heat.[3]

As unsatisfactory cipher telegrams about Afghanistan continued to arrive, the queen suggested to Sir Henry Ponsonby that perhaps something could be done via Grand Duke Sergei. On 27 April, again at the government's request, Queen Victoria wrote a formal letter to Sergei begging him to ask the tsar to do all he could to promote peace and to 'assure the Emperor of my pacific intentions and hope that we may both be able to avoid war'. Although the queen was unable to see how this could be achieved, Sergei was also very anxious that war with Britain be avoided and Queen Victoria thought he seemed sad and preoccupied.[4]

A large-scale war in Afghanistan between Britain and Russia was in any case impracticable. Russia was anxious about a British invasion of the Black Sea and once the Russians were convinced that 'the Straits would remain closed and the Black Sea secure, they lost interest in being able to threaten the British in Afghanistan.'[5] On 4 May Russia backed down and agreed to settle the frontier question by arbitration. As a facesaver, it was later stated that the battle at Pendjeh had taken place in direct infringement of the emperor's instructions.

* * *

Then trouble arose over Bulgaria. In 1885 the southern Bulgars of Eastern Roumelia, still under Turkish rule since the war of 1878, declared their independence and were unified with the northern part of Bulgaria in direct defiance of the Treaty of Berlin.

Northern Bulgaria was under the rule of the tsar's cousin Prince Alexander of Battenberg ('Sandro'), who had been set up as sovereign prince in 1879 with the support of his uncle Tsar Alexander II. Unfortunately, the new tsar despised Sandro; Alexander III did not want a strong Bulgaria and was incensed by the Bulgarian unification. He resented Sandro's plans to govern without Russian interference and did not give him the same support as the previous tsar had done. Alexander III now did all he could to discredit Sandro throughout Europe.

To make matters worse, Sandro was hoping to marry Queen Victoria's granddaughter Princess Victoria of Prussia (known as Moretta), daughter of Vicky and Fritz, a marriage championed by the queen and Vicky but opposed by Fritz, the German Emperor, and Chancellor Bismarck.

The queen had strong family reasons for supporting Sandro, the prince she had once regarded as a Russian spy when he visited Prince Alfred on board his ship. Sandro's brother Louis had married Queen Victoria's granddaughter Princess Victoria of Hesse; while another brother Henry had recently married the queen's youngest child Princess Beatrice. She was now afraid that the tsar would force Sandro's abdication so that he could place a Russian vassal on the Bulgarian throne.

The action of the Bulgarians aroused the aspirations of the Greeks, who began to demand their share of the territory they felt should have been allotted to them at the Congress of Berlin. They were prepared to back their demands by action and seize what they wanted from the Turks. The Great Powers refused to help and insisted that Greece must give way. The Greeks replied by moving troops towards the Turkish frontier. By the end of April, a naval blockade by the Great Powers and the possible bombardment of Athens were becoming daily more likely. When the diplomatic representatives were recalled, only those from France and Russia remained. The situation was defused when the Greeks backed down and demobilised.

In Bulgaria, Sandro was not so lucky. Russia, the queen said in 1883, 'was never to be trusted'[6] and in this she was now proved correct.

* * *

In September 1885 the Russians tried to get a proportion of the Bulgarian people to vote for the deposition of Sandro but the attempt failed. The tsar then recalled the Russian officers serving in the Bulgarian army. Sandro, although determined that blood should not be spilled, could muster 10,000 men and he appealed to the sultan to prevent the advance of Turkish troops.

By 25 September the queen had heard that the tsar was 'very bitter against poor Sandro'. He had not wished to order the

Russian officers to leave but had done so after the sultan's direct appeal to him. She received a letter from Lord Salisbury, saying that the tsar stipulated that the 'insurrection must be localised and Turkish troops kept out of Roumelia.' She noted that Salisbury 'fears [the] power of Russia will increase at Constantinople.' If Russia proposed Sandro's deposition, it was now a question of how far the other Great Powers would go to oppose the tsar.[7]

More than ever now Victoria felt the separation from Ella. On her granddaughter's birthday, 1 November, she recorded sadly, 'Alas! she is so far away, that she is almost lost to us.'[8]

A week later news came that the tsar had dismissed Sandro from the Russian army. There was great indignation in Britain at Alexander III's behaviour, with many newspaper articles appearing on the subject. The queen's relationship with the tsar, never very good, now deteriorated further over Alexander's treatment of his cousin.

King Milan of Serbia was determined to deny Bulgaria its recent gains. Encouraged by Austria he declared war and on 13 November his army attacked Bulgaria. The Serbians were defeated by the Bulgarians (whose commanders were mere junior officers) at Slivinitza the following week and Austria ordered Sandro's men to halt.

The Bulgarian matter dragged on and on. The queen told Vicky that the 'stupid tsar' could not possibly depose Sandro, 'who I am sure will never and ought never to desert his people...'[9]

Italy proposed that the Governor Generalship of Eastern Roumelia should be confided to Sandro for an indefinite period in a personal union. Although Sandro accepted the proposal Russia was not satisfied and the tsar refused any further concessions, which the queen thought very wrong.

By August 'cruel calumnies' were being circulated about Sandro. Queen Victoria knew who was to blame. 'The Russians are at the bottom of the whole thing, I fear.'[10]

The queen was at Balmoral on 22 August when alarming news arrived in a cipher telegram. 'Sandro has been deposed and taken prisoner, a provisional government being formed by the union of the Ministers and opposition! The army has taken the oath!' With all the royal family in a state of shock the queen immediately telegraphed Lord Salisbury, only to find that he had no news at all because direct communication with Sofia had been cut. Later, to her intense relief, news arrived that Sandro was safe and believed to be in Romania. This last statement turned out to be untrue. In fact

Sandro had been kidnapped from his palace in Sofia on 21 August and forced to abdicate at gunpoint. He was then taken by boat to Russian Bessarabia.

On 25 August a telegram arrived from Sir Robert Morier in St Petersburg, which the queen copied into her journal: 'The Russian government received last night a telegram from the commanding officer at Reni (in Russian territory) to say that [the] Bulgarian prince's yacht had just arrived with [the] Prince of Bulgaria on board. The captain presented a note to the Russian authorities, and had orders to deliver His Highness to them. Instructions from St. Petersburg were at once sent that the *prisoner* (!) was to land and regain liberty, but I gathered that it was strongly hinted he should proceed by railway to the Russian frontier!'

The queen called this behaviour 'monstrous' and a clear indication that the whole episode had been planned by the Russians. She was sickened by this treachery, writing from Balmoral that she 'really could hardly have felt much more for my own son.'[11]

They then heard from Sandro's father, Prince Alexander of Hesse, that Sandro was free, having being handed over to a Russian general.

As telegrams continued to arrive, reports came that there was a counter-revolution in Sofia. Sandro was proclaimed sovereign prince again and the East Roumelian government, the army and the people were eager for his return. The Bulgarian government, however, cautioned him to wait a while. The Russians were sending an agent to Bulgaria, saying that under no circumstances would the Prince of Bulgaria be allowed back. Even the Turks were afraid to encourage Sandro's return for fear of displeasing Russia. 'How wretched, and how foolish, playing into Russia's hands. This is ruining all!' exclaimed the exasperated queen.[12]

Although reports indicated that there would be no interference from the tsar at the moment, the queen recorded further telegrams which indicated that the Russian diplomat Alexander Nelidov had told the Turkish government that they would never allow the Prince of Bulgaria to return as complications would ensue. The German Ambassador agreed, saying it would be a misfortune. 'These two men have done all the mischief!' Victoria wrote angrily.[13]

Sandro received a warm welcome in Bulgaria but his return to Sofia was brief. On 2 September the queen received a copy of a placatory message sent by Sandro to Alexander III and the emperor's brutal and offensive answer. Only Sandro's abdication would restore friendly relations between Russia and Bulgaria.

All the royal family were startled and questioned the authenticity of Sandro's message, which seemed too humble. The following day there was indignation in the British newspapers, who stated that the country should not tolerate what had happened. The queen received a petition from many members of parliament to the same effect.

The humble tone of the telegram to Alexander III made Sandro's position in Bulgaria untenable. Completely disillusioned, he confirmed his abdication and left the country on 8 September.

While the queen hoped a middle course of action could be found until passions cooled and the tsar came to his senses, she told Vicky that 'I am, and always have been, of the decided opinion that the tsar is merely saying he won't have Sandro as he dislikes him, which is not a reason for Europe, or part of it, humbly to submit.'[14]

In her frustration, the queen turned on her ambassadors. She had already asked for her ambassador in Russia, Sir Robert Morier, to be recalled and now she demanded that Lord Salisbury do so too. Salisbury refused to be cowed, replying that he could find no justification for such a startling step.

As delegates from Bulgaria toured Europe in search of a new ruler, Sandro forgot any idea of marriage with Moretta and retired into private life as Count Hartenau. He made a morganatic marriage in 1889 and died in 1893.

Queen Victoria never forgave the tsar, whose sanity she often questioned; and Alexander III was offended by an attack made against him by Lord Salisbury. By February 1887 he was contemptuously referring to England as a weak country, unable to engage in European politics and certainly not to be feared by Russia.

Relations between Britain and Russia continued to be fraught.

* * *

It was probably fortunate that between 1886 and 1889 the Duke and Duchess of Edinburgh were living in Malta, where Alfred was commander-in-chief of the Mediterranean Fleet. This took Marie away from the cold, damp English weather and out of Queen Victoria's orbit at this critical time in Anglo-Russian relations. In Malta she really could be mistress of all she surveyed, for a while at least, but although she entertained lavishly Marie soon became bored with life in the confines of the small island.

By this time a truce had been declared between the queen and her daughter-in-law. Alone among all Queen Victoria's relations, the Duchess of Edinburgh was the only one she did not attempt to dominate, and Victoria certainly did not get the 'unswerving obedience' from the duchess that she demanded from her own children. Significantly, Marie's portrait was the only one of family to be hung in the queen's private breakfast room at Windsor.[15]

* * *

Marital concerns raised their head again in February 1886, when the queen heard that Princess Irene of Hesse and her father Grand Duke Louis were going to visit Ella in St Petersburg. She was afraid that the whole visit was a plot by the tsar's aunt Grand Duchess Olga Feodorovna, who wanted Irene to marry her son Grand Duke Michael Michaelovich, known in the family as Miche-Miche. The queen exploded. 'I shall *never* forgive it, if she also is to go to that horrid, corrupt country – and I should break with Papa if he did it!' she told Princess Victoria of Battenberg firmly.[16]

She was also concerned about Ella. After three years her marriage remained childless and was the cause of gossip in St Petersburg. There were rumours that she was unhappy and that Sergei, an officer in the Preobrajensky Guards, was having affairs with some of the junior officers. He also seemed to exert a controlling influence over Ella, who was seven years his junior. He had a quick temper, demanded order and discipline, stood for no opposition and controlled the household with a rod of iron. Proud Ella used her siblings to try and scotch the rumours, constantly mentioning in letters to them and her grandmother how happy she was. The queen was not deceived. 'Ella's constant speaking of her happiness I don't quite like,' she wrote. '*When* people are very happy they don't require to *tell* others of it.'[17]

Ella's diaries are unfortunately lost. Yet she loved her husband, and the couple's niece Grand Duchess Maria Pavlovna, who later lived with them, wrote in her memoirs that her aunt and uncle always shared the same bed.

* * *

Meanwhile, there was trouble brewing and it again concerned Russia.

Since the annexation of the Punjab in 1849, the deposed Maharajah of Lahore, Duleep Singh, had been living in England as a 'guest' of the British government, who were paying him a pension. Their relationship had recently soured over money and the refusal of Britain to return the maharajah's family estate in the Punjab.

Forty-nine-year-old Duleep Singh was now Britain's implacable foe and was threatening to go to India and raise the Sikhs in rebellion. The queen called it 'perfect madness!' He tried to get to India but the British took him off the ship at Aden and told him he would lose his pension unless he returned to London. Instead he abandoned his wife and children, moved to Paris and tried to regain his throne. To do this, he turned towards the tsar. When Queen Victoria heard this she was astounded, fearing he was 'quite off his head'.[18]

On 21 June Duleep Singh wrote to the Russian Ambassador Baron George de Staal (who succeeded von Mohrenheim in 1884) offering his services to Alexander III and requesting a passport to enable him to travel to St Petersburg. If the tsar received him kindly, Duleep Singh intended to go to the border with India. The maharajah then wrote to the Duke of Grafton telling him what he had done. The duke passed his letter to Windsor.

On 6 July 1886 Queen Victoria wrote to Duleep Singh saying she had received 'extraordinary reports of your resigning your allowance ... and of your intending to transfer your allegiance to Russia! I cannot believe this of you who always professed such loyalty and devotion to me...' She asked for assurances that the reports were not true.[19]

The queen received Duleep Singh's reply a few days later. He confirmed that he had indeed offered his services to Russia but had not yet received a response. The British Embassy in Paris then began mounting a discreet surveillance operation on the maharajah.

Duleep Singh had been convinced by intermediaries in Moscow that Alexander III was keen to invade India, the 'jewel' in Queen Victoria's crown. If Russia invaded through Lahore in the north-west of India, Duleep Singh said he could hold open the door with a force of 45,000 Sikhs and start a rebellion to enable the tsar to supplant the queen/empress.

In July Duleep Singh was received by Prince Kutzebue, Counsellor of the Russian Embassy in Paris. During a prickly interview he was asked what he expected to obtain from Russia. The response, as reported by Kutzebue to his Foreign Minister de Giers, was: 'A large sum of money ... he hopes to extract up to three million pounds sterling from the English government.' The Russians believed the maharajah was trying to blackmail the British 'and make them pay by threatening them with the prestige that he would gain' if he placed himself under Russian protection.[20]

The tsar was not told about the incident. Instead a letter was sent to the maharajah informing him that the Russians were not interested in fomenting trouble in India. On 7 September the *Journal des Débats* in Paris published a report about 'An uprising of the people of north-eastern India against British rule and in favour of Russian invasion.' Other newspapers published the story and the maharajah denied that he had proclaimed any such revolution. Following this, Duleep Singh visited Kotzebue again, convinced that a war between Russia and England was imminent. He said a proclamation had been made (without his knowledge) calling on people in the Punjab to revolt in his name, with assurances that Russia would back them. Again, he was shown the door.

This time Alexander III was informed. He minuted on Kotzebue's report 'maybe some time it will be useful.'[21]

The Maharajah Duleep Singh was now in open revolt against the Empress of India.

* * *

On 10 March [NS] 1887 Duleep Singh wrote to the tsar, to whom he had been introduced by the Prince of Wales in 1873, imploring him to grant him asylum in Russia. 'I am offering my loyal allegiance to Your Imperial Majesty. I do not ask any pecuniary gain whatsoever, as my loyal subjects have already furnished me with sufficient means and are further largely providing for my future maintenance, so that I am entirely independent of everybody in this respect.' Enclosed with this letter was one to the maharajah from Queen Victoria.[22]

Duleep Singh could not get to Russia without a British passport. While he waited for a reply to his letter, there was an attempt on the emperor's life.

* * *

Every year on 1/13 March the imperial family travelled by train to the capital to attend the commemoration service for Alexander II in the SS Peter and Paul Cathedral. After the service they returned to the station in an open carriage along a route heavily guarded by police. As their train was about to leave, the tsar was informed that some students carrying crude bombs concealed in hollowed out books had been arrested on one of St Petersburg's main streets. They had intended to hurl them at the carriage as the imperial family passed. The tsar remained silent and grimly boarded the train.

Queen Victoria received the details from Sir Robert Morier in St Petersburg. '[The] emperor went to church first, and conspirators were arrested near Anichkov Palace, 5 minutes before [the] emperor left it. His Imperial Majesty breakfasted on his return from church with the Grand Duke Paul, and there learnt the danger he had escaped. Dynamite bombs were smeared with some virulent poison, intended to cause death even in case of a slight wound. The conspirators are all Russian students, the eldest being only twenty-three,' Morier wrote. He added, 'I have just seen Their Majesties at a party given by the Grand Duchess Vladimir. The emperor was in glad spirits – the empress seemed depressed. The utmost consternation prevails, as it was thought the end of such conspiracies was past, and it is believed the present one has important ramifications...'[23]

Sir Robert later reported to the Prime Minister, Lord Salisbury, that he had been told by the Russian Foreign Minister Nicolai de Giers that the attempt on 13 March would be followed by 'more serious operations and that the tsar was doomed'.[24] The rumour, which proved false, had emanated from Berlin.

Duleep Singh arrived in Russia in March imagining that his presence would galvanise the tsar to see him and finalise plans for the invasion. With him was his mistress Ada Wetherill and they were travelling as Mr and Mrs Casey. All this was being reported back to London by Foreign Office spies.

Meanwhile, Alexander III was given the maharajah's dossier and he authorised him to come and live in Russia. The British Ambassador was instructed to express to de Giers 'the very serious view Her Majesty's government would take should the maharajah be allowed to make any move towards Central Asia.'[25]

By May Duleep Singh was sending out seditious letters, including one to the tsar which was nothing less than 'a detailed blueprint for war'. The letter was translated into Russian and the tsar minuted his observations at the side. It was 'desirable' that the maharajah become a Russian subject; it was necessary to verify whether the Indian princes would rise in revolt; and it would be possible 'to send English-speaking emissaries to test the ground'. He told Pobedonostsev that he believed Duleep Singh could be useful to them one day in India, 'where we have no shortage of questions to debate with the English'.[26]

The Foreign Office spies were reporting that in order to maintain a pretext for war, Russia was going to send Duleep Singh to the Indian frontier. The plan was to wreck the talks about the boundary with Afghanistan then, at an appropriate moment, the maharajah would be produced 'like a rabbit out of a hat'. If the Bulgarian dispute could be resolved, Russia would 'attack in Asia.'[27]

In June the tsar refused to renew the Three Emperors' League, which had linked Austria, Germany and Russia since 1881 and been renewed for three years in 1884. Bismarck, afraid Russia would turn towards France, offered a Reinsurance Treaty instead, giving Russia a 'certain amount of influence' in the Balkans. Russia pledged neutrality towards Germany unless the Germans invaded France but Germany would remain neutral towards Russia unless the Russians attacked Austria. Relations between them continued to be strained. Anti-Germanism became the way to favour and promotion as Russian foreign policy began to turn away from Germany.

Sir Henry Ponsonby sent a summary of events to Queen Victoria. It detailed Duleep Singh's plot, how they feared that if he came to India with a Russian army the Sikhs might rise up and join him (although most of them were loyal), and how the plot was broken up. It also detailed several assassination attempts against the tsar. In Russia the maharajah was now impatiently awaiting the tsar's answer.

Not until January 1888 did he receive it. Alexander III, hearing that the maharajah was living with his mistress, a former chambermaid who was expecting their child, refused to see him. Duleep Singh must leave.

The tsar had no intention of invading India.

* * *

In December 1887 Lord and Lady Randolph Churchill set out on a visit to Russia armed with a letter of introduction to the tsar and tsarina from the Princess of Wales. The queen was concerned. Lord Randolph had resigned as Chancellor of the Exchequer the previous year and Victoria was anxious that it be made known that this was a purely private trip which had no political implications.

During the Churchills' stay they were granted an audience with the sovereigns at Gatchina. While Jennie was taken on a tour of the palace, Randolph met the tsar. To his disappointment the monarch began the conversation in French, talking rather low into his beard so that Randolph, whose hearing was not perfect, missed some of his remarks. Randolph advised him to take no notice of the British press, as nobody in public life cared what they said anyway, but then the tsar surprisingly broached the Eastern Question. 'With regard to the Black Sea and the Dardanelles,' he told Lord Randolph, 'if you desire peace and friendship with Russia, you must not mix yourselves up there against us. We will never suffer any other power to hold the Dardanelles, except the Turks or ourselves; and if the Turks ultimately go out, it is by Russians that they will be succeeded.' Following this warning, Alexander added: 'You have a great task before you on your return to England – to improve the relations between Russia and England.'[28]

As *The Times* reported on 3 January 1888, the Russian newspaper *Novosti* took up this call, hoping that Lord Randolph could 'convince his countrymen of the peaceful and harmless character of the Russians' and that he would try and convince other members of Lord Salisbury's cabinet (which they regarded as a traditional enemy of Russia) to resign.

But Lord Randolph's hasty and ill-conceived resignation had ruined his political career for good and, anyway, after the Bulgarian fiasco, improving Anglo-Russian relations would be easier said than done.

Strained Relations

'A sovereign whom she does not look upon as a gentleman.'
– Queen Victoria

In June 1887 Queen Victoria celebrated her Golden Jubilee. No similar occasion had occurred since the reign of her grandfather George III in 1809, although there could be no proper celebrations of his fifty years on the throne because Britain was at war with France.

In a letter to Vicky in March the queen listed all the relatives she wished to invite for the celebrations. Among them were Ella and Sergei, although she was still upset about the Russian marriage. She was glad her granddaughter was happy but, as she wrote to Princess Victoria of Battenberg, 'it is the *whole* position in such a *corrupt* country where you can trust *no one* and where politics are so antagonistic to one's own views and feelings which is so sad and distressing to us all.'[1]

Ella was delighted when Alexander III agreed to send her and Sergei to London as his representative. 'The idea of seeing you so soon is most delightful and although our visit will be short, it will be most pleasant,' she wrote on 7/19 May.[2] She and Sergei had sent Queen Victoria a shawl for her birthday, knowing how often the queen wore one when she was out driving.

The grand ducal couple arrived in London on 16 June and stayed at Clarence House with Alfred and Marie, who had returned briefly from Malta to take part in the celebrations. The following evening they all attended a reception at the Russian Embassy and on 19 June they lunched with the queen at Windsor Castle.

The queen left for London on 20 June. Among the many Jubilee honours conferred by the queen, *The Times* recorded on 21 June, Sergei was made an Honorary Knight Grand Cross of the Order of the Bath.

Jubilee day was proclaimed a public holiday and by early morning crowds had already gathered in front of the palace to witness the spectacle, which commenced with the First Life Guards regiment and was followed by *aides-de-camp*, equerries and members of the volunteer forces. At Westminster Abbey guests had been arriving since nine o'clock in the morning. Many of the foreign representatives, including Ella, had gone on ahead of the queen and taken their places inside.

A huge roar rose from the crowds as the queen came into sight riding in an open barouche escorted by mounted *aides-de-camp* and equerries. Despite pleas from her children and the politicians she refused to wear a crown and insisted on a bonnet. Six more carriages followed containing other members of the queen's family, then seventeen princes on horseback, including the tsar's representative Grand Duke Sergei of Russia, the Prince of Wales and Crown Prince Frederick of Germany who, unknown to the crowds, was already mortally ill with the cancer that would kill him the following year.

The royal procession culminated in a Service of Thanksgiving in Westminster Abbey attended by fifty foreign kings and princes, including forty-three members of the queen's family. Among the Heralds in their tabards and the colourful traditional costumes of the Indian princes and their ladies, the queen stood out as she entered in her black dress, relieved only by the Order of the Garter and the Star of India.

That evening there was a grand dinner at Buckingham Palace for which the queen wore a black dress embroidered in silver with roses, thistles and shamrocks. She retired exhausted at ten o'clock, leaving the others to enjoy the spectacular firework display.

The festivities continued for several more days and included reviews of the army volunteers in Hyde Park, the army at Aldershot, and the Grand Fleet at Spithead.

One of the offshoots of the jubilee was the appointment to the queen of two Indian attendants. One of them, the good-looking Abdul Karim, became a favourite with Victoria and the following year was promoted to the role of the Queen's Indian Secretary, or Munshi, to teach her Urdu, a form of Hindustani. Although the Household and most of her family disapproved he accompanied her when travelling and continued the lessons, the queen having maintained that 'there is no hatred to a brown skin.'

After many of the visitors had left, Ella and Serge remained behind for a private visit to the queen at Windsor Castle. Their final engagement was the queen's garden party at Buckingham Palace on 29 June.

Their time spent with the queen seems to have allayed concerns in Victoria's mind over the couple's happiness. Thanking her grandmother for some photographs Ella, who thought of the queen almost as a mother, wrote, '...all I can always repeat is that I am perfectly happy and yet in my new house and life will never forget my old home and those which are all so dear to me...'[3]

***

In March 1888 Queen Victoria took a spring holiday at the Villa Palmieri in Florence. Among those in the area that year was the tsar's aunt Queen Olga of Württemberg, the only surviving daughter of Emperor Nicholas I.

Olga arrived at the Villa Palmieri after lunch accompanied by her niece the Duchess of Edinburgh. It had been thirty-five years since Olga and Victoria had last met, just before the Crimean war when the then crown princess came to England with her husband Carl. Victoria remembered her as a handsome, although frail, young woman. Now although she was still 'terribly thin and pale, ... her features are still beautiful.' Relations between Olga and her husband were at an all-time low, Carl having fallen under the influence of an American adventurer called Charles Woodcock whose appointment to the nobility as Baron von Savage caused a scandal in Württemberg. As the queen recorded, Olga 'remained a short while, speaking most kindly of many things.'[4]

The tsar's aunt may have called on the queen but the Anglophobe tsar did not. Alexander III was the only Russian monarch who Queen Victoria did not meet during his reign, although they had met in the 1870s when he was still the tsarevich. Personally, the queen regarded him as 'a sovereign whom she does not look upon as a gentleman'.[5] Although Victoria was grateful to him for his warm welcome to Ella, relations between the monarchs remained strained. She even warned her grandson, who since the deaths of his grandfather William I and father Frederick III in quick succession had now become Kaiser William II of Germany, against going to Russia. William ignored her and whilst in Russia he and his entourage wasted no time in criticising Queen Victoria to Alexander III, who needed no encouragement to pass judgment on her anyway.

Yet Russia was moving away from Germany. Under Alexander III the Russian court became more nationalistic. All the palace staff were required to be Russian, a new 'Russianised' army uniform was introduced, those with German names were removed from government and high commands in the army and, most significantly, the German language was forbidden at court.

The tsar was notoriously anti-Semitic (a trait later passed on to his eldest son Nicholas but not shared by Queen Victoria), and persecution of the Jews was the most severe until the time of Hitler. The Jewish people had been granted some privileges during Alexander II's reign following his reforms in the 1860s but these were reversed when in 1882 the Minister of the Interior, Count Ignatiev, introduced new laws which forbade the Jews to live outside the Pale of Settlement on Russia's western borders and restricted their rights still further. Jews left Russia in their thousands. Many of those who stayed were converted to revolutionary ideas and there were frequent pogroms, when the non-Jewish population were incited against the Jews, beating them up and destroying their property. The situation for Russia's Jews now deteriorated considerably as the tsar forbade any improvements in their lifestyle and even refused to promote officers if they were Jewish. This persecution inflamed public opinion in Britain and 'ruined Russia's image in Europe'.[6]

Alexander also turned his attention towards the Imperial family and in 1886 a new imperial decree was issued. This limited the rank of grand duke, which carried an allowance of £20,000 per year, and grand duchess, with a dowry of £100,000, and the title of 'Imperial Highness', to the sovereign's children and grandchildren in the male line only. The next generation would be princes and princesses with the title of 'Highness' and a lump sum of £100,000 at birth. Great-great-grandchildren would be 'Serene Highness' and would be allowed to marry suitable non-royals with the tsar's permission. In 1889 male members of the imperial family were forbidden to marry anyone not already of the Orthodox religion, a decree which in time would affect some of Queen Victoria's descendants.

The arts, however, flourished. The tsar appointed Carl Fabergé to the post of Supplier to the Imperial Court in 1885. Fabergé quickly caught the mood of refined elegance, producing objects of fantasy whose emphasis was more on the visual impression than on the value of the materials – jewelled and enamelled cigarette cases, picture frames, bell pushes and parasol handles; sprays of flowers in gold or enamel with diamond centres and nephrite leaves, set in rock crystal to simulate a vase of water; tiny animals and birds with precious stones for eyes. In 1885 he was asked to design an Easter egg as a surprise for the empress. Eggs symbolising life and the Resurrection were a traditional Russian Easter gift and this was the beginning of the famous Fabergé Easter eggs, of which fifty were produced for the imperial family between 1885 and 1916. Many of these beautiful Fabergé *objets* found their way to the British royal family.

But even the Okhrana failed to stop attacks on the tsar. While at Balmoral during October 1888 Queen Victoria received a Reuters' telegram saying that the emperor's train had been involved in a nasty accident while returning from a trip to the Caucasus.

On 17/29 October as the imperial train approached Borki in the province of Kharkov it gave a sudden lurch. There was a mighty bang and several more jolts, followed by the sound of clanging iron as the coaches at the rear of the train crashed against those in front and the train was derailed. The wheels of the dining car had been ripped off and part of the train rolled down the embankment. 'Many people were killed and wounded, twenty-one of the former, and up to now, thirty of the latter. Too awful! It looks as if some terrible attempt had again taken place,' the shocked queen wrote in her journal.[7] Although the imperial family escaped more or less unscathed, the emperor's dog Kamchatka was among the fatalities.

The Commission of Enquiry found that the accident was caused by the excessive speed of a train that was too heavy, on rails that were too light and sleepers that were old. However, rumours persisted that a bomb had been smuggled aboard and the terrorists' ringleader died in the explosion. Some members of the imperial family also inclined towards this view.

The events at Borki increased the nervous tension of the emperor and, especially, the empress. Alexander now became more moody and unsociable, shunning public functions to an unprecedented degree. He began to drink more heavily and the effects of terrorism, together with worry over his wife, took their toll on his own health. Marie Feodorovna, whose nerves had never recovered from the shock of seeing the mangled body of her father-in-law in the Winter Palace, now became prone to fits of nervous prostration. Official entertaining was cut down even more – but there would be no liberal concessions to appease the terrorists.

It was these security concerns, allied with political considerations, which prevented the tsar and tsarina coming to England. The tsar's meetings with foreign monarchs were anyway now kept to a minimum and his most frequent foreign trips were to visit his wife's family in Denmark, where he was at least able to relax.

When the political climate finally allowed the widowed Marie Feodorovna to visit London again in 1907, long after Victoria's death, she had been absent for thirty-four years.

***

Instead of going to England himself, in May 1889 the tsar sent his cousin Grand Duke Alexander Michaelovich as his personal representative. The grand duke was to convey Alexander III's greetings to the queen and try and ease some of the tension between Russia and Britain.

'Sandro', as he was known in the family (not to be confused with the Battenberg prince who had ruled Bulgaria), was in the navy and just returning from a long voyage. Stopping off in England, he was staying at the Buckingham Palace Hotel in London. His first call was on the Prince and Princess of Wales at Marlborough House. Then on 14 May he was invited to lunch at Buckingham Palace. 'I had heard a great deal about the alleged coldness of the powerful queen and was prepared to be frozen,' the grand duke recalled in his 'self-serving' and not always accurate memoirs.[8] Filled with apprehension, he arrived at the palace where after a few moments he was shown into the queen's presence, only to be 'slightly taken aback by the very pronounced cordiality of her manner'.

According to the grand duke's memoirs, while visiting Agra in India he had met Abdul Karim, the queen's Munshi, whose family came from the town, and 'accepted an invitation to dine at his house'. This encounter had been reported back to Queen Victoria and it explained her warm reception of the tsar's cousin.[9]

After lunch, at which the Prince and Princess of Wales and other immediate family members were present, the queen questioned Sandro about the political situation in South America, China and Japan where he had recently travelled. Afterwards he was present at the queen's Drawing Room (which was also attended by his cousin the Duchess of Edinburgh) and the family dinner party which followed.

Sandro would doubtless have been pleased to hear the queen's impression of him when she wrote her journal later that evening: 'The grand duke, who is twenty-three, very tall and good looking, is particularly pleasing and amiable. He has travelled in India,' she added with significant approval.[10]

Yet when Tsarevich Nicholas visited India as part of his Far East tour towards the end of 1890 Victoria assigned Sir Donald Mackenzie Wallace, Foreign Correspondent of *The Times*, to his suite, instructing that the Russian party must be watched carefully and certainly not left alone.

* * *

In 1891 tragedy struck the family of the tsar's brother Grand Duke Paul Alexandrovich with the death of his twenty-one-year-old wife Princess Alexandra of Greece. The couple, already the parents of a young daughter Maria, were staying with Sergei and Ella, who had moved to Moscow on Sergei's appointment as Governor General earlier that year. (It was said that he only consented to go provided the tsar expel Moscow's Jews.)

Accounts of what happened differ. The generally accepted version is that one morning in September Alexandra, who was seven months pregnant, walked down to the river near Ella and Sergei's country home Ilinskoie and jumped into a boat moored by the landing stage. Some say she then collapsed into a convulsive fit. Another version says that the following evening she fainted during a ball and was carried to her room, where she suffered severe labour pains. Whichever is correct, there was no doctor for miles and the only help that could be obtained was from the old village midwife. A son, Dmitri, was born prematurely on 6/18 September but by the time the doctors arrived Alexandra was in a coma. A telegram was immediately sent to her parents King George and Queen Olga, who hurried to Russia and reached her bedside just in time. Six days after the birth of her son she died without regaining consciousness. Paul was distraught. Malicious rumours then attributed Alexandra's death to suicide, after she was alleged to have learnt of a liaison between Paul and Ella.

Queen Victoria, anxious to know all the facts, asked Victoria of Battenberg what had brought on the fits and whether the medical report could be obtained. Alexandra had been very ill and anaemic during her daughter's birth the previous year, so the queen thought that the state of her blood was probably not good and her heart was weak, which she said Ella telegraphed was '"flatulency" of the heart,' so poor Alexandra was unable to stand any shock and consequently her kidney disorder triggered blood poisoning.[11] The queen felt that Alexandra's health had been neglected before her marriage.

Soon Ella was able to report that 'Paul's children are both well and the baby [Dmitri] getting on so nicely... The christening will take place on 29 October (old-style calendar) 10 November, their engagement day only three years ago. Such perfect happiness to be broken up like that is too sad...'[12]

The Duchess of Edinburgh said that Alexandra's health was so bad that she would not have lived long anyway. Queen Victoria was now concerned that her granddaughter Princess Alix of Hesse should have at least a year to gain strength before there was any thought of *her* marriage.

* * *

For some time Ella had been campaigning to have her sister Alix (known as Alicky in the family) join her in Russia as the bride of the tsarevich. Nicholas and Alicky had met at Ella's wedding in 1884, and then again in the spring of 1889 when the seventeen-year-old princess stayed with Ella and Sergei in Russia. Alicky was beautiful with red-gold hair, pale skin and blue-grey eyes and Nicholas had fallen in love with her. He naturally shared this news with his Aunt Ella – but there was a problem. The match did not find favour with Alexander III and Empress Marie, both of whom felt that Alicky was too stiff, shy and unimportant to marry the heir to the Russian throne. Also, as Ella well knew, there would be opposition from Queen Victoria over yet another Russian marriage. This was one instance when Queen Victoria and the tsar were in agreement.

The union between Alfred and Marie had not been a success and the omens for another Russian union were certainly not good. Marie Feodorovna already had her own candidates lined up for Nicholas. She opposed a marriage to Alicky and in this she found an unlikely ally in Queen Victoria, who now faced the very real fear that Alicky would go to 'horrid' Russia. 'It would not do on account of the religion,' the queen told Victoria of Battenberg, 'and I know moreover that Minny [the empress] does not *wish* it.'[13]

Writing to her brother Ernie and determined to remove her grandmother's prejudices, Ella primed him carefully about what he should (and more importantly what he should *not*) say about the burgeoning romance between Alicky and Nicky. 'Through all the idiotic trash in the newspapers she [the queen] gets impossible untrue views and founds all her arguments on facts which probably never existed,' Ella told him.[14]

It soon became obvious that Ella was the chief matchmaker. She had thrown Alicky and Nicholas together as much as possible and in letters to her grandmother she stressed the happy family life of the emperor and empress. Despite Victoria of Battenberg's assurance that there was nothing to worry about, the queen returned to the charge in December.

She had heard through the Princess of Wales, who in turn had been informed by her sister Empress Marie, that Ella and Sergei 'do *all* they can to bring it about, encouraging and even urging the boy to do it!' The empress was annoyed. The queen felt strongly that for the younger sister to marry the emperor's eldest son would not lead to happiness and she was adamant that Alicky must *not* visit Russia again. She wrote to Alicky's father Grand Duke Louis to insist that he put his foot down over the matter. The wife of the tsarevich would be 'in a most difficult and precarious position' and at any moment something dreadful could happen in a country whose state was 'so bad, so rotten'.[15] Still, the queen said, there were other princes and grand dukes, and she knew by now that Ella would move heaven and earth to get her sister married in Russia.

To Queen Victoria's annoyance Alicky had already turned down a proposal from her cousin Prince Albert Victor (Eddy), heir to the throne after his father the Prince of Wales. Now the queen hoped that Alicky would marry Prince Max of Baden.

Religion was the big stumbling block to marriage with Nicholas as far as Alicky was concerned. The wife of the tsarevich was required to convert to the Russian Orthodox faith. Alicky had already been confirmed into the Lutheran Church and felt that to abjure her religion for a crown would be a sin. Ella, though, had taken a different decision. A journey she and Sergei made to the Holy Land in 1888 had a great influence on her and, although she had no obligation to do so, at the end of 1890 she announced her decision to convert to Russian Orthodoxy so that she would be of the same faith of her husband. Her father was disturbed and upset by his daughter's choice but it seems that Ella obtained support and understanding from Queen Victoria.

The queen's response to Ella's announcement is unfortunately not in existence but Ella's reply, covering seven pages, has survived and shows her relief and gratitude for her grandmother's words. 'You cannot think how intensely and deeply touched I was by all you say,' she replied. 'I was so afraid you might not understand this step and the comforting joy your dear lines gave me I shall never forget... The Greek Church reminds me so much of the Eng[lish] Church ... also to have the same religion as one's husband is such a happiness.'[16]

Ella's conversion took place during Easter 1891. She kept the name of Grand Duchess Elisabeth Feodorovna but chose the Saint's Day of the Righteous Elizabeth, mother of John the Baptist, which is kept on 18 September. 'The ceremony went off so well and is very beautiful,' she told her grandmother on 12/24 May. 'I sent it in German to papa who was to send it to [my] sisters; they shall send it to you, if you would like to read it.'[17]

* * *

It had been arranged that Prince Alfred, Duke of Edinburgh, would eventually succeed his childless uncle Ernest as the Duke of Saxe-Coburg-Gotha. In 1889 he, Marie and their four daughters took up residence in the Palais Edinburgh in Coburg where their son Alfred was already being educated in preparation for one day succeeding his father. The love of Coburg, a place Alfred and Marie could call their own, was at least something that the grand duchess had in common with Queen Victoria.

By the spring of 1892 Alfred and Marie's eldest daughter 'Missy' was sixteen and her stunning beauty was attracting attention. She soon had two suitors – Grand Duke George Michaelovich of Russia and Prince George of Wales. The Duchess of Edinburgh, noting that Missy was drawn to Russia, quietly refused the grand duke's proposal. Her own father's extra-marital affairs had turned her away from the idea of a Romanov son-in-law. Missy's other suitor was not so easily disposed of.

Prince George (who, following the death of his elder brother Eddy earlier that year, was now second in line to the British throne) very much wanted to marry Missy, with whom he had fallen in love when he stayed with the Edinburghs in Malta. Alfred approved of this match and was backed by the Prince of Wales and Queen Victoria but Missy's mother was opposed. She was determined that the queen would *not* domineer her over the question of her daughter's marriage. When George proposed to Missy the duchess dictated a letter of refusal and looked for a bridegroom outside of Queen Victoria's orbit. To thwart the queen she had to move fast and, as a fervent Germanophile, her eye fell on Romania, whose royal family were relatives of the kaiser.

The Romanian throne was founded in 1866, when Prince Karl of Hohenzollern-Sigmaringen (the Catholic branch of the Hohenzollern family) was invited to become ruling Prince. In 1878 he wrested independence from Turkey, becoming King Carol I of an autonomous Romania. He and his wife Elisabeth, who wrote under the name of Carmen Sylva, had a daughter but this only child died at the age of four. Their unprepossessing heir was Carl's nephew Crown Prince Ferdinand, ten years Missy's senior. A marriage with him would extend the influence of the Romanovs in the Balkans and also earn the gratitude of the Germans, who were anxious for the Romanian Crown Prince to have a suitable royal wife. But above all it would be revenge on the British royal family for not treating the Duchess of Edinburgh with what she considered sufficient respect.

On 2 June 1892 Queen Victoria was 'dumbfounded' to receive a telegram from Prince Alfred which read: 'Missy engaged to Ferdinand of Roumania [*sic*] today.'[18]

The betrothal took place at Potsdam and was engineered by Missy's mother. Neither the queen nor Alfred had been in favour of this match. Although Ferdinand was believed to be a nice young man with charming parents, as Queen Victoria told Victoria of Battenberg when she announced this *fait accompli,* Missy would be going to an insecure country in whose capital, Bucharest, the immoral society was '*quite awful!'* The Duchess of Edinburgh then pretended that she and her husband had wanted Missy to marry Prince George but Missy had refused him. 'It was the dream of Affie's life,' the queen lamented.[19]

Very briefly, Queen Victoria was taken in by her daughter-in-law's machinations. 'I fear Bertie is very angry,' she wrote, '– but he is unjust and wrong. Affie and Marie wished for George...' It soon became apparent from the duchess's 'happy, expectant face' that this was not true and the queen began speaking of Missy as 'a great victim ... to be enormously pitied'.[20] Moreover, she was still a child.

By 24 June Missy and her mother were at Windsor where the Duchess of Edinburgh found that Queen Victoria was not very cordial, preferring to avoid a long talk with her daughter-in-law. 'She holds me entirely responsible for having allowing Ferdinand to make his proposal in Berlin when custom demanded that this should have happened in England, under the eye of the grandmother and my husband,' she told King Carol on 24 June. According to the duchess, Victoria did not congratulate her granddaughter and when Prince Alfred brought Ferdinand to see her she gave him a very cool reception and 'did not say a friendly or encouraging word to him'. Marie, aware that the queen always behaved like this, was not at all worried, ascribing it to the jealousy of the English family over her daughter's brilliant prospects. The queen 'is discontented and unhappy, accusing me of sacrificing my daughter's youth and happiness to an uncertain future', the duchess continued in her letter to the Romanian king.[21]

The queen's journal says nothing about her reception of Ferdinand beyond recording that Alfred brought him to see her at Windsor on 23 June. Another account says that she spoke to him kindly in his native German and saved him from embarrassment the next morning at breakfast when he broke his bread rolls into his coffee in the German fashion. Noting that no one else was doing so, Victoria said he must come to her private apartments where they could do that together. Ferdinand had one thing going for him in the queen's eyes. His maternal grandfather had been her cousin Prince Ferdinand of Saxe-Coburg-Gotha, the King-Consort of Portugal.

The engagement caused shock and surprise in the royal courts of Europe, where it was expected that the lovely Missy would be a future queen of England. There were also considerable difficulties over the wedding, as Ferdinand came from the Catholic branch of the Hohenzollern-Sigmaringen family and their children would have to be raised in the Orthodox religion of Romania. The queen naturally wanted her granddaughter to be married at Windsor like other members of the family but there were problems. Two ceremonies, Roman Catholic and Protestant, would be required and neither church was prepared to relinquish the honour of their church celebrating the first marriage service.

The queen discussed the difficulties with the Bishop of Rochester, who then went to see the Archbishop of Canterbury. The queen thought the marriage should either take place quietly in England, or in Coburg.

A quiet wedding was the last thing the Duchess of Edinburgh wanted. Marie hoped for a grand ceremony in Coburg where, as the wife of the Duchy's heir, she would be one of the leading ladies. This idea was foiled by Missy's English relatives, who refused to travel to the court of Prince Albert's 'wicked' brother Grand Duke Ernest. It was finally decided that the wedding would take place in Sigmaringen in January, by which time Missy would be seventeen. The Duchess of Edinburgh was delighted; at least the ceremony would take place far from the influence of her all-powerful mother-in-law.

In another letter to King Carol, written on 10 October, the Duchess told him that she did not see any political importance in the marriage. 'Before my own marriage,' she continued, 'in Russia and above all in England, there was so much ... shouting out in celebration of the enormous political importance of the union and what have been the results? None whatsoever!'[22]

* * *

In the wake of all this, on 23 November Sergei and Ella (the latter 'as sweet and lovely as ever', rhapsodised the queen) arrived at Windsor Castle after a lengthy absence.[23] During the summer Ella told the queen how much she and Sergei wanted to visit England again and Victoria wasted no time in issuing an invitation.

As the queen feared, the Russian climate was not conducive to her granddaughter's health. 'One gets so sensitive to the cold and last year I had all the winter rheumatics in my shoulder,' Ella wrote on one occasion.[24] The death of her father Grand Duke Louis in March 1892 exacerbated all this.

A few days after their arrival Ella and Sergei went to the Russian Church in London to attend the service for the Empress Marie Feodorovna's birthday. Then there were the usual walks and drives with the queen, as well as visits to the kennels. They attended a performance of the opera *Carmen* in the Waterloo Gallery and also spent a night at Sandringham.

At the beginning of December Ella and Sergei drove with the queen to Farnborough Hill in Hampshire, the home of Victoria's old friend the widowed Empress Eugenie of France, who had moved there in 1881. Over tea in the Red Parlour Eugenie and Victoria called each other 'dear sister' and then argued about who was to be first to pass through the door, each wishing to cede precedence to the other. Eugenie was said to be the only person who could reduce the queen to uncontrollable laughter. Their friendship dated from 1855, when the queen and Prince Albert paid a State Visit to Napoleon III's court in Paris.

On 7 December Sergei left for London to see his sister Marie, who was arriving that evening in advance of a visit by the Romanian royal family. 'He expressed himself so pleased with the short "*séjour*", and hoped to come again next year,' Victoria wrote approvingly. 'It is a pleasure to see how he loves dear Ella and how happy they are together. Dined with her, (alas! her last evening, which she was very sorry for)...'[25]

As Ella left the following day to meet Sergei at Dover, Queen Victoria prepared to meet the Romanian contingent and also discussed Missy's marriage contract with Lord Rosebery.

Alfred, Marie, Missy and Ducky arrived at Windsor Castle on 9 December, followed the next day by Crown Prince Ferdinand.

King Carol of Romania, his brother Leopold (Ferdinand's father) and the crown prince met the queen on 12 December. The king was proud to receive the Order of the Garter from Victoria but was less pleased at being told he had to wear knee breeches at dinner that night. Ferdinand was made a Knight of the Order of the Bath and was given a silver gilt basket as a wedding present. The queen also gave Missy her presents, which she listed as 'a handsome emerald and diamond pendant, and earrings to match, Honiton lace and stuffs, an Indian shawl and Scotch cloak.'[26]

The queen did not attend Missy's wedding, which took place at Sigmaringen on 10 January 1893. Later she heard that the ceremony had gone extremely well and that the bride looked lovely.

Yet again, the Duchess of Edinburgh had her way.

* * *

On 22 August 1893 Duke Ernest died. Alfred became Duke of Saxe-Coburg-Gotha and moved into Schloss Ehrenburg, the official residence of the Duke, where Marie now held court. 'Marie will love being No. 1 and reigning Duchess, I am sure,' Vicky wrote to her daughter Sophie, the Crown Princess of Greece.[27]

For Marie life in Coburg was infinitely preferable to life in London and what she described as Britain's 'hideous climate'. In April 1890 she told Missy that she found the city cold and dark, describing Clarence House as like 'going into a dark grotto, all yellow and smoky'.[28] Now she could do as she wished, taking her orders from nobody. More important still, she was free from the strictures of her mother-in-law, as she had been during the carefree days when they lived in Malta. She 'was her own mistress; it was a small kingdom perhaps, but her will was undiscussed, she took her orders from no one, and could live as she wished,' Missy wrote in her memoirs. Alfred, however, was less enthusiastic. He found Coburg 'deadly dull' and missed his life in the Royal Navy.[29] Relations between the couple remained difficult.

* * *

In 1892 the change of Cabinet in England gave Russia an opportunity to push forward troops in Afghanistan towards the Indian frontier. As Vicky warned her mother on 16 August, the British needed more men in India. 'It behoves us to be on the watch and not to part with anything which can strengthen our arm – whereas any weakness will only tempt our enemies to attack us,'[30] she insisted. By the following year it appeared that the Russians were trying to incorporate into their empire the countries which they had helped to liberate from the Turkish yoke.

Alexander III could not stand the bombastic young German Emperor William II, Vicky's son, who after he succeeded sacked Chancellor Bismarck. Russia had been slowly moving towards France ever since the tsar's refusal to renew the Three Emperors' League. In July 1891 some French warships paid a ceremonial visit to Kronstadt and the emperor stood bareheaded while the 'Marseillaise', previously banned in the Russian Empire, was played. The following month a formal agreement was signed between France and Russia. The renewal of the alliance between Austria, Germany and Italy led to suspicions in some Russian quarters 'that England might become linked in some way with the three central powers', an outcome which would have 'imperilled both France's ambitions in the Mediterranean and Russia's hopes for the Dardanelles'. These suspicions led Russia and France to 'seek mutual protection'.[31]

In 1893 Russia signed a secret military treaty with France; the following year they signed a full military alliance. Now Russia would not have to confront the mighty German army (or the combined forces of Germany and Austria) without an ally.

Europe was split into two opposing camps: the Triple Alliance of Germany, Austria and Italy on one side; France and Russia on the other. As Europe took sides, England would eventually have to choose between them.

In this climate of mutual suspicion it remained to be seen whether England would form any kind of alliance with Russia. For the moment she pursued her policy of 'splendid isolation'.

Betrothal in Coburg

'The more I think of sweet Alicky's marriage the
more unhappy I am.'
— Queen Victoria.

At the end of June 1893 royal guests converged on London for the
wedding of the queen's grandson Prince George, Duke of York and
Princess May of Teck. Among them was George's cousin Tsarevich
Nicholas of Russia.

Twenty-five-year-old Nicholas was shy, extraordinarily polite,
with enormous charm and a streak of obstinacy. There was no
trace of the vivacity of his mother Empress Marie Feodorovna,
nor of the enormous physical strength of Alexander III. Nicholas
had been to England as a small boy in 1873 but this was his first
visit as an adult. Again, he stayed with the Prince and Princess of
Wales at Marlborough House. Although he remembered one of
the rooms from the earlier visit, 'he does not feel quite at his ease
at Marlborough House and finds the hours quite dreadful,' the
Duchess of Coburg told Missy.[1]

The numerous wedding festivities would now form the
opportunity for Queen Victoria to meet Nicholas again and assess
the future ruler of Russia. There was a subtext to this encounter.
In Russia the search for a suitable bride for the tsarevich was
continuing but, to his parents' dismay, Nicholas would not marry
anyone except Queen Victoria's beautiful granddaughter Princess
Alix (Alicky) of Hesse. Although Alicky returned his love, she still
steadfastly refused to convert to Orthodoxy saying it was against
her conscience. Nicholas hoped she would attend George's wedding
and he could change her mind.

He was aware that Queen Victoria had taken the four young Hesse princesses under her wing after the death of Princess Alice in 1878. He probably also knew that Queen Victoria disliked the fact that Alicky's sister Ella had married his uncle Grand Duke Sergei and that the queen detested the Russians, who she said possessed a '*bourgeoiserie*' which she disliked intensely.[2] It was therefore vital that Nicholas make a good impression if he had any hope of marrying Alix.

He arrived at Windsor Castle shortly before 2 o'clock on 1 July to find the queen waiting at the top of the staircase to greet him. In order to show him every possible honour all the men were wearing uniforms. Whatever the queen expected, she was pleasantly surprised as her journal shows: 'He is charming, and wonderfully like Georgie [The Duke of York]. He always speaks English and almost without a fault, having had an English tutor, a Mr Heath, who is still with him.' She noted that he was always called Nicky and, something that really impressed her, 'he is very simple and unaffected'.[3] Another surprise was that he was small, around 5 foot 6 inches, quite unlike his giant of a father who stood over 6 feet tall. He was also diffident; the domineering personality of Alexander III stunted any attempt at initiative by his son.

The tsarevich briefly recorded his impression of Victoria in a letter to his mother: 'She is very friendly [and] talked a lot.'[4] To his great surprise the queen gave him the Order of the Garter, something which he certainly had not expected. (His heraldic plate remains in St George's Chapel at Windsor above Stall N7.)

In his diary Nicholas was not exactly complimentary about Victoria's appearance, describing her as 'a round ball on unsteady legs'.[5] He found her remarkably kind when he lunched with her and the Battenbergs, and noticed that she had two Indian attendants.

On 5 July he was seated next to the queen at the state banquet at Buckingham Palace. Victoria again described him as 'charming' and commented on his facial resemblance to the Duke of York, 'which leads to no end of funny mistakes, the one being mistaken for the other!'[6]

The tsarevich's visit went some way towards softening the queen's attitude to Russia. There had been a dispute over the Pamir Mountains which bordered Northern India and Afghanistan, and the Foreign Secretary Lord Rosebery threatened to send troops to defend Britain's interests. Later that year the tsar sent several Russian Orders to the Duke of York, including the Order of

St Andrew which George told his 'dearest Uncle Sasha' that he was 'pleased and proud' to have.[7]

In the main object of his trip Nicholas was disappointed. Alicky did not go to the wedding and after attending the ceremony on 6 July he left England the next day.

* * *

In the autumn of 1893 the queen invited Ella, Sergei and his brother the widowed Grand Duke Paul to Balmoral. They arrived in bright sunshine and were met at Ballater station by Princess Beatrice's husband Prince Henry of Battenberg, who accompanied them on the drive to the castle. At the bridge near Balmoral they were joined by the Highland regiment but the skirling bagpipes could not alleviate Paul's distress. 'Poor Paul looks very sad,' the queen noted as she greeted them at the door.[8]

While Paul and Sergei went out on a deer drive with Prince Henry, the queen drove out with Ella and quizzed her about the death of Paul's wife Alexandra, who had been staying with them when she died. Victoria later took the opportunity for a private conversation with Ella's lady-in-waiting, who she asked about her granddaughter's life in Russia. One afternoon they all had tea in the Dantzig Shiel, a single-storey gabled cottage built on the estate by the queen about 5 miles west of the castle.

On 3 October there was a double celebration. Prince Maurice, the son of Princess Beatrice and Prince Henry, celebrated his birthday with a cake with two candles and some toys. It was also the thirty-third birthday of Paul, and the queen made sure he was not left out. Before they all went to Princess Louise of Fife's home at nearby Mar Lodge she gave Paul 'a nosegay, a wrapper [probably tartan] and a cigarette case'.[9]

Their stay came to an end all too soon, and on 10 October Victoria recorded with sadness that 'I had alas! to take leave of dear sweet Ella,' as well as Sergei and Paul 'whom we liked very much.'[10]

The Russians returned home early the next morning loaded with gifts. The queen also sent some things for Paul's children, including a doll and a pretty white dress for three-year-old Grand Duchess Maria with which he said his daughter was enchanted.

Paul's letter of thanks is preserved in the Royal Photographic Collection at Windsor: 'You had the kindness during my stay in Scotland to ask me for a photograph of my children. I hasten to carry out your request by sending the most recent photograph ... taken at my home shortly after my return to St Petersburg. It is with profound gratitude that I often think of my charming stay at Balmoral and of the extreme kindness which Your Majesty showed to me.'[11]

Once back in Russia, Ella resumed her campaign to see Alicky married to the tsarevich. The queen of course was not in favour of this match. 'I perfectly understand all you say,' Ella wrote to her grandmother, '... only my wish for it is because I like the boy, his parents lead a model life, all heart and religion which gives them strength in the difficult moments of life and brings them nearer to God.'[12]

Ella and Sergei still encouraged Nicholas to hope and they even planned for him to meet Alicky at Coburg, where they were staying during the autumn of 1893. This fell through because Nicholas had just returned from Denmark and the emperor did not want him to travel again so quickly. Sergei was annoyed, believing that Nicholas was now wavering.

On 14/26 October he sent Nicholas a stinging rebuke: 'My wife [Ella] was so disappointed and outraged by your letter that she asked me to tell you she considers this case decisively finished... If you have no strong character, no will or your feelings have changed it's deplorable you haven't told me or my wife.'[13]

But Nicholas had not given up and circumstances in Russia were soon to undergo a dramatic change.

* * *

At the end of January 1894 Queen Victoria learnt that the tsar of Russia was very ill with a bad case of influenza, bronchitis and a lung infection. Soon news arrived that he seemed a little better and it appeared the crisis had passed. It was the calm before the storm.

In April the queen travelled to Coburg for the wedding of two of her grandchildren, Alice's son Grand Duke Ernest Louis of Hesse and Alfred's daughter Princess Victoria Melita ('Ducky') of Edinburgh and Saxe-Coburg-Gotha. The Duchess of Coburg had naturally hoped that Ducky would marry one of the Russian grand dukes but Queen Victoria, backed by Prince Alfred, engineered the Hesse marriage. She told Victoria of Battenberg that 'she had it out' with the Duchess of Coburg and had written to her 'kindly but strongly'.[14] Ernie and Ducky were first cousins but, in the Protestant church this was no bar to their marriage.

Although the queen won this round in her battle to thwart her daughter-in-law, neither bride nor groom was really enthusiastic; Ducky was in love with her Russian cousin Grand Duke Cyril, while Ernie seemed more anxious to ensure that the queen would attend his wedding and less keen to propose to Ducky.

In December 1893 the Duchess of Coburg told Missy that Ducky's engagement would take place at Coburg in April 1894, with the marriage at Windsor in the summer. The duchess was concerned about the queen's influence. 'They will want to have it all their own way, as a revenge for your engagement,' she continued. 'So nothing to take place until April, when granny will probably indicate the exact day, hour and minute and even the room, when and where Ducky is to be engaged after [i.e., according to] all the rules!'[15]

In the event, the engagement took place in January and in the following month (possibly forestalling what the duchess referred to as the 'mischief' the queen and Vicky could do) Ernie travelled to England.

It was left to the queen to set the date of the marriage, which she decreed would take place on 19 April. The duchess wanted the wedding to take place at the end of the month, but as she told Missy: 'Granny [Queen Victoria] would not admit it [i.e. agree to it] saying she was to be back in England by that time, so no powers on earth would have made her change the date. And now the capricious old lady wanted to have it two days later, but papa positively refused.'[16]

The Duchess of Coburg was worried about Ernie's closeness to his grandmother and as the wedding day approached, she complained to Missy about what she called his 'constant Anglomania'.[17] 'I had a long talk with Ernie ... about the English family, about granny and explained to him why we could not really like them and how often they had been nasty and spiteful to me,' she wrote. 'I don't think Ernie quite believed me, but all the same *it must be said* [she wrote these words in German] because he must not always be dragging Ducky to England in perpetual adoration of granny and [must] quite understand the reasons why we can never adore her. Otherwise I fear conflicts...'[18]

The queen arrived in Coburg in state. When her train pulled into the station she was met by Alfred and Marie and two of their daughters – Crown Princess Marie of Romania (Missy) and the unmarried Princess Alexandra (Sandra). All the gentlemen were in uniform and the kaiser had sent a squadron of the queen's regiment of Prussian Dragoons to form a guard of honour. The queen drove with Alfred and Marie through gaily decorated streets to Schloss Ehrenburg, where a large number of what she called 'the Royal Mob' were waiting to greet her in the salon. Among them was the tsarevich, who had come with his uncles Grand Duke Sergei, Paul and Vladimir as well as his Aunt Ella. That night Sergei and Ella were among those who dined with the queen; Nicholas was not present.

The tsarevich was desperate to persuade Alicky to marry him. His cousin Grand Duke Constantine Constantinovich recorded in his diary that the empress suggested he seek assistance from the queen, 'who has a great influence on her granddaughter'.[19] Perhaps the Empress Marie was unaware of Victoria's strong feelings about another Russian marriage – but was she aware of the risk of Alicky bringing haemophilia into the direct line of the Russian imperial family?

Alicky's brother Friedrich ('Frittie') was thought to be a haemophiliac; he died from a haemorrhage after falling through an open window when he was three. Her sister Irene proved to be a carrier, giving birth to a haemophiliac son in 1889; there would be another one in 1900. The empress's original opposition to the marriage may, in part, have been due to her uncertainty about this, although it is unlikely that the genetic pattern of the disease (already known in medical circles) was understood in the more sheltered atmosphere of Europe's royal courts.

***

The wedding of Ernie and Ducky took place on 19 April in the chapel of the Schloss, following a private civil ceremony in the queen's apartments. At the wedding breakfast afterwards Nicholas was seated next to the queen, who again commented on his charm.

The following day Queen Victoria learned from Ella that Nicky and Alix were engaged. 'I was quite thunderstruck,' Victoria recorded, 'as though I knew Nicky much wished it, I thought Alicky was not sure of her mind.' In fact the queen had been positive that Alicky would not accept him. They came into her room, the queen kissed them both and 'told Nicky he must make the religious difficulties as easy as he could for her, which he promised to do'. News of the engagement seemed popular, the queen noted, although she also recorded the drawbacks – 'Russia is so far away, the position is a difficult one, as well as the question of religion.'[20] But on the whole, now that Ernie was married and his wife would be acting as hostess in Darmstadt, Queen Victoria accepted the *fait accompli* as Nicholas and Alicky were so obviously fond of one another.

She called in the Munshi to share the good news and congratulate the tsarevich. Nicholas had not been impressed when he visited India. 'How stifling it is to be surrounded again by the English and to see red uniforms everywhere,' he wrote in his diary at the time.[21] Now he wisely kept these thoughts to himself.

The following morning Victoria sent the band of the Dragoon Guards to play under Nicholas's window, an attention which touched him enormously. He and Alicky had breakfast with the queen who gave them a small present (without, unfortunately, noting in her journal what it was). She was impressed with the tsarevich, calling him 'so natural simple and kind',[22] in contrast with his gruff father.

Later that morning all the royals crammed onto the steps at the rear of the Edinburgh Palace to be photographed by the Coburg court photographer Professor Uhlenhuth and other English and German photographers. That evening the newly betrothed couple were among the small select group of people who dined with the queen and a toast was drunk to their health.

Nicholas and Alicky had coffee with the queen nearly every morning. 'Now I must call her granny,' he recorded in his diary a few days later.[23]

After lunch on 26 April Nicholas went to the queen's room for a talk. She thought him 'so sensible' and immediately agreed to his request to be allowed to come to England privately to visit his fiancée at the end of June.

Many people thought a marriage between the tsarevich and a granddaughter of Queen Victoria would be good for Anglo-British relations. Lord Salisbury told the queen that he felt sure it would 'have a good influence for peace'. The Archbishop of Canterbury wrote in a similar vein and even the Munshi agreed. At the end of the year he wrote in Urdu in Victoria's Hindustani journal: 'The marriage ... occasioned the greatest joy as it led to more love between England and Russia.'[24]

It remained to be seen whether this would be true.

***

There is no doubt that Victoria liked the tsarevich very much and was susceptible to his charm. The words sensible, amiable, natural and nice recur often in the queen's journal when she wrote about him. As the queen had noticed, Nicholas's command of English was almost perfect thanks to his English tutor Charles Heath. In fact it was so good that for many years Alexander III asked his son to help him write his own letters to Queen Victoria. Now Nicholas began to correspond with her himself.

On his return to Russia he sent her the book written by Prince Esper Ukhktomsky (a member of the Imperial Geographical Society) when he accompanied Nicholas on the journey to Egypt, India, Singapore, Java, Siam, China and Japan between November 1890 and August 1891. Victoria naturally wrote to thank Nicholas for the splendid volume (which she later also acquired in the English translation), at the same time making clear the responsibility she felt towards Alicky and signing herself 'your affectionate (future) Grandmama'. Not only was the queen concerned for her granddaughter's health but she considered herself Alicky's guardian, as she made clear. 'As she has no parents, I feel I am the only person who can really be answerable for her. All her dear sisters after their beloved mother's death looked to *me* as their second mother, but *they* had *still* their dear *father*. Now poor dear Alicky is an orphan and has *no one* but me *at all* in that position. Anything you wish, I hope you will tell me *direct*.'[25]

Poor Nicholas was having trouble with the queen's writing, which was sprinkled with abbreviated words, capital letters and frequent underlinings. He found it very difficult to decipher and complained to Alicky that it took a long time for him to work it out. To his brother George he was less complimentary. 'The old queen (belly woman) often writes to me – that's nice, isn't it?'[26]

Alicky had gone to Harrogate to take the waters in the hope of curing the sciatica of which she had been complaining since her father died in 1892. The queen wrote to Nicholas enclosing a copy of the doctor's letter about his fiancée's treatment and health. The following month Victoria received another letter from Nicholas, thanking her for her kindness to him at Coburg and her concern over Alicky's wellbeing.

The queen was also worried about Alicky's 'nerves'. Her face and hands flushed red when she was agitated, a problem which seemed to manifest itself when the princess was confronted by people she did not know. With all these issues, how would she cope with the bitter St Petersburg winter and the glittering social occasions of the Russian season?

Victoria was not just concerned about Alicky's health, as is most evident from a letter she wrote to Victoria of Battenberg on 25 May. 'The more I think of sweet Alicky's marriage the more unhappy I am! *Not* as to the personality, for I like him *very* much but on account of the country, the policy and differences with us and the awful insecurity to which that sweet child will be exposed.'[27]

Plans were now in hand for Nicholas to visit England on board the *Polar Star*. 'You don't know, dearest grandmama, how *happy* I am to come and spend some time with you and my beloved little bride,' he wrote on 2/14 June. 'What a different impression for me this time – with my stay in London last year for Georgie's wedding.' He signed himself, 'your most loving and devoted (future) grandson.'[28]

***

Queen Victoria was meanwhile engaging in a tussle with her Russian daughter-in-law. The previous year when Missy was expecting her first child in Romania the queen was quick to recommend suitable medical attendants. The Duchess of Coburg feared that the nurse the queen wanted would report everything back to Windsor. 'I had terrible fights with granny-dear about an English ... nurse for you,' Marie told Missy on 17 July 1893, 'but will not give up the admirable one I have already engaged and will bring her with me, instead of the old gossip granny wants you to have.' Then there was another battle because the queen insisted on an English doctor who Marie said she did not know at all and, moreover, it would be a 'monstrous expense'.[29] The duchess's nurse attended Missy during all her confinements, as did her personal physician Dr Playfair who was acceptable to the queen as he was the brother of one of her lords-in-waiting. He brought to Romania a telegram from the queen demanding that he be allowed to attend her granddaughter. 'We want to be on the safe side, so near the East you know ... most uncertain,' Victoria wrote.[30]

Now the tussle was repeated in Darmstadt, where Ducky was expecting her first child in the spring of 1895. Ernie wanted to have a German doctor in order not to upset local prejudices but the Duchess of Coburg wanted her daughter to have a *Russian* nurse. Queen Victoria, although concerned, decided that she could not really object as it was her first baby but, as she told Victoria of Battenberg, the English were the best in the world when it came to dealing with childbirth and women's illnesses, 'more skilful and *much* more *delicate*. Aunt Marie does not *know* this, as she never had *but* one English doctor...'[31]

It may have been due to Marie's financial independence, but Queen Victoria found that her Russian daughter-in-law was the only member of the family she was unable to intimidate.

The Fateful Year of 1894

'I wish she had *not* gone to Livadia.'
– Queen Victoria.

Nicholas arrived at Gravesend on 20 June. From there he travelled to Walton-on-Thames, where Alicky was staying with her sister Victoria and her husband Prince Louis of Battenberg. They spent three idyllic days boating and picnicking before going to visit the queen, who had returned from Balmoral to Windsor.

Every morning the queen had breakfast at Frogmore with Alicky and Nicholas, who usually joined them after his early morning ride. One afternoon Alicky used her birthday present from the queen, as Nicholas recorded seemingly impressed: 'We went onto the grass where we made tea, Alix did everything since she has a superb new tea basket from granny.'[1]

Nicholas brought with him a casket of jewels for his bride, including a pink pearl engagement ring, a chain bracelet containing a huge emerald and a necklace of pink pearls. From the emperor came a 'marvellous sapphire and diamond brooch', and a sautoir of pearls created by Fabergé; and from the empress an emerald bracelet and a magnificent jewel-encrusted Easter egg. Looking at all these fabulous treasures the queen cautioned her granddaughter not to 'get too proud'.[2]

The queen took the couple and some other guests to visit the Duke and Duchess of Connaught at neighbouring Bagshot Park. Prince Arthur, an army officer, served in India between 1886 and 1890 and was anxious to show off his Indian-style billiard room wing, which had been pre-fabricated in India and installed by Indian craftsmen. Queen Victoria, who remained fascinated by India and had recently added an Indian-style Durbar Room to Osborne, was impressed: 'They took us to a tent, an Indian Shamiana, where we took tea. After that [we] went into the house and looked at the beautiful Indian room designed by Ram Singh, much of the carving having been executed by him. It is full of beautiful things they brought back from India, and so is the corridor leading to it. The rhododendrons were out splendidly in the grounds.'[3]

Dinner at Windsor Castle that night was a formal affair. Normally when the queen held a large dinner with illustrious guests the band played the National Anthem from the terrace as she came into dinner – but things did not always go to plan.

At five o'clock on the evening of one state dinner it was realised that the ageing equerry had forgotten to order the band. The regiment was encamped in Windsor Great Park, so a swift horseman was despatched to the commanding officer and three wagonettes were ordered to convey the bandsmen to the castle. So far so good – then another equerry realised that to reach the castle's terrace the band would have to go through the dining room, which would be impossible if the royal family were already in there. Four ladders were therefore borrowed from the castle fire brigade so that if the musicians were late arriving they could scale the outside walls onto the terrace. Queen Victoria processed into dinner that night to the sound of dead silence but, as the guests took their seats, figures could be seen climbing onto the terrace and before the soup was served the band had struck up an overture. The next morning, Victoria sent a note to the equerry saying that the band should be instructed to *always* play the National Anthem as she entered the dining room.

There was no such mishap when Nicholas dined with the queen, although to his horror she insisted he dress in the Windsor Uniform introduced by her grandfather King George III in 1779 for members of the royal family and distinguished guests (a version is still worn today). 'I have to appear in a tail coat with red collar and cuffs and breeches and pumps – how ghastly!' he wrote disapprovingly to his brother George.[4] To make matters worse the shoes rubbed his feet and he was exhausted from standing around all evening. He was not even allowed to smoke in the queen's presence, as she objected to the habit. In order to light up, Nicholas had to go to the billiard room (which was some distance from the drawing room) after Victoria had retired to bed.

The tsarevich spent a couple of days with the Prince of Wales at Sandringham, where among the guests were the prince's good friend the Jewish millionaire Baron Maurice de Hirsch and some horse dealers. Although Nicholas bought two horses in a local horse sale he tried to socialise as little as possible with Bertie's friends.

He was relieved to return to Alicky at Windsor. Archduke Franz Ferdinand of Austria had just arrived and on 29 June there was a dinner in his honour. Nicholas, who Victoria thought 'most affectionate and attentive', had the privilege of leading the queen into the dining room. 'Dear Nicky is very amiable and quite at home with us,' she told Vicky.[5]

By now Nicholas was feeling like part of the British royal family. In the morning he and Alicky went to Frogmore with the queen, where a table was set up in the shade of the elm trees and liveried attendants served tea. After lunch, rain or shine, the queen insisted they accompany her on a carriage drive. 'I have become almost as indispensible to my future grandmother as her two Indians and her Scotsman [the queen's attendants],' he told Grand Duke George who, having been diagnosed with tuberculosis, was living in the Caucasus.[6]

Nicholas was enjoying himself just being with Alicky. 'Granny has been very friendly,' he told his mother, 'and even allowed us *to go out for drives* without a chaperone! I confess I didn't expect that!'[7]

The queen took Nicholas to a service in Frogmore mausoleum, which he claimed to have enjoyed very much. He introduced her to Charles Heath, 'an oldish man, kind and plain spoken',[8] who was now teaching English to the emperor's youngest son Michael. She also met Father Yanishev, the emperor's confessor, 'a very enlightened and wide minded man' who was preparing Alicky for her conversion to Orthodoxy. 'He is a very fine looking man with long grey hair and beard.'[9] Both Mr Heath and Father Yanishev remained to dinner that evening.

The one low point of the visit was when Nicholas became locked inside the lavatory. After half-an-hour of yelling and trying to open the door with the key, Alicky managed to open it from the outside.

To his great regret Nicholas had to decline a dinner invitation from the Guards' mess at Windsor because, as he recorded, the queen and Alicky did not like him to miss dinner at the castle.

***

As a Russian army officer, Nicholas was probably delighted to accompany Queen Victoria and Alicky to Aldershot, a small town in the south of England where the British army's military camp had been established in the 1850s on a nearby heath. Victoria and her guests stayed at the Royal Pavilion, a single-storey house constructed around three sides of a square, with a large reception room in the middle and a drawing room to the right. The royal family and their attendants occupied the west wing; the east wing housed the dining room and the gentlemen-in-waiting. The kitchens were in a separate block, connected to the main house by an underground passage. The royal party arrived in time for tea on 11 July, although to the queen's regret it was too cold and wet to take it outside.

Nicholas described the camp to his sister Xenia as 'the English Krasnoe Selo', the military camp near St Petersburg where the Imperial Guards held their summer manoeuvres. The pavilion, he told her, was a wooden one-storey structure 'like an Indian bungalow' and the walls were so thin that every sound could be heard through the walls. Moreover, to his amazement, they all had rooms opening off the same corridor. That evening there was a large dinner. The queen had already asked several times when Nicholas was going to wear his red Circassion coat, so he wore it that evening. Despite his telling Xenia that it 'will absolutely drive granny wild,'[10] if the Cossack uniform did impress Victoria she made no comment about it in her journal.

It was a fine, clear although not very warm night, so afterwards there was a torchlight tattoo. 'It was a very pretty sight and very successfully carried out, though the bands were not very good of themselves, particularly not the trumpets...' the queen recorded with an air of disappointment.[11]

The following day Nicholas, wearing full Hussar uniform, followed the queen's carriage on horseback to Laffan's Plain where they watched the parade of 10,000 men.

They left Aldershot in time for the christening of the infant son of George and May, the Duke and Duchess of York, on 16 July. Nicholas and Alicky were among the godparents and accompanied Queen Victoria to White Lodge, Richmond Park, for the ceremony. Little Prince Edward (the future King Edward VIII) wore the Honiton lace christening gown made for the queen's eldest daughter Vicky (and used in the royal family until 2004).

Back at Windsor there were concerts to entertain the company. The Polish opera singers Jean and Edouard de Reszke (particular favourites of Nicholas's mother the Empress Marie) sang for the guests one afternoon, and after dinner on 17 July selections from the opera *Signa* were performed.

On 19 July the queen and her guests embarked on the royal yacht *Alberta* for Osborne House. 'It is funny to think that I lived here twenty-one years ago,' Nicholas recorded thoughtfully after visiting Albert Cottage on the Osborne estate, 'but I remember almost nothing.'[12] Victoria's life was exactly the same as at Windsor. For Nicholas there was the added attraction of being near the sea and in his diary he noted that the view across the Solent to the mainland was 'surprisingly beautiful'.

Nicholas and Alicky took tea in the Upper Alcove with the queen. The sailors from the imperial yacht *Polar Star* were walking around the grounds and later the queen invited them onto the terrace. 'They drew up, and I bowed to them, all calling out a greeting in Russian. Nicky then told them I was pleased to see them and they answered and then marched off. They were fine looking, tall men,' Victoria wrote approvingly.[13]

Nicholas's departure was set for the following day, as he had to return to Russia for his sister Xenia's marriage to Grand Duke Alexander Michaelovich (the 'Sandro' the queen had received at Buckingham Palace a few years earlier). He and Alicky spent their last day together in Cowes, shopping in the town's main street for little enamelled pins and brooches.

After dinner Nicholas changed into the uniform of the Guard Corps. '....he took leave of me in the Hall,' Victoria recorded, 'thanking me much for all my kindness, and kissing me very affectionately.'[14] After leaving some lovely presents for Victoria, Nicholas drove away to the strains of the Russian imperial anthem. Alicky remained with the queen at Osborne.

Nicholas seems to have enjoyed the final days on the Isle of Wight far more than Windsor. Writing from the army camp at Krasnoe Selo to thank Victoria for her kindness, he told her how happy he was to be allowed to think of himself as her grandson. 'I loved Osborne so much,' he continued, saying how delighted he was to be asked to spend five days there.[15]

* * *

Victoria was at Balmoral in September when more alarming news of the emperor's health began to arrive. Although Alexander III was very ill in January it was thought he had recovered. He was still only forty-nine and it could be expected that he would live for many more years. Yet at Xenia's wedding that summer all the splendour of the uniforms, the sumptuous court dresses and the blazing jewels could not conceal the seriousness of the emperor's condition. He looked old and tired, his clothes hung off him and his mighty frame sagged.

On 26 September the Princess of Wales arrived back from a visit to her parents in Copenhagen saying she was very anxious about Alexander's health. He had never recovered fully from the bout of influenza and she told the queen that Empress Marie was very worried. The empress was also concerned about her son George, who had tuberculosis and was now spitting blood.

The tsar was clearly very ill. From the imperial hunting lodge at Spala in Poland, where they had gone to hunt, Nicholas reported to the queen that the air there seemed to have done his father a lot of good but the doctors insisted he leave for the Crimea. Victoria became even more anxious when she heard that Nicholas had abandoned his plans to join his fiancée in Darmstadt in order to accompany his parents to Livadia, where it was hoped that the warmer southern climate would help the tsar's health.

On 10 October a telegram arrived at Balmoral. The emperor's condition had not improved and the empress had once more summoned the German doctor. As Alexander's condition deteriorated, the telegrams received by the queen indicated that his strength was diminishing. He was sometimes a little better, sometimes worse. As anxiety increased, Ella and Sergei left Moscow for the Crimea.

At the end of the month Queen Victoria sent another enquiry about the tsar's condition. The reply was not reassuring: 'Heard from Nicky that his dear father was weaker, and that he had asked Alicky to come.'[16]

Queen Victoria was upset that her granddaughter would soon very likely be placed on an unsafe throne and that when this happened she would be able to see her only rarely. 'Do explain what I have said to Nicky,' she wrote to Victoria of Battenberg, 'and also to both that I *do* pray that (at any time) she will come to see me once more before she marries.'[17]

By 28 October the queen was receiving daily updates from Nicholas and Alicky, as well as the bulletins from St Petersburg. Ella reported that the emperor was 'weaker, the action of the heart being so feeble'.[18] As he began to grow gradually weaker, the Prince and Princess of Wales left for Russia, the princess to support her sister.

Then on 1 November (Ella's thirtieth birthday) a telegram arrived from Nicholas and Alicky. It was the worst possible news: 'Dearest beloved father has been taken from us. He gently went to sleep.' The queen's thoughts immediately turned to 'poor Minny' [the empress] and 'poor dear Nicky and darling Alicky'. That night Victoria wrote in her journal: 'May God help them All! What a terrible load of responsibility and anxiety has been laid upon the poor children! I had hoped and trusted they would have many years of comparative quiet and happiness before ascending this thorny throne.'[19] To Vicky she wrote that it was a 'horrible tragedy'. Her heart also went out to the widowed empress, who she heard was 'calm but broken hearted'.[20] Knowing the pain the empress was feeling, having been through the same herself, Victoria immediately sent her a message and despatched some comforting books.

Marie Feodorovna replied by telegram: 'Your loving and deepest sympathy soothes my broken heart in my immense misfortune. I thank you with all my heart, my dearest aunt,' and she signed herself, 'your sincerely loving, despairing Minny'.[21]

This was followed by a letter. 'You can really understand my feelings, because the Lord imposed the same dreadful loss on you, the greatest loss on earth, to lose the one who was everything for me, for I loved my dearest Angel above all else and I can't imagine how I will live without him. And my poor, beloved Nicky, apart from the irreplaceable loss of his deeply beloved father, has to carry the heavy lot on his young shoulders so early, this cuts me deeply to the heart. Thank God, he's so happy with his charming Alicky. She's his greatest comfort in his great misfortune and is certainly more and more loving and faithful in sharing everything with him.'[22]

Victoria also dashed off a letter of sympathy to Nicholas, hardly able to summon up the words to express her feelings. 'The best I can find are comprised in "God bless you." ... May our two countries ever be friends, and may you be as great a lover of peace as your dear father.'[23]

This illustrates the change in the relationship between Queen Victoria and Nicholas. The queen's twenty-six-year-old future grandson was now Nicholas II, Emperor and autocrat of all the

Russias, ruler of a mighty empire – an event which the seventy-five-year-old Victoria had not expected to happen during her lifetime. The family connection would now have to be balanced alongside the political relationship between their countries and this could cause problems.

* * *

The queen now received daily reports about Alexander's death, the arrangements for the funeral and Alicky's conversion to the Orthodox faith. Victoria had already been questioning Ella about the Orthodox religion and received the encouraging reply that 'the questions you asked me in your last letter have not in the least troubled Alix...'[24] Alicky's conversion took place quietly on the morning after Alexander III's death, in the presence of Nicholas, Empress Marie and Ella. She took the name of Grand Duchess Alexandra Feodorovna. They all took communion after her confirmation which, Ella told Queen Victoria, 'was so beautiful and touching. She [Alicky] read very well.'[25]

Meanwhile the Prince and Princess of Wales had arrived. Hurrying to Russia to support Empress Marie, they heard the news of Alexander III's death when they reached the British Embassy in Vienna. On reaching Livadia they discovered that no arrangements had been made for the funeral. Nicholas, overwhelmed by his new responsibilities and overawed by his uncles, seemed reluctant to make any decisions; Empress Marie, consumed with grief, was also unwilling, while apparently not encouraging anyone else to make them either.

The Prince of Wales immediately took charge and reported daily to Queen Victoria in a series of telegrams, beginning on Monday, 5 November [NS] 1894: 'Thanks for telegram. We are all well. Minny [Marie Feodorovna] wonderfully resigned in her grief. We leave here Thursday, arrive Moscow Sunday, leave Monday. Arrive Petersburg Tuesday. Am writing. Albert Edward.'[26] Queen Victoria obviously did not receive this, as the following day the prince telegraphed again: 'Sorry my telegram did not reach you yesterday. Leave Thursday. Stay Sunday Moscow, arrive Petersburg Tuesday. Written to you yesterday at some length [Ella?] telegraphed. Albert Edward.' Bertie then telegraphed his son George, Duke of York, asking him to come to Russia, not only out of respect for his uncle the late tsar, but as a support for Nicholas. As a close friend of the new monarch it was felt that he would be an enormous moral support for his cousin.

The queen was now demanding regular reports from Livadia and, to the despair of the Prince of Wales's equerry Arthur Ellis, who privately called her 'the old tiresome woman at Windsor Castle', she was constantly telegraphing asking for more letters. Later on 6 November the Prince of Wales sent another message: 'Have announced George's departure on 12th [he] cannot reach Petersburg before 15th. Should you wish to see him [he] could be with you in Balmoral for 24 hours.' Victoria apparently then telegraphed Bertie again, anxious to know the date of the tsar's wedding. There was also the question of who would represent her at the funeral. 'Thanks for telegram,' the Prince of Wales replied on 7 November. 'Will let you know about wedding from Petersburg. Date not yet settled. Will gladly represent you at funeral. [The] Lord Chamberlain [Lord Carrington] should arrive not later than 17th. Just starting for Sevastopol.'

Alexander III's coffin was carried to the jetty at Yalta by sailors from the imperial yacht along a path strewn with cypress sprays and laurel leaves, followed by the imperial family on foot. It took two-and-a-half hours for the long procession (which included the emperor's charger, without trappings) to reach Yalta harbour where the coffin was placed on board the warship *Pamiat Merkuria*. Accompanied by an escort from the Black Sea fleet and a final salute of cannons it sailed for Sevastopol where a train was waiting to take them north. Three days and 1,400 miles later the slow-moving train reached Moscow, where snow was on the ground and the wind was biting. In a silence broken only by tolling bells and guns firing in salute, the coffin was borne through streets lined with thousands of sorrowing people. Ten times they stopped at churches along the route for a Litany to be sung on the steps before they finally reached the Archangel Cathedral in the Kremlin, where Alexander III lay in state for 36 hours. Still the interminable masses for the dead continued. One was repeated thirty-nine times.

The whole process had to be gone through again when the coffin was borne back to the station for the final journey to St Petersburg. Bertie later described the journey as 'very fatiguing, though most impressive, with the constant religious services in the open air at the different places where the train had to stop.'[27]

Nicholas's time was no longer his own but, in the middle of the numerous funeral services he tactfully wrote to his dearest grandmama from Moscow on 30 October/11 November, saying how her telegrams had touched them all deeply and explaining that his wedding had to take place as soon as possible because his mother would soon be going south to the Caucasus with his brother George. It was also impossible, Nicholas continued apologetically, for Alicky to go and stay with the queen before their hasty wedding but he promised that as soon as the opportunity arose they would both pay her a visit and he hoped that this would occur soon.

The announcement that the wedding would take place in the very near future gave the queen a terrible shock, although she realised it would be impossible for Alicky to return to Darmstadt as she would worry so much about Nicholas. In a burst of frustration, she told Victoria of Battenberg that she feared the next time she saw Alicky she would be the great empress of Russia. '*Cela me revolte* to feel that she has been taken *possession* of and carried away as it were by those Russians. I wish she had *not* gone to Livadia and *yet* that was also impossible!'[28]

In her reply to Nicholas, after speaking about his devotion to his mother and the dreadful time she had gone through, Victoria returned to what was uppermost in her mind – her certainty that he would make Alicky a good husband. The queen was reassured by Nicholas's love for her granddaughter, knowing she would be safe and well looked after. She sent some Indian embroidery as a wedding present from the Munshi.[29]

* * *

Queen Victoria was travelling from Balmoral to Windsor by train and had reached Carlisle when Bertie's telegram from St Petersburg was handed to her. 'Arrived here at 10 this morning,' the Prince telegraphed on 13 November. 'Funeral procession on foot on Friday [from the station to the SS Peter & Paul Cathedral] lasted 4 hours, then service nearly an hour. Last ceremony probably Monday or Tuesday. Damp and dark weather...'

By now telegrams were flying between Windsor and St Petersburg. 'Glad to hear of your safe arrival [at Windsor],' Bertie telegraphed two days later. 'Alfred, Irene, Ernie and Georgie [Duke of York] just arrived, all well. Funeral on Monday. Wedding probably 25th.'

In fact it was decided to hold the wedding on 26 November, the forty-seventh birthday of Empress Marie, a day when it was permissible for the court to briefly come out of mourning. 'Minny and Alix [the Princess of Wales] will of course be present at wedding on 26th and Alix delighted to represent you if you will let her know your wishes,' Bertie telegraphed to his mother, also on 15 November. At the queen's request, the Danish artist Laurits Tuxen was despatched to St Petersburg to paint the marriage ceremony. The painting hung at Osborne until 1901.

Meanwhile the funeral services continued. On 16 November Bertie telegraphed again. 'The service on Monday commences at 10 and will last 2 or 3 hours. My father-in-law [King Christian IX of Denmark] and Waldemar [his son] arrived today.'

On Monday, 19 November the queen held a memorial service at Windsor to coincide with the final funeral service in St Petersburg. 'The music was beautiful and a fine Russian Hymn always sung at funerals throughout the Greek Church, was sung without accompaniment, and was very impressive,' Victoria recorded in her journal. 'The service lasted half an hour.'[30] Later that day a telegram arrived from Bertie. 'Funeral service just over. Most impressive. Dear Minny bore up with wonderful fortitude.'

As preparations for the new tsar's wedding commenced, the Empress Marie's uncle Prince Hans of Glücksburg wrote to thank Sir Hugh MacDonell, the former British Ambassador to Denmark, for his sympathy on Alexander III's death. After telling him that they had 'very good news of the poor empress who though still in isolation still is in very good health,' Prince Hans continued: 'We are glad to hear how perfectly well her amiable son the now present young emperor acts and thinks and speaks, so the whole world has hope that he will follow his lamented father's footsteps, to maintain the world peace and to live for his country's and people's civilisation... The empress is very satisfied too with the young imperial bride! She knew her only little before but the empress as well as the poor late emperor liked her from the first arriving at Livadia...'[31]

If Queen Victoria had been informed of these last comments she could only have been reassured.

* * *

'Tomorrow morning poor dear Alicky's fate will be sealed,' the queen wrote to Vicky on 25 November with a prescience she could never have imagined in all her wildest fears. She had already received a letter from Ella dated 5/17 November, enclosing a description and sketches of Alicky's wedding attire. Ella also said that, contrary to the usual custom, the wedding ceremony would not be followed by a banquet and ball because of mourning for Alexander III.[32]

The next day, returning to the castle from her customary drive, the queen received a telegram from the Prince of Wales. 'Wedding over at 2, most impressive. Alicky looked lovely. Great enthusiasm amongst the people.' Similar telegrams soon arrived from the Duchess of Coburg and the Princess of Wales. 'Oh! how I do wish I had been there,' Victoria lamented. A large dinner was given at Windsor that evening in honour of the wedding. The menu included *Escalope de Turbot à la Crème, La Mousse de Faisans* and *Le Boeuf à la Mode.* Queen Victoria proposed a toast to 'the healths of their Majesties the Emperor and Empress of Russia, my dear grandchildren' and remained standing while *God Save the Tsar* was played. 'How I thought of darling Alicky and how impossible it seemed that that gentle little simple Alicky should be the great Empress of Russia!'[33]

It would take a long time for Queen Victoria to accustom herself to the new situation.

* * *

The Prince of Wales and the Duke of York left Russia in early December. 'We leave here on 2nd [and] stay 24 hours at Berlin with Vicky. Shall be back on 6th. Have written to you plans [?] by Thursday's messenger. Minny and Alix will (just) remain here for the present,' Bertie told Queen Victoria on 24 November.

A few days later he reported news of Grand Duke George, Nicholas's brother who was now heir to the throne until the new tsar had a son. Although George had been at Livadia when his father died the doctors had forbidden him to accompany the others to the cold of Moscow and St Petersburg and he left for the Caucasus on board the *Orel*. 'Last accounts of Nicky's brother better, [you] must not believe accounts in newspapers,' he telegraphed on 30 November.

The queen had appointed the tsar Colonel-in-Chief of the Scots Greys, the regiment he had so greatly admired at Aldershot during the summer. From the Anichkov Palace he sent a letter of surprise and thanks with Lord Carrington, the queen's Lord Chamberlain who was about to return to Windsor, telling the queen he would be 'happy and proud' to wear the uniform in her presence one day.[34]

Alicky also wrote to thank her grandmother for the items for her trousseau – a pendant with the queen's portrait and 'the lovely ring I wore for the wedding and ever since and when I look at it I have to think of the beloved giver.' The queen also sent her the Order of Victoria and Albert.[35]

Bertie and his son George arrived at Windsor on 6 December while the queen was having tea. They remained for almost an hour while the Prince of Wales told her about Alexander III's illness, the journey back to St Petersburg, the various religious services and the great courage of Empress Marie, now the dowager empress. He then spoke of the new tsar, 'how well he had begun, & how kind & absolutely devoted he was to darling Alicky', the queen noted with pleasure.[36] He probably did not tell her that Nicholas looked pale and tired throughout the long marriage ceremony and that Alicky, as solemn and unsmiling as ever, was struggling under the weight of her heavy dress and robes which prevented her from moving without assistance. General Arthur Ellis, in his report to the queen, said that in some people's eyes the beautiful bride was possibly eclipsed by her even more beautiful sister Ella, Grand Duchess Sergei. He also remarked that 'everything had the appearance of a forced air of mock festivity' and that unsurprisingly, 'a shadow of sadness seemed to hang over the whole ceremony.'[37]

The queen departed for Osborne, where on 21 December she received Baron George de Staal, who was being reaccredited as the Russian Ambassador, and General Tchertkoff, the special envoy sent officially to announce the death of Alexander III and the accession of Nicholas II. That night both were invited to dinner in the Durbar Room. '[Baron] de Staal, who is very agreeable, sat next to me, and talked much of the poor emperor's death, of Nicky and what satisfaction his reception of the Poles had given, and his promise that the observance of their [Catholic] religion would no longer be interfered with. Both ... de Staal and General Tchertkoff, were full of anxiety that Nicky should not overwork himself and begged me to write & urge this on him.'[38]

The Russian Empire was now governed by an inexperienced young man of twenty-six who was totally unprepared for the task. Victoria naturally hoped that, with the strong family connections between them, he would lean towards England. But those who hoped the accession of the new tsar would herald a more liberal regime were doomed to disappointment. Nicholas dismissed as 'senseless dreams' the hope that the representatives of the Zemstvo (local government councils) would be allowed to participate in internal government and declared that, like his father, he would reign as an autocrat.

Although Nicholas may have had the best of intentions, the Russians were still not to be trusted. As Vicky wrote to her daughter Sophie, Nicky could 'kill nihilism with one blow, and rest in safety, if only he could take up the plan his grandfather [Alexander II] had prepared all ready. But who can tell him?'[39]

Meetings on the Riviera

'She was so kind and amiable.'
— Empress Marie Feodorovna.

On 15 March 1895 Queen Victoria arrived at the Grand Hotel, Cimiez, in the hills above Nice. She had been travelling to the Riviera since 1882 when she visited Menton near the Italian border and drove through Monte Carlo (of which she thoroughly disapproved). In 1887 she spent a few nights in Cannes to see the villa where her son Leopold died. Four years later she stayed at the Grand Hotel at Grasse, visiting a perfume factory during her stay; and the following year her destination was the Hotel Costebelle in Hyères. Since then the queen spent a few weeks every spring on the Riviera but although flags waved, flowers were presented and local dignitaries welcomed Victoria, on none of these occasions does she record any contact with the Romanovs. This situation was about to change.

The French Riviera had been a favourite haunt of the Romanovs since 1856 when the Dowager Empress Alexandra Feodorovna (widow of Nicholas I) stayed in the Villa Acquaviva on the Promenade des Anglais in Nice. Since then a regular Russian colony had grown up in the towns and villages between Marseilles and Menton and many members of the imperial family and Russian high society owned villas in the vicinity. Among them was Queen Victoria's daughter-in-law the Duchess of Coburg, who owned the Chateau Fabron in one of the most prestigious areas near Nice. It was therefore no surprise that the queen received many Russian visitors.

The queen usually travelled in the second week of March, returning to England in the last week of April. On no account would the superstitious monarch cross the Channel on a Friday.

With her went between sixty and a hundred people, including her Indian attendants and the grooms who cared for her donkey. The number varied depending on how many of her daughters, grandchildren and their suites accompanied the queen.

Cimiez was much favoured by the British aristocracy. The queen enjoyed the warm sunny weather and the beauty of the mountains and the sea but her incognito as 'Madame la Comtesse de Balmoral' when she travelled fooled nobody. The hotel's gardens were transformed, repairs and alterations carried out to the queen's rooms, her horses and carriages arrived and the other hotel guests departed. Nobody would be allowed to invade Victoria's privacy.

Whether or not it was because she was now the grandmother of the Empress of Russia, from 1895 the Romanovs began to beat a path to the queen's door. Among the first was Princess Eugenie of Oldenburg, who the queen had once considered as a bride for Prince Alfred. Victoria had not seen Eugenie since she visited Osborne in 1873 but now the princess and her relatives became regular callers. Sometimes when Eugenie dined with the queen she was accompanied by her son Prince Peter.

Eugenie's brother Prince George of Leuchtenberg and his second wife were also staying in the vicinity. George's first wife had been Princess Theresa of Oldenburg, the sister of Princess Eugenie's husband Prince Alexander. The marriage, which was against the laws of the Orthodox Church, took place in secret in 1879 and their son Alexander was born in 1881. Theresa died from consumption in 1883 and four years later George married Princess Anastasia (Stana), daughter of Prince Nicholas, the ruler of Montenegro.

Also at Cimiez were Grand Duke Peter Nicolaievich of Russia (a grandson of Tsar Nicholas I) and his wife Militsa (Stana's sister), who were staying at nearby Beaulieu. Peter was a talented painter and an avid reader with a passion for the arts and architecture but he had been forced to resign from the Lancers Life Guards regiment for health reasons. He suffered from tuberculosis and during the early 1890s he and Militsa often travelled to the warmer climates of Italy, the Mediterranean, Egypt, North Africa and Palestine, where they indulged their love of classical architecture and art to the full. Militsa and Stana were described by the queen as handsome and pleasant. Both were dressed in white (a mourning colour in Russia) in deep mourning for Alexander III. A few days later the queen met George and Stana's children, Sergei born in 1890, and Elena born in 1892. On 15 April Peter and Militsa, with her sisters Hélène and Anna of Montenegro, dined with the queen.

The presence of the imperial family in Nice over many years ensured that there were several Russian Orthodox churches in the area. One evening the 140 members of the choir of the Imperial Chapel, which had been built in memory of Alexander II's eldest son Nixa, sang for Victoria and her guests in the hotel's large dining room. The queen was impressed both with the Russian compositions, beautifully sung without accompaniment, and the deep bass voices of the men. They wore Russian national dress 'as it used to be worn in olden times'.[1]

Princess Eugenie left Cimiez early but the Leuchtenbergs and Grand Duke Peter and Grand Duchess Militsa were at Nice station to see Victoria off when her train left for Darmstadt on 23 April. On the train she noted that Princess Beatrice read her 'a very pretty Russian story'.[2] Perhaps the queen was beginning to warm towards Russia after all.

* * *

The old queen was fond of the young tsar and on a personal level things were going well. The political climate was unfortunately not so good. The on-going dispute between Russia and Britain over the boundary between Russian and Afghan territory in the Pamir Mountains was finally settled by a boundary commission and a convention eventually ratified the formal acknowledgement of Russian and British possessions in Central Eurasia. The British agreed also to the use of the name 'The Nicholas Range' on maps in honour of the tsar; in return Russia agreed that Lake Zorkul should be referred to as 'Lake Victoria' in honour of the queen. Problems elsewhere proved more difficult to solve.

There was war between China and Japan and, after being soundly defeated, the Chinese sought intervention from the Great Powers to obtain an armistice. Russia, Japan's neighbour, was unwilling to allow the Japanese to obtain a foothold in China. When they realised that Japan meant to annexe Manchuria (a North China province for which they had their own plans), the Russians demanded Britain back the plan to evict them. Britain, whose interests were not involved, refused.

The queen then wrote a diplomatic letter to the tsar explaining that it was impossible to take Russia's side because of the strong feeling in the country. Derogatory comments about England had been appearing in the Russian press and Victoria complained to Nicholas, saying they were apparently written by Prince Alexander Utkhomsky, who was a journalist known to him. Nicholas replied, saying rather disingenuously (in view of the fact that the Russian press was subject to the strictest censorship in the world) that he could not prevent the newspapers publishing people's opinions and pointing out that the English papers often contained some unfair comments about Russia. Furthermore, he continued, books which erroneously misconstrued the actions of Russia in Asia and the country's internal politics were frequently sent to him from London but he was sure that there was as little aggression in them as there was in the newspaper articles that the queen had complained about. Later, in a conversation with the departing British Ambassador, Nicholas said that the Russian press were of 'very little importance'.[3]

In Europe there was great concern at what would happen when the Ottoman Empire crumbled. Russia continued to pursue her aims of obtaining the Dardanelles and Constantinople. In August there was an insurrection in Crete but the Russians obstructed any solution and seemed determined to humour the Turks. Germany was annoyed at Britain's good understanding with Russia. Queen Victoria was anxious that both personally and politically all was well with Russia.

Alfred and Marie were often at Windsor that May, having come from Germany for a few weeks. By now the queen probably knew that Alicky was expecting her first child and the presence of the Duchess of Coburg reminded her about the battles over the doctor and nurse for Missy and Ducky's confinements. By mid-October Queen Victoria was very anxious about Alicky. 'I dread that Russian doctor!' she told Victoria of Battenberg.[4]

On 15 November, while the queen was on the train from Balmoral to Windsor, she received good news from Nicholas. 'Darling Alix has just given birth to a lovely enormous little daughter, Olga,' he telegraphed. 'My joy is beyond words. Mother and child doing well.'[5] Although many people were disappointed that the child was a girl and not the longed-for heir, Queen Victoria was both thankful and relieved. The tsar and tsarina asked her to be their daughter's godmother and she gladly accepted.

* * *

In March 1896 the queen was back at the Grand Hotel in Cimiez, where once again she had many Russian visitors.

Princess Eugenie, her husband Prince Alexander of Oldenburg and brother George of Leuchtenberg were at the station to greet the queen when she arrived. Victoria was annoyed when she reached the hotel because a new building now obstructed her view. 'We drove up the old road and through the Arènes, as the other is impassable owing to the building of an enormous new hotel, which has been most provokingly put up just in front of the Grand Hotel, taking away all the view and privacy,' she wrote in her journal on 11 March. It would be her last stay at this particular establishment.

At the end of the month the Dowager Empress Marie Feodorovna arrived at the Villa des Terrasses at nearby La Turbie with her son George, whose new yacht the *Tsarnitsa* was moored in Villefranche harbour. On 6 April the dowager empress (whom the queen still called Minny) visited the queen accompanied by her younger children, seventeen-year-old Michael and thirteen-year-old Olga. Victoria immediately noticed how young the dowager empress looked (she was forty-eight) and how sad. 'She talked much of dear Alicky, and the baby,' Victoria recorded. The queen mentioned her unhappiness that, since the death of the previous Foreign Minister, Nicolai de Giers, in January 1895, Russia had not been so friendly to England and she asked the empress to speak to Nicholas about it. 'She said she would do so, and could not understand the coolness.'[6]

Lord Salisbury was received by the queen on 8 April. They discussed 'the incredible behaviour of Russia', whose new Foreign Minister Prince Alexei Lobanov-Rostovsky (who was thoroughly prejudiced against England) was trying to unite other foreign powers against her, including urging and encouraging France against England with regard to Egypt. Furthermore, the prince refused to co-operate with Lord Salisbury's government, suspecting them of trying to create tension in Europe in order to take some of Turkey's territory on the demise of the Ottoman Empire. Salisbury told the queen that all sensible statesmen were anxious for England and Russia to have a good understanding, 'but there is a feeling amongst our people against her [Russia], and if she shows herself to be so unfriendly, it will make it very difficult for the government.'[7]

The following day the queen had another Russian visitor. Countess Hélène Sheremetev was the daughter of Grand Duchess Marie Nicolaievna, Duchess of Leuchtenberg, by her second, morganatic, marriage to Count Gregory Stroganov. In 1879 aged just eighteen, Hélène married Vladimir Alexeievitch Sheremetev, a commander in His Imperial Majesty's Own Convoy, the special military unit who protected the tsar. Apart from Empress Marie Feodorovna, with whom Hélène remained a favourite, most members of the imperial family and the court disliked the Sheremetevs. They tried to live a grand lifestyle in their house on the fashionable English Quay helped by subsidies from various relations. After Sheremetev squandered all Hélène's money they were forced to let the house and live on an allowance paid by the tsar and Hélène's half-sister Princess Eugenie of Oldenburg. Sheremetev, who one member of the court described as a 'dedicated scoundrel', then 'borrowed money and profiteered on the patronage of his own miserable men by the empress'. After he died in 1893 Hélène married another officer, Gregory Nikititch Miklashevich, a Colonel of His Imperial Majesty's Own Convoy.[8]

Hélène, the queen recorded, 'is tall and handsome, very like her grandfather the Emperor Nicholas, and speaks English very fluently'. Probably because of her unpopularity with members of the imperial court, Victoria noted that 'she seemed much pleased at my wishing to see her.'[9]

Other visitors included the dowager empress's brother-in-law Grand Duke Alexei Alexandrovich, and Charles Heath, the English tutor to young Grand Duke Michael Alexandrovich, with whom Victoria had what she described as an interesting conversation.

On 10 April the queen paid a return call to the dowager empress at La Turbie, driving through 'indescribably beautiful scenery' accompanied by her daughter Princess Helena, *her* daughter Princess Helena Victoria (Thora) of Schleswig-Holstein and members of the suite. At the Villa des Terrasses the queen admired the 'fine Cossack' wearing a uniform of blue velvet, who helped them alight from the carriage. After greeting Empress Marie they were shown inside, 'where we found the Cesarewitch [*sic*] George, who looks too dreadfully ill, so thin, and weak.'[10] He did not join Empress Marie, Michael and Olga when they lunched at the hotel with the queen on 22 April. The empress 'seemed very sad and anxious' about George,[11] who was unable to join in many of the family's activities. During their stay he suffered another haemorrhage, which caused more concern about his health. The dowager empress was therefore pleased that the Princess of Wales was coming to visit her at La Turbie.

Alexandra arrived with her daughters Victoria and Maud to stay at the Villa de Masse and after lunch on 26 April she called on the queen in the company of her sister. 'Poor George of Russia is a little better,'[12] the queen recorded. It was a beautiful warm day, so at four o'clock they all went for a carriage drive. The queen, Alix and Empress Marie occupied one carriage, followed by another containing Princess Beatrice, Victoria of Wales, Michael and Olga.

'I accompanied Aunt Alix from Villefranche to see dear granny, where we spent about an hour,' the dowager empress told Nicholas, 'and then the queen drove us in her carriage to Beaulieu, where ours was waiting. She was so kind and amiable and in good spirits, but from time to time poked me in the eye with her parasol which was less pleasant.'[13]

* * *

In May 1896 the tsar's coronation took place in Moscow. As uncle and aunt of the Russian sovereigns Alfred and Marie would naturally be attending, so the queen discussed with Lord Salisbury her proposal to send Prince Arthur, Duke of Connaught, to represent her at the ceremony. This upset Prince George, the Duke of York, who hoped to be able to attend his cousin's coronation as the queen's representative. George was certain he would be selected and wrote to Nicholas saying he regretted most deeply that the Connaughts, whom Nicholas and Alicky hardly knew, would be going in his place.

Victoria, who had seen the splendour of Marie's jewels, was determined that Arthur's wife Louise Margaret, a Prussian princess by birth, would not be overshadowed in Moscow. She therefore lent a collection of her own jewels, including a diamond necklace and a several large stars which the duchess wore linked together as a tiara. Prince Arthur then wondered whether he would be expected to insure them, a slightly worrying prospect as they would have to be covered to the value of £30,000.

The duke compiled an album of his own Russian photographs and also sent the queen an account of the festivities, including the procession into Moscow and the 'glorious and impressive' 4-hour ceremony in the cathedral, which he called 'the most magnificent pageant one could ever see'. Alicky, he said, looked 'perfectly lovely' and both seemed 'much moved by [the] solemnity of the occasion', but after the long coronation ceremony she and Nicholas seemed 'terribly tired'. Three days of receptions followed, during which Arthur escorted seven different princesses, attended various embassy balls and a gala at the opera. Both sovereigns bore up well but the duke later told the queen that he thought Nicholas looked more tired than Alicky.[14]

At Balmoral the queen, whose eyesight was failing, had all the accounts of the magnificent ceremony read to her, lamenting. 'Oh! could I but have seen darling Alicky! She must have looked so beautiful.'[15]

The queen's impressions of the occasion were marred by reports of a disaster in Moscow. On 30 May the traditional fête for the people was held at Khodynka Meadow. By the early morning over 500,000 peasants were camped in the field singing, dancing and playing the balalaika. Soon the wagons arrived with the free food, beer and mugs which were to be distributed to everyone. Suddenly, at about six o'clock in the morning there was a stampede after rumours spread that there would not be enough for everyone (the estimate of people attending was 400,000, based on the 1883 figure). As the people behind pushed forward, those in front fell into the military trenches which criss-crossed the field, or were trampled underfoot where they fell. In no time thousands of dead and wounded men, women and children were lying on the ground. Trenches were hastily covered with branches to hide the bodies; others were flung unceremoniously onto carts; more bodies were thrust under the pavilion where the tsar was shortly to be received. The official estimate was 1,389 dead and 1,300 wounded. The true number was undoubtedly much higher. That night, persuaded by his uncles not to upset Russia's only European ally, Nicholas and Alexandra attended the ball at the French Embassy. The peasants murmured about their heartlessness, condemning them as callous and insensitive.

Again, the accounts were read aloud to the queen. 'The amount of people killed at Moscow amounts to 3,000, and there are grave accusations against the police and others,' she recorded. 'The accounts ... of the funerals of the victims, which of course could not be carried out quickly enough are too distressing. Nicky and Alicky have repeatedly visited the hospitals.'[16] The queen immediately sent a message of sympathy to the wounded and also contributed to the relief fund. (She later received from her ambassador a cup, bowl and plate which had been intended for distribution that day.)

Although Nicholas paid for the victims' funerals out of his own purse, the damage was done. It was not an auspicious start to the new reign.

The question of responsibility divided the imperial family. The Minister of the Court, Count Vorontzov-Dashkov, was in charge of the general arrangements for the coronation; Grand Duke Sergei was in charge of the arrangements in Moscow. Nicholas initially agreed to an enquiry headed by Count Constantine Pahlen, former Minister of Justice to Alexander III and a protégé of the dowager empress, but he revoked the mandate when Sergei threatened to resign. Many, including the dowager empress, could not understand why the police were not at Khodynka Meadow all night and they blamed Sergei. Alicky sided with Sergei, whose conduct was criticised by the family. The issue was never resolved. The Chief of Moscow Police was dismissed but no action was taken against the grand duke. Ella mentioned none of this in her letters to Queen Victoria, probably not wanting to cause her grandmother further distress.

Sergei was now accused of having too much influence over the tsar but he was not the only person advising Nicholas. People were trying to stir up trouble by saying that Ella and Sergei did not get on with Nicholas and Alexandra. As Ella explained to Queen Victoria, 'People will intrigue and lie as long as the world exists and we are not the first nor the last who have been calumniated...' Although outranked by her younger sister, Ella insisted that this did not worry her and that Alicky was 'already dearly loved in her new home'.[17] This was not entirely correct.

The newspapers had been hinting that the empress was again pregnant, and in June the queen asked Victoria of Battenberg, who had attended the coronation with her husband Louis, whether it was true. As Grand Duchess Tatiana was not born until the following summer it appears that either the report was false or the Empress may have miscarried. Prince Louis told the queen that Nicholas was devoted to her and 'anxious to do anything to keep on good terms with England'. The French alliance, Nicholas said, had been a necessity forced upon Russia by the Triple Alliance of Germany, Austro-Hungary and Italy.[18]

In a bid to maintain better relations with Russia, when Prince Lobanov-Rostovsky died at the end of August the Prince of Wales tried to persuade the queen to suggest Baron George de Staal, the current Russian Ambassador, as his replacement.

Both Queen Victoria and Lord Salisbury were against this, feeling that interference in Russia's affairs would be resented in St Petersburg. De Staal remained as ambassador, but the appointment of Count Michael Mouravieff as Foreign Minister caused concern in Vienna, where Emperor Franz Joseph saw it as a result of Victoria's influence on the tsar. On 15 September *The Times* reported that, of all the Great Powers, 'Great Britain alone continues to be the object of unabated mistrust and ill-will.'

The Russian Occupation of Balmoral

'It seems quite like a dream...'
– Queen Victoria.

It was in this climate of mistrust that Nicholas and Alicky were to undertake what he described to his brother George as a series of 'intolerable foreign visits', which would take them to Austria, Kiel (to see the empress's sister Princess Irene), Germany, his grandparents in Denmark, then England, France and Darmstadt. 'On top of it, we shall have to drag our poor little daughter with us, as all the relatives want to see her.'[1]

Lord Salisbury had suggested to the queen that an invitation to the new tsar and tsarina to visit Balmoral might persuade Nicholas 'to sweeten the rest of Europe towards British exertions in the Sudan',[2] where an Anglo-Egyptian campaign to reconquer the territory lost by the Khedives of Egypt in 1884 was underway despite the protests of the Russians. The tsar, in conversation with the British Ambassador Nicholas O'Conor, had been diplomatic, expressing a keen wish to see Balmoral, which he had heard so much about from the tsarina. He also recalled his earlier visits to Britain with fondness.

Queen Victoria was delighted at the chance to see Alicky again after an absence of two years, during which her granddaughter's life had undergone many changes. She was now anxious for Ella and Sergei to visit for a week or ten days, either just before or after Alicky and Nicky, as she was longing to see them too. That, however, proved impossible, but on the queen's birthday Ella sent her grandmother a new painting of herself. As the queen told Princess Beatrice, 'It is a profile, very like and beautifully painted in pastel.'[3]

Arrangements for the tsar's stay were soon being discussed. The queen favoured a quiet, family visit but the Prince of Wales disagreed. Nicky was the ruler of a mighty empire, he and Alicky should therefore be received with full honours. Bertie 'considered it necessary to impress Russia and foster good relations on account of British military action in the Sudan'.[4] The queen eventually came around to this way of thinking and decided that the Prince of Wales would receive the Russian sovereigns in state when they landed at Leith. It was decided for security reasons to have a small travelling escort when they drove from Ballatar station to Balmoral, as it would be dark.

The imperial entourage was so enormous that it felt more like a foreign occupation than a visit. Some of the Russian and English suite would be lodged at nearby Abergeldie Castle for reasons of space, while some Russian servants would stay at local inns and farmhouses. This would later present its own problems when the Russians had difficulty understanding the Scottish accents of their hosts, while the Scots spoke no Russian.

For several days before the tsar and tsarina's arrival the queen was preoccupied with preparations. Alterations were made to the interior of Balmoral Castle. The rooms the Russian sovereigns would occupy were redecorated in the imperial colours of black and yellow; the queen inspected the temporary passage, made 'with a staircase from the little anteroom next to the dining room, so as to enable the company, during Nicky's visit, to go to the ballroom, which will be used for all meals, without passing through the narrow passage into which open so many of the offices.' Then she went to see the temporary Humphrey Huts which had been put up near the stables to accommodate servants, many of whom had been forced to vacate their rooms in the castle to accommodate the Russians. 'The rooms are very comfortable,' the queen noted,[5] although the laundry maids, four of whom had to share a bed, probably would not have agreed.

The queen was terrified that Russian anarchists would make an attempt on Nicholas's life while he was staying with her. A large cache of dynamite had recently been discovered hidden in the basement of an anarchist's house in Antwerp by Okhrana agents working alongside officers from Scotland Yard. Security would therefore be tight. A pilot train would precede the imperial party on the railway journey from Leith to Ballater in case a bomb had been planted on the tracks; and local police and railway officials would patrol the railway line. The tsar, of course, brought his own security detail, which would work alongside dozens of Scotland Yard detectives. Every time the tsar left the castle, detectives would hide behind the bushes and trees to guard against attacks by terrorists.

* * *

The imperial visitors were due to arrive on 21 September. The queen had already received a telegram from Alicky on 11 September saying that 'Nicky agrees to all,' meaning the arrangements outlined in the queen's letter. Things were ploughing ahead when another message arrived, this time from the Princess of Wales in Denmark, where Nicholas was enjoying himself bicycling around the countryside near Bernstorff with his relatives. The tsar and tsarina had been to the Burmeister & Wain shipyard in Copenhagen where the new imperial yacht was about to undergo its first sea trials. As the Princess of Wales telegraphed, they were 'much distressed that on account of new ship will not be able to start till Sunday arriving 22nd.' The princess hoped the queen would not mind.[6]

The queen did mind. Anything that altered her planned schedule was always a 'great inconvenience' and this was no exception, even though the delay was only one day. Maybe she minded because the 'new ship' was the tsar's sumptuous imperial yacht *Standart,* while her own *Victoria and Albert* was old, dating from 1855, despite her repeated lobbying of parliament to have a new one. (The *Victoria & Albert III* was launched in 1899 and not completed during her lifetime.)

During the afternoon before they arrived the queen drove to inspect the preparations at Ballater station, which had been very prettily decorated. A portico and a glazed room had been built over the platform and these improvements would remain after the imperial couple had departed. Several of the local people had decorated their houses in anticipation of the tsar's arrival and Venetian masts and festoons, which would be illuminated, lined the approach to Ballater.

* * *

Nicholas and Alicky arrived at Leith on the *Standart* on the morning of 22 September. Despite a message from the Prince of Wales's private secretary Sir Francis Knollys at the beginning of September saying that the weather in Scotland was likely to be warm when they landed, it was pouring with rain. On the quayside the British flags and the black and yellow Russian imperial flags flapped in the wind and the bunting was soaked by the rain. The tsar and tsarina were greeted by the Prince of Wales, the Duke of Connaught and other dignitaries, who defied the weather to reach the *Standart* in a small tender. Nicholas had kept his promise to the queen and arrived in the uniform of the Scots Greys, although with some reservations. '… you will understand how unpleasant it was to have to say goodbye to our officers and crew in a foreign uniform!' he wrote to his mother.[7] Alicky was dressed all in white, with a large hat and an ostrich feather boa, while the Prince of Wales wore his Russian Dragoons uniform.

After lunch on board the *Standart* the royal party landed at the jetty in Leith, where a guard of honour of the Argyll and Sutherland Highlanders and the Royal Scots Greys stood to attention as the Russian and British national anthems were played. The imperial couple were presented with an engraved golden box by the Lord Provost, while his wife gave the empress a bouquet of orchids. Lady Lytton noted the emperor's few shy words of thanks and thought he ought to have done it better.

As a gun salute thundered out from Leith Castle, the royal party drove in open carriages to the railway station. There they boarded the queen's train for the four-and-a-half-hour journey to Ballater, which was punctuated by frequent stops to allow local dignitaries to present loyal addresses and bouquets. Nicholas later told his mother that the train was so rocky it nearly made Alicky feel ill.

When they finally reached Ballater station they were greeted by the Duke and Duchess of York and the Duke of Cambridge, the queen's cousin. A guard of honour was formed by the Black Watch and the Queen's Own Highlanders wearing their regimental kilts. The weather was appalling and 'all the decorations … looked sadly dashed by rain,' the queen's doctor Sir James Reid told his mother.[8] Still the interminable journey continued. It was 7 miles and another hour's drive in pouring rain to Balmoral Castle. Bonfires blazed on every hill as, escorted by the Scots Greys, Highlanders carrying flaming torches and accompanied by the pealing of church bells, the tsar and tsarina drove in an open landau pulled by eight white horses along the Deeside Road. Little Grand Duchess Olga followed in a separate carriage with her two attendants. It was nearly eight o'clock that evening before they reached Balmoral Castle. The skirl of the bagpipes playing 'The Campbells are Coming' heralded the arrival of the procession, vying with the pealing bells of Crathie Kirk. As the Scots Greys came into view, followed by the queen's pipers and the torchbearers and then the tsar and tsarina's carriage, the queen, her family and household came to the door to greet them. The Marquis of Carisbrooke later said the sovereigns' arrival was 'one of the most impressive sights he had ever witnessed'.[9]

After embracing the imperial couple and introducing them to her household Victoria led them inside where, like his aunt Marie, the Duchess of Coburg, the tsar discovered that tartan was everywhere, as were statues of Prince Albert. There was also a rather tactless exhibition of trophies won from the Russians in the Crimean War, to mark the anniversary of the fall of Sevastopol in 1855, which coincided with their visit.

Nicholas presented his suite – Count Vorontzov-Dashkov, Prince Galitzine and Count Benckendorff – and little Grand Duchess Olga was brought in, 'a most beautiful child, and so big', the queen enthused. Nicholas wrote to his mother that the queen 'is marvellously kind and amiable to us, and so delighted to see our little daughter!'[10] The castle was so crowded that the Duke and Duchess of York had to stay at Glen Muick, but they were present for dinner at nine o'clock that evening. It was a family affair, with only twelve people present and, to his great relief, Nicholas finally changed out of his Scots Greys uniform at 11 o'clock.

***

The following morning was again wet. That day, as the queen noted, she had reigned longer than any previous English sovereign (a record broken by her great-great-granddaughter Elizabeth II in 2015). The bad weather confined the ladies to the castle but as soon as the rain stopped Victoria took her granddaughter for a late afternoon drive.

Despite the bad weather Nicholas went out with the Prince of Wales's shooting party for a deer drive in the Abergeldie woods. The tsar had always been an enthusiastic hunter and the imperial family maintained several hunting estates in Poland, among them Bialowieza and Spala where they went out in all weathers. Nevertheless Nicholas was soon complaining to his mother that the weather was awful, the Prince of Wales dragged him out shooting every day in the cold, wind and rain, and he saw less of Alicky than he did in Russia. They had no luck with the deer and only managed to bag a brace of grouse. When the grouse hunt was called off on one occasion because of bad weather he was relieved. There was worse to come. At some point Nicholas was obliged to wear a kilt ('I never before exposed my knees,' he told a friend later[11]) and when he wanted to smoke he was obliged to go to a small room near the servants' quarters, which (thanks to the queen's son-in-law the late Prince Henry of Battenberg) was at least fairly comfortably furnished.

The next day the weather improved, so Alicky took her husband to The Merchants, the small shop in the nearby village of Crathie. The proprietor Mrs Symons had taught the future empress to bake scones when she was a child and Alicky took the traditional Scottish recipe with her to St Petersburg. On this visit to Mrs Symons the empress went on a spending spree, making what *The Times* described as 'a large number of purchases'.

Later that afternoon the Princess of Wales arrived from Copenhagen with her unmarried daughter Victoria (Toria), after a terrible sea crossing on the Royal Yacht *Osborne*. Although they stayed only a short time, the tsar was pleased to see them.

Nicholas and Toria had history. During the family reunion at Fredensborg Slot in Denmark in 1883 fifteen-year-old Nicholas had developed a teenage crush on Toria, who was the same age. 'I am in love with Victoria, and she seems to be with me, but I don't care,' he wrote in his diary. 'Yes, it is still more pleasant if she loves me.' He and Toria sat together at mealtimes, had their Danish lessons together, went for walks in the park or sat sketching. He enjoyed her company and discovered that it felt dull if she was not there. In the evenings they chased each other through Fredensborg's galleries, had what Nicholas called 'romps' in a small corner room of the palace, or played hide and seek with their cousins, using it as a good excuse to be together. 'Victoria and I went around together all the time, pretending we were still seeking them,' he recorded. To the amazement of the adolescent Nicky, the less he appeared to care for Toria the more she followed him, 'and I secretly rejoiced. In the evening I tried to be alone with her and kiss her: she is so lovely.' The following day their roles were reversed. 'The more Victoria torments and teases her prey, the more the prey loves her. This prey is ME.'

With other members of the family they visited Copenhagen, embarked on yachting trips, went for walks in the forest and had parties but inevitably the day of parting came too quickly. 'Still more and more I love Victoria, awfully sorry we'll have to leave soon. They'll be no playing or romping with her in the small corner room,' he wrote sadly. When he returned home Nicholas missed her. He read and re-read the regular letters he received from England but he must have known that nothing could ever come of this teenage crush, as marriages between first cousins were prohibited by the Orthodox Church. The following year at Ella and Sergei's wedding he met twelve-year-old Princess Alix of Hesse. Toria was forgotten, but ten years later she was still writing Christmas cards to 'my darling Old Nick' and they remained the best of friends.[12]

***

Although the queen wanted this to be a private, family visit, there was no escape from politics. Britain was Russia's chief rival and the state of affairs in the Ottoman Empire, where Sultan Abdul Hamid II seemed to have lost all control, was causing the queen much concern.

The Ottoman Empire was beset with nationalist uprisings, to which the sultan responded by massacring the Armenians, earning himself the nickname of 'Abdul the Damned'. (Figures vary between 30,000 and 100,000 people killed.) As indignation erupted all over Europe the Armenians believed that Russia and other Christian countries would come to their aid, but Kaiser William provoked outrage by supporting the sultan. Britain professed great sympathy with the Armenian cause. The Russians certainly did not share this concern, worried that any control over the Ottoman Empire by the European Powers would diminish Russia's substantial influence in Constantinople. Baron George de Staal suggested to the queen that she speak to the tsar about the more important points.

Victoria broached the subject with Nicholas while returning from a visit to Braemar Castle, saying that the Russian Ambassador in Constantinople had told the British Ambassador 'that he hoped some agreement would be come to with England' during the tsar's visit, 'as affairs were very critical and some catastrophe was dreaded.' Nicholas replied that 'he quite saw this and would see what he could do, though it was most difficult.' The queen then said that 'if England and Russia went together there must be peace, and something ought to be done to bring this about.'[13] Nicholas made no mention of this rather awkward conversation in his diary.

The following day the weather was again cold and wet. The highlight of Nicholas's day was lunch in the forest after an unsuccessful deer drive. Meanwhile, the queen and Alicky had lunch in the castle, followed by a concert by Paolo Tosti, the Italian composer and singing master to the royal family.

Saturday proved milder and while Nicholas was again out hunting, the queen had lunch with her granddaughter Alicky and the children of the Duke of York. 'Georgie's dear little boys [David and Bertie, the future Edward VIII and George VI] came in, as well as little Olga,'[14] Victoria recorded with pleasure.

The arrival on 26 September of Lord Salisbury, who felt it very important that Britain remain on good terms with Russia, did not pass unnoticed in the Russian press. 'Certainly nobody here desires to raise a systematic opposition to every attempt at a *rapprochement* between Russia and Great Britain,' reported the *Novoe Vremya* on 24 September, 'but the bitter experience of many a long year has taught the Russians that such a *rapprochement* is extremely difficult to reconcile with their own national interests. If the British government could prove the contrary, not by words but by actions, everybody in Russia would sincerely hail so complete a change, but at present we see no indication of anything of the kind.'

Salisbury had been a reluctant guest, only agreeing to go after his secretary had obtained a guarantee that his normally ice cold rooms would be properly heated. He was received by the queen after lunch and she recorded the outline of their conversation. 'I told him how well disposed Nicky was, and how anxious to speak to him. What Lord Salisbury is most anxious to avoid is anything which could appear as an attack on the Mahomedans, [*sic*] or encouragement of a propaganda against Moslems, which would be most dangerous on account of the enormous number of our Mahomedan subjects. He fears that the only thing which could do any good would be the removal of the sultan, but a Mahomedan would have to be placed in Constantinople.'[15]

* * *

On a stormy Sunday morning the royal family went to Crathie Kirk for the service. A new modern kirk had been dedicated on 18 June 1895, the third church on this site. It was funded by private donations and the proceeds of a bazaar which, with princesses and duchesses among the stallholders, raised £2,400.00. The queen visited the bazaar several times.

The tsar and tsarina were, of course, Russian Orthodox. 'It was very interesting seeing the two pews full of the royalties and the emperor and empress standing by the queen even in the Scotch Kirk, where all is simple and reverent,' wrote Lady Lytton.[16] The queen's lady-in-waiting Marie Mallet was surprised to see the Russian monarchs in the church of another denomination, something which a Catholic monarch would never do. The service was taken by Dr Colin Campbell of Dundee, who the queen thought 'preached very well'.[17] Lady Lytton thought the sermon dull.

After lunch the rain cleared and they had tea at Abergeldie Castle 3 miles away, which was leased by the queen and lent to the Prince of Wales. (In 2016 severe flooding in the area would nearly cause the castle to collapse into the river.)

According to the queen, Nicholas had appeared well disposed and anxious to speak to Lord Salisbury about Turkey. Nicholas, despite complaining about the time he was forced to spend away from Alicky, told his mother that 'it's good at least for him to learn from the source what the opinions and views of Russia are.'[18] The two men met for an hour-and-a-half after tea on Sunday. Lord Salisbury put forward the suggestion that their countries should 'act together as a stabilising force' and thought the only answer was to depose the sultan. The tsar, the prime minister reported, 'seemed favourable to a consultation between the ambassadors of the Powers and their respective governments as to what could be done...' Now that Lord Salisbury had lost faith that the sultan would keep the Straits closed to Russia, he threw in the carrot of the opening of the Straits to warships of all kinds. But the tsar wanted them kept closed; he was not in favour of allowing foreign warships into the Black Sea. Despite some disagreement, Salisbury 'was much struck by [Nicholas's] great candour and desire to be on the best of terms' with England. The tsar also spoke about his desire for an Extradition Treaty between England and Russia, and 'disclaimed in the strongest manner any unfriendly intentions against India'.[19]

* * *

The queen was immensely pleased by the family aspect of the visit. '... apart from their being so dear and simple and unchanged, I think the charming visit will have done great good. I had a very frank conversation with dear Nicky who I think very good and very thoughtful,' she told her daughter Vicky, the widowed Empress Frederick of Germany. One of the ladies-in-waiting, however, thought that the queen 'influenced the emperor and empress to be too much on their majesterial [*sic*] dignity.'[20]

On Monday while Nicholas went out shooting grouse (he bagged two), the queen took Alicky back to The Merchants, where the empress again made several purchases. After lunch 'the dear fat beautiful baby was brought in as usual,' and on one occasion the queen recorded that Olga sat on the floor playing with Princess Beatrice's son Maurice. One morning the queen went to see the baby grand duchess have her bath, describing her as 'a splendid child and so merry and full of life'. To Victoria of Battenberg the queen wrote that Olga was 'too delicious'.[21] Sir James Reid remarked on the 'pretty sight' of the empress playing with her 'beautiful child'. Reid weighed the little girl, recording that at ten-and-a-half-months she was '30 and a half lbs. less clothes 3 and a half lbs'.[22]

Nicholas and Alexandra's two-year-old godson Prince Edward of York, known in the family as David, was full of solicitude for his little second cousin Olga in whom he found an ideal companion. If she fell over while they were playing, he gallantly helped her up before giving her a kiss. The Princess of Wales was probably not alone in thinking that Olga would one day make her grandson David a suitable bride.

During their stay the empress found time to sit for a head-and-shoulders portrait, although to the queen's regret there was no time for Nicholas to be painted as well. Also, on 29 September despite the dull weather, a photographer from Messrs W. & D. Downey came from Ballater to photograph members of the royal party. Nicholas was photographed outside in his Scots Greys uniform, both on his own and with the Duke of Connaught, who compiled his own album of pictures of the visit. The Prince and Princess of Wales arrived for lunch with their daughters Toria and Maud and the latter's husband Prince Carl of Denmark. They had married in July so this was the first time Nicholas had seen Maud and Carl as a married couple. Maud, who was eighteen months Nicholas's junior, always teasingly called him 'Mr Toad' or 'darling *little* Nicky' when they were children.[23] One of the most famous pictures was taken that day by photographer Robert Milne – four generations of royals. The queen, the Prince of Wales, the tsar, tsarina and baby Olga (on the front of the book jacket).

Nicholas had a second, not altogether welcome, conversation with Lord Salisbury, who now found him unenthusiastic about plans to topple the sultan. They also had a brief non-committal discussion about a British occupation of Egypt. Lord Salisbury briefed the queen, saying he would try to do what he could to meet the tsar's views. Victoria then took the opportunity to talk politics to Nicholas again as they returned from the afternoon drive and tea at the Danzig Shiel.

The following afternoon a large party drove over to Mar Lodge, the home of Princess Louise (the eldest daughter of the Prince and Princess of Wales) and her husband the Duke of Fife. All the Prince of Wales's family were present, including the Fifes' two little daughters Lady Alexandra and Lady Maud Duff.

Back at Balmoral, Alicky showed the queen her beautiful jewels, 'of which she has quantities, all her own private property,' Victoria noted.[24]

Nicholas was absent from dinner that evening, a fact attested to by the seating plan, which shows the queen flanked by the Empress of Russia and the Duchess of Connaught. Among those present were the Duke of Connaught, Prince Francis Joseph of Battenberg, the queen's granddaughter Princess Helena Victoria (Thora) of Schleswig-Holstein and Princess Beatrice (the widowed Princess Henry of Battenberg). According to the queen's journal Nicholas was suffering from a swollen face but in fact the tsar, who had a horror of dentists, had toothache. Sir James Reid was summoned and found that Nicholas's 'left cheek was swollen from irritation at the stump of a decayed molar'. He prescribed some iodine for the gum.[25]

The following morning the swelling had subsided and the tsar came down to breakfast. To his great relief both Lord Salisbury and the Prince of Wales had left, which at least freed him from the obligation going out shooting every day. It seems that Nicholas also could not wait to be gone. He had already started packing, although he and Alicky would not depart for another two days. The morning's excursion was to the top of Craig Gowan. A cairn had been built there in 1852 to commemorate the queen and Prince Albert's taking possession of Balmoral and in 1855 a bonfire had been lit, pipers played and the villagers and servants danced to celebrate the fall of Sevastopol – something that probably was not mentioned to Nicholas. Nearby was a seven-bedroom house also called Craig Gowan which, had Nicholas but known it, would be home to his exiled sister Xenia during the Second World War.

Lunch, at the 'ungodly hour' of 12.15, as Nicholas recorded, was followed by the usual afternoon drive and tea in one of the many small houses on the estate. At least the weather that day was 'beautiful'.[26]

* * *

On 2 October Nicholas went to the queen's room for a private meeting, described by Victoria as 'a very satisfactory conversation'.

Russia had refused Britain's request to exert pressure on the Ottoman Empire, which had been partially responsible for the massacres of the Armenians. Nicholas was 'strongly against deposing the sultan, which he considers would be very risky and I agree,' the queen recorded, 'but he does not object to the various ambassadors consulting together, and reporting as to what necessary measures should be taken to prevent further massacres.' If the sultan refused to agree to their decision then they would have to use force. They also spoke about Russia's intimacy with France, the country that was next on the tsar and tsarina's itinerary (a visit the queen regretted). 'Nicky told me that Russia finding herself isolated, owing to the Triple Alliance, which was formed behind her back, she formed an alliance or treaty with France, but purely military and defensive. If one or other should be attacked, they should help one another, but not in the event of one of them attacking anyone else.' The queen put the subject of their conversation in a detailed memorandum to Lord Salisbury; Nicholas's diary entry was brief: '...sat with granny and had a talk with her about political matters.'[27]

After consultation, the European Powers sent a telegram warning Sultan Abdul Hamid that unless he stopped the Armenian massacres immediately his throne would be in peril.

As for France, the queen never received any assurance from Nicholas, and she was left with no idea what his own feelings about England were.

* * *

The final day of their stay, 3 October, came round all too quickly for the queen, but probably not for Nicholas. At midday they went down below the terrace, near the ballroom where a photographer from Messrs W. & D. Downey was waiting. Among the party were the Duke and Duchess of Connaught, with their daughters Princesses Margaret and Patricia. 'We were all photographed by the new cinematograph process, which makes moving pictures by winding off a reel of films,' the queen wrote in her journal. 'We were walking up and down and the children jumping about. Then [I] took a turn in the pony chair...'

The tsar and tsarina each planted a tree near what Queen Victoria described as the Garden Cottage. The trees selected were Cumbrian Pines but Nicholas, who seemed confused by the whole process, had to ask the head forester Mr Michie what he was supposed to do. Having been told to shovel some soil round the roots and then use the watering can to sprinkle water on it, Nicholas duly planted his tree and was followed by Alicky. There are unfortunately no plaques to show where these trees might have been or whether they in fact survive.

That afternoon they took a drive ('alas! for the last time!' lamented the queen) in dark, showery weather. Later there was a family dinner. 'At 10 dear Nicky and Alicky left to my regret, as I am so fond of them both.' They were accompanied by Highlanders holding torches, although this time there were no skirling pipes.[28]

Before departing from the castle, Nicholas left £1,000 to be distributed to the servants as some compensation for the discomfort they had been forced to endure. There was also the usual shower of presentation gifts to other members of the court, including 'a gold cigarette case with his imperial arms in gold and diamonds in the corner', to Dr Reid for curing the tsar's toothache.[29]

'Here we have not had the finest weather,' the empress wrote to her former governess Miss Jackson. 'My husband has not shot one stag, only a brace of grouse.' Nevertheless, she said goodbye to the queen with a heavy heart. 'Who knows when we may meet again and where?'[30]

'Granny was kinder and more amiable than ever,' Nicholas told his mother. 'She sent Lord Salisbury to see me, and I had two very serious talks with him.' Yet Nicholas had remained non-committal and politically the visit was a failure. Russians, Lord Salisbury said, 'cling to the "old traditions" despite the friendliness of the emperor.'[31]

As the empress wrote to her sister Victoria of Battenberg, 'family ties don't count in politics.'[32]

* * *

The queen had written to Nicholas asking him to tell the French not to be so unfriendly towards England. She hoped that he would express his disapproval of such sentiments while he was in Paris. With matters in Turkey becoming more and more threatening and danger of fresh massacres by the sultan, the queen was anxious to hear from him about this and about France – but the following month she was astonished to receive a letter from Nicholas about Egypt, a country towards which Britain was turning as Russia veered towards the Far East and where England was Russia's only real rival.

As Russia's interests in the Far East developed she had become an important user of the Suez Canal, which Britain had obtained control of in 1870. Both Britain and France wanted possession of the Upper Nile Valley and 'the Russian representative on the Egyptian Debt Commission supported the French in making difficulties for the British administration in Egypt.'[33]

In October Nicholas wrote to Queen Victoria from Darmstadt explaining the Russian viewpoint. 'As to Egypt, I must own, dearest grandmama, the question is of a very serious character, as it does not only concern France alone, but the whole of Europe.' He explained that Russia needed her shortest sea route to East Siberia 'free and open'. Egypt's occupation by British forces was proving a continuous threat to Russia's sea routes to the Far East because Britain controlled the Suez Canal. For that reason Russia and France were opposed to Britain remaining in Egypt and they wanted the real integrity of the Suez Canal. 'Politics alas! are not the same as private or domestic affairs and they are not guided by personal or relationship feelings.' He ended by saying that Baron de Staal would be happy to give a clear explanation of the Egyptian difficulties if the queen would give him the chance to speak to her openly.[34]

The queen recorded her astonishment at this letter, as Nicholas had barely mentioned Egypt during his visit to Balmoral. It was, she said, 'the one thing to which Russia takes exception' but after a conversation with de Staal, she learnt that 'it was really of no consequence, and was past.' She decided not to answer about Egypt, or to press Nicholas on the subject of Turkey, because things 'were made rather difficult for him sometimes'.[35]

In December, the queen heard that the tsar had sent a strong warning to the sultan to follow the advice of the Powers, otherwise they would have to take coercive measures. 'This sounds very encouraging...'[36]

Nevertheless, although she realised that Nicholas's character was not strong like his father's, the queen did not live long enough to form any definite impressions about him.

* * *

That Christmas the tsar and tsarina sent Queen Victoria a red and oyster guilloché enamel and moonstone notebook made by the court jeweller, Carl Fabergé, 'to dearest grandmama from Nicky and Alix, Xmas 1896'.[37] Unlike her daughter-in-law the Princess of Wales the queen was not a particular admirer of Fabergé's work. In the Royal Collection there are only three pieces *known* to have belonged to her. In 1894 the Lord Chamberlain, Lord Carrington, is believed to have given the queen a Fabergé raspberry plant; and in a 1900 the tsarina sent her grandmother a Fabergé desk clock of rock crystal, gold, enamel, silver, diamonds and rubies, which is now in the Royal Collection.[38]

After the tsar and tsarina's visit the queen was left with the feeling that Alicky 'had become a little aloof', and she had even had to talk to her granddaughter 'about the importance of smiling and appearing pleasant'.[39] In their regular correspondence (most of which was unfortunately destroyed in 1917 to prevent it falling into the wrong hands) the queen voiced these fears and gave her granddaughter some wise advice.

> There is no harder craft than our craft of ruling. I have ruled for more than fifty years in my own country, which I have known since childhood, and, nevertheless, every day I think about what I need to do to retain and strengthen the love of my subjects. How much harder is your situation. You find yourself in a foreign country which you do not know at all, where the customs, the way of thinking and the people themselves are completely alien to you, and nevertheless it is your first duty to win their love and respect.

Her well intentioned words fell on deaf ears. 'You are mistaken, my dear grandmama,' the empress replied. 'Russia is not England. Here we do not need to earn the love of the people. The Russian people revere their tsars as divine beings, from whom all charity and fortune derive. As far as St Petersburg society is concerned, that is something which one may wholly disregard. The opinions of those who make up this society and their mocking have no significance whatsoever.'[40]

Here lay the seeds of the dynasty's downfall which, thankfully, Queen Victoria would not live to see.

Diamond Jubilee

That 'old policy of unfortunate distrust and opposition...'
– Queen Victoria.

In March 1897 Queen Victoria left for her spring break at Cimiez accompanied by her daughter Princess Beatrice and granddaughter Princess Helena Victoria (Thora) of Schleswig-Holstein. This time she would be staying at the huge new Excelsior Hotel Regina, where although her party had a whole wing to themselves with a private entrance and an electric lift, Victoria felt all at sea. She missed her old, familiar rooms at the Grand Hotel.

Not only that, but before they all left England the queen's Household had threatened to resign over her insistence in bringing the Munshi to Cimiez. This meant that he would dine with the Household, something they could never accept. Although the queen backed the Munshi and the Household did not resign, the tension when they arrived in Cimiez was palpable.

By this time the queen's spring holiday had developed into a routine. She worked at her state correspondence from ten o'clock for an hour, then after putting on a garden hat and a silk cloak, she was assisted into her donkey carriage by one of the Indian attendants. The rest of the morning was spent driving round the grounds of the neighbouring villas or working on more papers in the shade of a tree. The owners, among them the extremely wealthy Baron von Dervis, were always delighted to make an alteration to their entrance if necessary so that the queen's donkey cart could pass through.

The biggest event of the day was the two-hour afternoon carriage drive, when Victoria scattered loose change to the poor and needy who appeared at intervals along the route. The queen liked to attend all the local festivals and was especially fond of the Battle of the Flowers, where Princess Beatrice's children encouraged her to 'make spirited attacks on French officers and participants on the floats'.[1]

State business, however, was never far away. When the queen returned to her room one evening she found a cipher telegram awaiting her. It concerned affairs in Crete.

In February 1897 the people of Crete rebelled against their Turkish overlords and demanded union with Greece. The tsar's uncle King George I of Greece sent troops to help them. The Great Powers would not permit the Ottoman Empire to be dismembered and sent an international force to Crete. When the Greeks were ordered to withdraw their troops they refused. By the following month the situation was deteriorating. 'German and Austrian ambassadors pressed today for blockade of Volo,' read the cipher message the queen received on 19 March. 'French Ambassador does the same and fears war on the frontier.' Sir Nicholas O'Conor telegraphed from St Petersburg that the emperor feared Britain's abstention would 'break up the concert and lead to war between Greece and Turkey'.[2] The newspapers were reporting fighting near Crete and the queen feared impending trouble at Constantinople. The situation progressed slowly and news was scarce, so Victoria continued her holiday. One day, driving in the vicinity of Nice, she stopped briefly before the memorial chapel erected on the site of the Villa Bermont, where Alexander II's son Nixa had died in 1865.

She also received large numbers of foreign royalties who were staying in the area. Among them were George and Stana of Leuchtenberg, who dined with her on 19 March. Stana, the queen recorded, 'was in great good looks'. Most evenings the queen dined with the Leuchtenbergs, Grand Duke Peter and his wife Militsa, or their Montenegrin relatives. Afterwards local musicians gave a concert.

Another visitor was the tsar's elderly great uncle Grand Duke Michael Nicolaievich, the former Viceroy of the Caucasus, who Victoria had not met for thirty-seven years. The grand duke, 'a very amiable old man',[3] was accompanied by his son Grand Duke Michael Michaelovich with his morganatic wife Sophie, Countess de Torby, and *their* son Michael (known in the family as 'Boy'). Grand Duke Michael Michaelovich had been banished from Russia by Alexander III after his marriage to Sophie because she was of lower rank, despite the fact that she had an impressive list of royal relations. From 1895 Michael and Sophie spent every winter in the Villa Lotus in avenue du Roi-Albert in Cannes and the remainder of the year in England. Eventually Michael bought the villa and renamed it the Villa Kazbek after the highest mountain in the Caucasus. They moved into the villa, 'a great white terraced structure full of jardinières and with ferns hanging from the walls', in 1899. The staff of thirty-five included 'five footmen, a butler, a valet, a lady's maid, a governess, a nursery maid and six chefs'.[4]

Another of the queen's Russian-born visitors was Grand Duke Michael Nicolaievich's daughter, Grand Duchess Anastasia of Mecklenburg-Schwerin, who arrived with *her* daughter Alexandrine and the latter's fiancé Prince Christian of Denmark (later King Christian X), the tsar's cousin.

Tragedy struck Anastasia's family while the queen was in Cannes. Early in the morning of 10 April Anastasia's husband Hereditary Grand Duke Friedrich Franz of Mecklenburg-Schwerin was found severely injured at the Villa Wenden, his Italian-style home which dominated the bay in Cannes. He had fallen over the balustrade of an 8-foot high wall onto the street below and died soon afterwards. Although the family insisted it was an accident, the grand duke's poor health led most people to believe he had committed suicide. The queen sent Princess Beatrice to the villa with a message of condolence.

***

The queen was still in Cannes on 18 April when Sultan Abdul Hamid declared war on Greece. The ill-equipped Greeks were no match for the German-trained officers of the Turkish army and they suffered defeat after defeat.

While Britain and other Great Powers sympathised with Greece, Russia (supported by Germany) favoured Turkey. This was another awkward situation for the queen, whose granddaughter Sophie was married to Crown Prince Constantine of Greece. At the request of Lord Salisbury, Queen Victoria sent a strongly worded telegram to the tsar 'urging him to do what he could for the restoration of peace'.[5]

The following day the queen recorded Nicholas's reply. Like her, he was anxious for the war to be brought to a swift conclusion and he did not object to the idea of an ambassadors' conference in Paris.

However, he 'suggested it would perhaps be more efficacious if the cabinets of England, France and Russia, as guaranteeing powers, considered directly between themselves the terms of peace, while at the same time using their influence to bring about an armistice.' The idea of Greece's three guaranteeing powers working together was welcome to him and he authorised Sir Nicholas O'Conor to telegraph London in this sense. The queen declared this 'very satisfactory'.[6]

On 26 April the Russian Foreign Minister Count Mouravieff declared that Russia would associate herself with the other powers if the French government was convinced that the time was right.

The queen left Cannes three days later and, once back at Windsor, she discussed the war in Crete with Lord Salisbury on 3 May. He told her that it was impossible to do anything because France could not act without Russia, and the Russians had changed tack, 'Nicky having evidently yielded to Mouravieff and pressure from Germany.' It was, said Salisbury, 'a terrible time'[7] and he was very worried. Later that day the Princess of Wales arrived straight from the railway station. She had received a telegram from her father King Christian IX of Denmark, who had heard from the tsar that he was trying to arrange an armistice.

On 18 May the queen was relieved to record that thanks to Nicholas's intervention hostilities had ceased. Nothing had been gained by Turkey.

* * *

The following month the queen heard that Alicky had given birth to her second child, another daughter, 'which is rather a disappointment, but both are doing well,' Victoria wrote in her journal on 10 June. They named her Tatiana. The queen was shocked that the Empress of Russia breastfed her children, thinking it 'a great mistake in her position'.[8] Victoria had a great aversion to mothers nursing their children, comparing them to animals. When her own daughter Alice had done so, the queen named one of her dairy cows 'Princess Alice'.

The queen wanted the Duchess of Coburg to come to England in May and stay for the Diamond Jubilee in June but Marie was having none of it. She did not like London and was determined to leave Coburg only at the last moment, brushing aside Missy's disappointment at being unable to go because Ferdinand had typhoid, and making light of the queen's great milestone of sixty years on the throne. Once in London, the duchess did nothing but complain to Missy 'about the English royal family, the dizzying schedule of festivities, the inferiority of English theatre versus German and the unseasonable heat in June'. Ella and Sergei were coming to Clarence House for a few days but then they had to stay with the queen. The duchess said they were 'furious' but 'are graciously allowed to come back [to us] .... after granny has left'.[9]

Although both Marie and Alfred enjoyed music, they now had little else in common apart from a love of their children. Alfred drank to drown his sorrows and found little or no support in his wife; the duchess was unhappy in her marriage.

* * *

By this time preparations were well advanced for the celebrations of the Diamond Jubilee. It was the biggest thing that had happened to the British monarchy so far, as no sovereign had ever reached such a milestone. Victoria was now a seventy-eight-year-old widow with failing eyesight and weak legs. It was therefore feared that any large celebration would be too arduous. There was also the question of the diplomatic problems which would be posed if the queen invited the crowned heads of Europe. The recent war in Crete, to name but one instance, had divided the family again. It was therefore decided that no foreign heads of state would be invited (to the annoyance of the kaiser) and that the jubilee would emphasise the might of the British Empire. It would be on a smaller scale than the Golden Jubilee and the main event would be a procession through London followed by a brief service at St Paul's Cathedral. Even this would take place on the steps, as the queen declared she was too lame to get out of her carriage and go inside. 'No!' gasped a surviving granddaughter of King George III incredulously, 'after sixty years' reign, to thank God in the street!!!'[10]

The tsar sent Ella and Sergei as his representatives. They arrived at Windsor Castle on 19 June to join the queen and the many other relatives assembled there, including Ella's siblings Ernie of Hesse and Victoria of Battenberg. That afternoon they had tea with the queen and other members of the family at Frogmore.

During the next few days, Ella and Sergei were frequently seen lunching, driving or having breakfast with the queen. At some time during her stay Ella sent for Sir James Reid, who used nitric acid to remove a small red spot from her face.

The accession day, 20 June, fell on a Sunday and was celebrated quietly with a family Thanksgiving Service at St George's Chapel, Windsor. A new Jubilee Hymn composed by Sir Arthur Sullivan was sung, along with Prince Albert's *Te Deum*. Afterwards the queen went to pray at Prince Albert's mausoleum.

On 21 June the royal party went by train to Buckingham Palace, where the queen's Hesse grandchildren and their spouses gave her a heart-shaped brooch set with diamonds, with the figure 60 in Slavonic characters inside it. A cabochon sapphire sat on top, and suspended below the heart were two more cabochon sapphires. It had been designed specially by Fabergé at the request of Nicholas and Alexandra. The queen wore the brooch during the official jubilee celebrations. Telegraphing their congratulations to the queen on reaching this milestone, the tsar and tsarina added that they were '… touched you wore our present'.

From Ella the queen also received a beautiful signed portrait of her in Russian court dress; and from Sergei a portrait of himself in more formal daywear. Both portraits now adorn the walls of Windsor Castle's Round Tower.[11]

That afternoon, 'seated in my chair, as I cannot stand long,' Queen Victoria received all the foreign princes who had come for the jubilee. In the evening she gave a dinner for 100 people in the Supper Room, where guests sat twelve to a table. Wearing a black dress embroidered down the front in gold, which had been specially worked in India, Victoria sat between Archduke Franz Ferdinand of Austria and the Prince of Naples. The Prince of Wales, Prince Alfred and Prince Arthur presided over tables at which royalty from all over Europe mingled with princes from Japan, Persia, Siam and Egypt.

After dinner, as the orchestra played in the gallery, Victoria sat on the throne in the Ballroom while the Colonial Premiers and their wives, the Special Envoys, Indian princes, officers of the Indian escorts and the various foreign royal suites were presented by the Lord Chamberlain. 'The Ballroom was very full and dreadfully hot, and the light very inefficient,' she noted in her journal.[12]

More than 3 million people poured into London for the jubilee and thousands slept on the pavements along the processional route to St Paul's. A quarter of a million pounds was spent on triumphal arches as well as red, white and blue street decorations with the novelty of electric light bulbs. A special jubilee mug was produced with a triple portrait of the queen, inscribed *The Centre of a World's Desire.* Hundreds of grandstands were erected and 25,000 colonial troops were billeted in tents in Hyde Park.

Tuesday 22 June was a Bank Holiday and the crowds were out early. The jubilee procession began with the Colonial Premiers, accompanied by soldiers from all over the Empire. Mounted troops from Australia, New Zealand, South Africa, Cyprus (wearing fezzes), Sikhs in their turbans, the Bengal Lancers and the Canadian mounted police, infantry from Ceylon, Jamaica, Sierra Leone and the Gold Coast all paraded through the streets of London in their colourful uniforms. A gun salute signalled the start of the royal processions. Mounted Dragoons, Hussars and Life Guards preceded the equerries, *aides-de-camp* and other male members of the Household wearing dress uniforms. Exotically dressed officers from the Indian Imperial Service Troops preceded the Sovereign's Escort of the Life Guards. The representatives of foreign powers included gorgeously dressed Indian princes, an emissary from China carrying a fan, colourful European princes and, in contrast, the envoy from the United States in black evening dress and hat. In open landaus came the queen's daughters, grandchildren and foreign royalties, followed by thirty-six European princes, their orders and decorations glittering as they rode along. Then as the strains of the national anthem echoed across the palace forecourt, the queen appeared in a state landau. Before setting out Victoria touched an electric button to telegraph a message to the British Empire. 'From my heart I thank our beloved people,' it read. 'May God bless them!'

Despite pleas from her family, Victoria refused to abandon her usual black dress but as a concession it was embroidered with silver thread and jet and her black cape was relieved by pieces of white lace. A plume of white ostrich feathers decorated the back of her bonnet, which had a spray of white acacias held in place by a diamond aigrette. Opposite Victoria sat the Princess of Wales and Princess Helena, with the Prince of Wales and the Duke of Cambridge riding alongside in their scarlet uniforms. As they drove through the dense, cheering crowds in brilliant sunshine ('Queen's Weather' people said) tears of happiness rolled down Victoria's cheeks. Alexandra leant forward and gently pressed the old queen's hand. At Temple Bar, the boundary of the City of London, the queen touched the Lord Mayor's sword as he welcomed her to the city, a tradition dating back to the reign of Elizabeth I.

A red carpet covered the steps of St Paul's, where the archbishops of Canterbury and York waited with the clergy, government, diplomatic corps and distinguished guests. All the colonial troops were drawn up on foot around the square but Victoria remained in her carriage. Five hundred choristers and two massed bands participated in the 20-minute service, which included Sullivan's Jubilee Hymn. A cinematograph picture was taken, which Victoria later said was 'very wonderful' but 'a little too hazy and too rapid'. As her landau drove away, the Archbishop of Canterbury called for three cheers for the queen. The response from the crowd was deafening.

The procession carried on through the City to the Mansion House, where the Lady Mayoress presented the queen with orchids in a silver basket. After crossing London Bridge they reached the poorer parts of London where the reception, the queen recorded later, 'was just as enthusiastic and orderly as elsewhere'. Victoria, remembering the accounts of the Khodynka disaster after the tsar's coronation the previous year, had been terrified that some such calamity would happen in London, but she need not have worried. By the time they arrived back at Buckingham Palace, where the royal princes lined up on their mounts in the quadrangle to greet her, the queen was extremely tired but happy.

The Diamond Jubilee banquet was held that evening in the Ballroom. Wearing a dress of black and silver silk, with a diamond trefoil necklace and the pearl and diamond brooch presented by members of her Household, Victoria entered with the Prince of Wales. The room was a mass of flowers, culminating in a 9-foot-high display of 60,000 orchids topped with a floral crown and the letters 'VRI'.

The guests were seated at eight round tables. Ella and Sergei were placed on the queen's table with the Grand Duke and Duchess of Hesse, the Princess of Wales, the Empress Frederick of Germany, the Archduke Franz Ferdinand of Austria-Hungary, the Prince of Naples, the Grand Duchess of Mecklenburg-Strelitz, Prince Albert of Prussia and the Crown Prince of Siam. Twenty-four chefs had come from Paris to prepare the fourteen-course dinner which included whitebait, salmon and roast beef. The Prince of Wales proposed a toast to the queen's distinguished guests. Afterwards, despite her fatigue, Victoria moved through the crowded room to speak to most of the princes and princesses before retiring to bed. That evening 2,500 beacons were lit on the hills around the country.

'A never-to-be-forgotten day,' the queen wrote in her journal. 'No one ever, I believe, has met with such an ovation as was given to me passing through those 6 miles of streets...'[13]

At Royal Ascot Ella and Sergei watched the races from the royal box with Prince Carl and Princess Maud of Denmark. To cheers from the delighted crowd, the Ascot Gold Cup was won by *Persimmon,* a horse owned by Maud's father the Prince of Wales.

On 27 June Ella and Sergei joined the queen for tea at Frogmore, followed by a drive. Although they left the following day ('both so dear and pleasant' was the queen's verdict)[14] there was still no rest for the queen as the services, receptions, parades and reviews continued. Delegations presented loyal addresses and congratulations, and garden parties were given at Buckingham Palace and Windsor Castle, the latter described by the Duchess of Coburg as 'a very dull affair indeed'.[15] There were concerts and investitures, reviews of the army at Aldershot, the Colonial troops at Windsor and the fleet at Spithead. A reception was held for members of the Indian escort, an audience was given to the United States special diplomatic envoy and a dinner for the queen's large family. The Colonial Premiers and their wives had to be entertained, as well as the Anglican Clergy and countless other dignitaries. 'Granny is gracious and I find her wonderfully well, but the life is impossible here and one loses one's whole day, especially now she is always at Frogmore,' the Duchess of Coburg complained to Missy on 5 July.[16]

During their stay in London all the royal guests signed the Fabergé visitors' book given to the queen by the tsar and tsarina for Christmas the previous year.

* * *

In the autumn of 1897 the queen received another first-hand report from Russia about the tsar and tsarina. In October her granddaughter Princess Helena Victoria (Thora) of Schleswig-Holstein was invited by Alicky to visit St Petersburg accompanied by her mother's lady-in-waiting Emily Loch. Thora and Alicky, who were both affected by shyness, were great friends and perhaps the empress thought that a Russian winter, with the added attractions of the Season which began in January, would help her twenty-seven-year-old cousin find a husband.

This was also a golden opportunity for Queen Victoria, who was becoming worried that Nicholas and Alicky were secluding themselves far too much at the Alexander Palace, Tsarskoe Selo, away from the capital and society. She asked Thora to report back her impressions. Soon after Thora arrived in Russia she sent the queen a reassuring letter: 'As to what you say about Alix and Nicky seeing so few people, Victoria and Irene both begged me to try and persuade Alix to have a few more, occasionally, and I have done my best. I think she quite knows how important it is [that] she should get to know more of the society but the truth is she and Nicky are so absolutely happy together that they do not like to have to give up their evenings to receiving people. I do really think however they will do more now.'[17]

This was the problem. The sovereigns were so happy in their marriage and family life that they did not want anyone or anything else to intrude. Also the empress was awkward in society and disliked the frivolous Russian court. St Petersburg matrons poked fun at the 'provincial' young empress, who was considered a prude. They said she lacked charm, was nervous and tongue-tied, danced clumsily and spoke poor French. She rarely smiled and her face and hands flushed red when she was agitated. Balls at the Winter Palace ceased as she withdrew further and further into her own cosy little world at Tsarskoe Selo. Later Thora was able to report that the tsar and tsarina had been asked to an evening reception at the British Embassy. As they had not yet visited any of the embassies she felt this would be a good beginning.

When the princess returned to London at the end of February she reported her impressions in person. Thora spent the afternoon with the queen on 1 March but beyond that there is no further comment in Queen Victoria's journal. Whether her anxiety was allayed is unknown.

* * *

As 1898 dawned there were still problems in Crete, with Russia pressing the candidature of the tsar's cousin Prince George of Greece for Governor, Germany objecting and trying to influence the sultan to object (although France, Italy and England were agreed on the choice) and Russia refusing to propose any other candidates. The queen thought that the only alternative would be to annexe Crete to Greece. By the beginning of February the sultan was refusing George of Greece's candidature without fear of the consequences and, because of this, Russia would not press for him more forcefully.

Then China declined a British loan, an action the queen felt damaged her country's prestige. After China's defeat by Japan in 1895 the Chinese found themselves paying a huge war indemnity and rumours surfaced that Russia had made them a secret loan of £8,000,000. In return, Russia demanded trading concessions and permission to extend the Trans-Siberian railway through Manchuria, the north-China province which extended into Siberia. The British government, which had often helped the Chinese with loans, then became suspicious of the Russo-Chinese arrangements. The last straw was when the Russians threatened China and stopped the British loan. 'This at the same time when Russia had declared (Nicky himself taking the lead) that they wanted to come to an understanding with us relative to China etc.,' the exasperated queen wrote in February.[18] She then received an encouraging telegram from Sir Nicholas O'Conor saying that the tsar had been friendly and wanted to come to an understanding with England. 'Heard this morning however that China would make the necessary concessions we asked for,' Victoria wrote.[19] A proposal from Lord Salisbury that Russia should enter into discussions about British views met with the tsar's agreement.

However much Victoria liked Nicky as a person it was clear that there was still a certain amount of distrust on both sides. 'Clearly Nicky was very anxious to be most amiable, but that the old policy of unfortunate distrust and opposition, would take long in being overcome,' she noted in her journal on 18 February. By the end of November affairs in Crete were improving and the queen had appointed Sir Charles Scott as Ambassador to Russia. 'Nicky likes him and is very friendly with him,' she recorded with satisfaction.[20]

In 1898 Russia obtained a ninety-nine-year lease on Port Arthur from the Chinese and began to build a strong naval base, giving Russia her first ice-free port on the Pacific. Count Sergei Witte, the tsar's Minister of Finance, was keen to export Russian goods to the Far East. As a first step, the Trans-Siberian railway was extended across north Manchuria and 'protected' by Russian troops.

Encouraged by the pacifist Bertha von Suttner (born Countess Kinsky von Wchinitz und Tettau) the tsar proposed a conference to discuss a limitation on armaments. Vicky, who was always suspicious of Russia, wrote to her mother that this action, which was 'so little in accord with their acknowledged national programme and their latest political moves, points to a sudden *fear* having arisen in their minds....'[21] and that the Russians were only acting in their own interests. The queen, however, thought the move was meant in a peaceful sense, although she had no idea how it could be carried out. She agreed that it would be a good idea to reduce the enormous armies of Russia, Germany and France although this would be impossible for Britain, with her large overseas Empire.

However, what later became The Hague Peace Conference was duly held between May and July 1899 and was attended by representatives of twenty-six governments.

***

In March 1898 the queen was back at the Excelsior Hotel Regina, Cimiez, where her arrival was greeted by a guard of honour formed by the 6th Alpine Chasseurs. In between driving out (even cold, wind and rain at the end of the month could not deter Victoria) and resuming her Urdu lessons in the hotel's garden with the Munshi, she received plenty of Russian visitors. Among them were Countess Tolstoy, who had once been governess to the queen's Russian daughter-in-law Marie; Prince George of Leuchtenberg; and the tsar's great uncle Grand Duke Michael Nicolaievich, who came at least twice with his son Grand Duke Michael Michaelovich and the latter's wife Sophie, Countess de Torby. The Court Circular also recorded that Grand Duke Boris Vladimirovich (the tsar's cousin) was among those who dined with the queen on 24 March.

On 25 April Victoria had a visit from another of Michael Nicholaievich's sons, 'Sandro', Grand Duke Alexander Michaelovich, who arrived with his wife Grand Duchess Xenia, the tsar's sister. Victoria remembered Sandro from their meeting at Buckingham Palace in 1889. 'He is very good looking,' she noted, still with an eye for a handsome man.[22] It was the first time that the queen had met Xenia, who she thought resembled her mother the Dowager Empress Marie Feodorovna to a great degree.

***

On 12 November Ella and Sergei arrived at Windsor, where Vicky was also staying. During their visit Sergei took the opportunity to visit Hampton Court with Vicky while Ella remained with the queen. They had the usual round of daily drives and the inevitable trip to lay wreaths at the mausoleum. Queen Victoria had lost none of her fondness for Ella, despite the hated Russian marriage, and found her visit a great pleasure. 'She is so lovely and so good and sensible,'[23] Victoria wrote, as Ella and Sergei left for a dreadfully rough crossing which made Ella, who was susceptible to sea sickness, very ill.

Victoria had come to the conclusion that the only way to keep Germany under control was to foster better relations with Russia. There was a strong feeling there that an alliance with Britain would be beneficial; this was partly fuelled by the tricky relationship between the tsar and the kaiser. 'Perfidious but pleasant in negotiation', was Lord Salisbury's summary of the Russian government. 'On the whole the results to which it arrives are not worse than the results of the German Emperor's unreasoning caprice, or of the violent popular passions by which France is divided.'[24]

In June 1898 the queen was informed by her ambassador Sir Charles Scott that relations between the countries were much better. In the final years of her reign Victoria sought to capitalise on that.

Final Years

'England without the Queen seems impossible.'
— Empress Alexandra Feodorovna.

In the previous difficult political climate correspondence between Queen Victoria and the tsar had lapsed. One thing they did have in common, however, was distrust of the kaiser and on 1 March 1899 Victoria wrote again: 'It is ages since you wrote to me and I to you, but I am sure you have not forgotten your old grandmama who wishes much we could see each other again... But I feel now there is *something* I *must* tell you, which you *ought* to know and which perhaps you do *not*,' and she went on to warn him about the conduct of her eldest grandson William, the German Kaiser, 'who takes every opportunity of impressing upon Sir F[rank] Lascelles [British Ambassador in Berlin] that Russia is doing all in her power to work against us.'

The queen stressed that neither she nor her ambassador believed such a thing but 'I am afraid William may go and tell things against us to you, just as he has done about you to us. If so, pray tell me openly and confidentially. It is so important that we should understand each other, and that such mischievous and unstraightforward proceedings should be put a stop to. You are so true yourself, that I am sure you will be shocked at this.'[1]

One of the things William had apparently told Lascelles was that Russia and France had invited Germany to join in a coalition against Britain. The kaiser, who in January 1899 celebrated his fortieth birthday, maintained that he had no intention of doing so.

Nicholas was grateful for the queen's candour. 'I am so happy you told me in that open way about William,' he replied on

13/25 March. 'Now I fully understand what he is up to – it is a dangerous double game he is playing at.'[2] The Russian Ambassador in Berlin, Count Osten-Sacken had said much the same to him about England and her policy as Sir Frank Lascelles in Berlin had told the queen and Lord Salisbury about Russia. Nicholas ended by saying that he and Alicky hoped to come to Balmoral in the autumn with their children Olga, Tatiana and the new baby expected in June.

On 11/23 May Nicholas wrote again, this time from Peterhof on the Gulf of Finland and slightly later than he had intended, to wish the queen a very happy birthday on 24 May and apologise that he and Alicky could not spend that day with her. The children, he added, had grown a lot and were flourishing while Alicky, in her eighth month of pregnancy, was feeling a lot better. She was enjoying being pushed around in her wheelchair, he added, 'which is done by her husband!'[3]

* * *

The queen's journey to the Riviera that spring was delayed by bad weather in the English Channel and it was not until 12 March that she arrived in Cimiez. Her journal recorded what was to be her last arrival in the town: 'Reached Nice at 4... Sir James Harris presented the Secrétaire Général, in place of the Préfèt, who was ill, and also the Général de Division Caze, and the Général de Brigade Joly, Governor of Nice. Youri Leuchtenberg was at the station and came into my saloon before we got out. May [the Duchess of York] and Thora [Princess Helena Victoria] drove with Beatrice and me. The streets were lined with troops and there were an immense number of people out, who were very enthusiastic. We had an escort as before. At the door of the hotel, the same little girl presented a bouquet and recited verses.'[4] Following all this, the queen was very tired and went to bed early that evening.

Once again the military guard mounted around the Hotel Excelsior Regina found it difficult to adjust to the English hours of 'breakfast at nine-thirty, lunch at one and dinner at a quarter to nine.'[5] Although they turned out to salute Victoria on her departure and return from the afternoon drive, they also had to be ready to receive visiting royalty appropriately. Yet again, many of these visitors were Russian and as usual Victoria saw quite a lot of George and Stana of Leuchtenberg. On 3 April the widowed Grand Duchess Anastasia of Mecklenburg-Schwerin (born Grand Duchess

Anastasia Michaelovna of Russia) came to lunch accompanied by her son the young Grand Duke Frederick Franz IV and her younger daughter Cecile. Her elder daughter Alexandrine had married Crown Prince Christian of Denmark the previous year.

On 1 May 1899 the queen recorded her final entry from Cimiez. 'Alas! my last charming drive in this paradise of nature, which I grieve to leave, as I get more attached to it every year. I shall mind returning to the sunless north, but I am so grateful for all I have enjoyed here.'[6]

Queen Victoria never visited France again.

* * *

In June the queen's daughter-in-law Marie arrived at Windsor with her pretty youngest daughter Beatrice. The Duchess of Coburg's relationship with Victoria had been ambivalent over the years. One moment she would describe the queen as 'very dear and kind' and the next she was complaining about her 'influence and interference'. In 1897 she told Missy, 'I let her telegraph and agitate herself, it is indifferent to me.'[7]

Marie and Alfred, whose marriage had long ceased to be happy, celebrated their silver wedding anniversary in January 1899 but the occasion was overshadowed by the illness of their only son 'young Alfred'. The twenty-four-year-old prince was reportedly in the grip of venereal disease and, with the doctors apparently not realising the seriousness of his illness, he was sent off to Meran in the Tyrol with his French tutor, a valet and a naval surgeon friend of his father. The court announced that he was suffering from nervous depression and there were reports that he also had self-inflicted shotgun wounds. Whatever happened, on 6 February a telegram arrived in Coburg announcing his death.

His parents were devastated and the relationship between them worsened, with Alfred blaming Marie (who had been largely responsible for his upbringing) for his untimely demise.

* * *

On 14/26 June another daughter was born to Alicky. Sir Charles Scott, the British Ambassador, told the queen that he feared the Russian people would be very disappointed at the birth of a third girl. He also deplored the fact that the tsar and tsarina still shut themselves away at Tsarskoe Selo and saw so few people.

News of the birth of Grand Duchess Maria Nicolaievna was soon marred by reports that Nicholas's brother George had died in the Caucasus. He had gone out alone on his motorcycle (which the doctors had forbidden him to ride) and some hours later, when he failed to return, his worried staff sent out a search party. By the time they found him it was too late. A peasant woman had discovered him collapsed at the side of the road, blood oozing from his mouth as he struggled to breathe. She supported him in her arms until he died. He was just twenty-eight. 'Only yesterday it was announced that he had renounced his right in favour of his younger brother Michael on account of the state of his health,' Queen Victoria recorded.[8]

Victoria realised what a terrible blow this would be and immediately sent her condolences to Nicholas and his mother. 'Thank you so [much] for kind sympathy in this terrible sudden bereavement,' the dowager empress telegraphed. 'My poor dearest son passed away quite alone[.] Am heartbroken.'[9] Nicholas also replied, thanking the queen for her warmth and sympathy on their terrible loss, which had touched them all deeply. He went on to report that Alicky and baby Maria were both well and that they passed most of the day on the balcony. 'Our plans for the autumn are not yet quite settled, but we hope you will let us come to Balmoral with our children about the end of August, new style.'[10] Nothing would have pleased the queen more. Alicky now had two children who Victoria had never seen (Tatiana and Maria) and the situation with Russia had become much easier during the summer. But there was no meeting at Balmoral.

Instead the tsar's brother Michael ('Misha'), whom Queen Victoria had met three years earlier in Cimiez, came to Scotland. On 8 October the queen's granddaughter Princess Louise came to Balmoral with her husband the Duke of Fife and sister Toria, and they 'brought over young Michael of Russia, Nicky's brother, who now, since the death of poor George, is the heir, but not called cesarewitch.'[*sic*] The twenty-year old grand duke was modest but considered not very intelligent. His sister Olga's rather telling nickname for him was 'dear, darling Floppy'. Nevertheless, the queen pronounced him 'remarkably nice and pleasing and pleasing looking'.[11]

Nicholas later wrote to thank the queen for her kindness to Misha, who had now returned to his relatives in Denmark 'perfectly enchanted' with his stay at Balmoral. He took the opportunity to commiserate with the queen about the terrible losses which her army had suffered in the Boer War in South Africa. 'God grant that [the war] may come to a speedy conclusion!' Nicholas added.[12] The tsar (like most of his family) supported the Boers, telling his mother that it was an 'unequal and unjust war'. Nevertheless, the British Ambassador reported that his tone was conciliatory, and early in 1900 the queen recorded that Nicholas 'had forbidden anything being done to embarrass us in our present difficulties'.[13]

In March she still believed that Nicholas was not hostile to England, despite the opposite attitude of the Russian Minister of War.

* * *

In spite of the political tensions between England and Russia there was always a flurry of gift giving for Christmas and birthdays. Empress Alexandra Feodorovna's Ledger of Parcels covering the years from 1897 has 713 individual entries in Russian, German, French and English (presumably entered by her ladies-in-waiting) but unfortunately it gives no indication of what the parcels contained. It shows three parcels sent to 'The Queen'. One was sent to Balmoral on 4 May 1898, in time for her birthday on 24 May; another was sent to Osborne on 5 December 1898, for Christmas; and a third was despatched on 6 May 1899 to Windsor. Another entry shows a parcel sent to Osborne on 18 December 1897, presumably also containing a Christmas gift for Victoria.[14]

In May 1900 the queen sent birthday wishes to the tsar. 'I thank you from the depth of my heart for all the love and great kindness you show me,' he replied, taking the opportunity to send good wishes to Victoria for her own approaching birthday. The queen invited the tsar and tsarina to visit England again and Nicholas reiterated that it was their ardent desire to come and visit her. Unfortunately, as he explained, the Shah of Persia was due to visit them in the summer and then there would be army manoeuvres in different areas of Russia but, he added, 'if there were a possibility of coming and seeing you we would be happy of doing so.'[15]

As the tsarina explained to Princess Bariatinsky, 'now is not the moment to be out of the country...' It was four years since she had seen her grandmother and they had never been separated for such a long period. She even thought of going 'all alone for a few days to see her', leaving Nicholas and the children behind, 'as she has been as a mother to me, ever since mama's death twenty-two years ago.'[16] Then one of the children became ill and the plan was never put into effect.

In July Nicholas consented to be godfather to the queen's great-grandson (and Alicky's nephew) Prince Louis of Battenberg, later Earl Mountbatten of Burma, who had been born the previous month.

* * *

Since the spring of 1900 Prince Alfred's health had been deteriorating. By the summer Marie was telling the queen that he was very unwell and suffering from a bad throat. The queen sent regular bulletins to Vicky, neither realising what was to follow.

Not until 25 July did Queen Victoria learn that her son's illness was incurable. A group of specialists in Vienna diagnosed a carcinomatous growth at the root of the tongue. He was unable to swallow and was being fed through a tube. An operation would be futile. This dreadful news was kept from the queen for as long as possible in order not to upset her further, as she was already depressed at the military reverses suffered by her army in South Africa.

Then at the end of July the eighty-one-year-old queen received the terrible news that Alfred had died in his sleep at the Rosenau, his father's beloved birthplace in Coburg.

Her heart went out to her daughter-in-law. The queen had already helped Marie settle Alfred's debts, which had run into such enormous amounts that creditors were threatening to repossess the Palais Edinburgh in Coburg. To forestall this Marie purchased the palace from her husband, who by that time was seriously ill, and settled everything with the help of the queen, who generously contributed £95,000. Now Marie was a widow. 'Poor darling Marie' lamented the queen, also feeling sorry for Alfred's four daughters who had adored him. 'I was greatly upset, — one sorrow, one trial, one anxiety, following on another. It is a horrible year, nothing but sadness and horrors of one kind and another.' The fact that the seriousness of Alfred's illness had been withheld from the monarch made the shock of his death all the more acute. 'I pray God to help me to be patient and have trust in Him, who has never failed me!' she continued, as telegrams poured in from stunned people as far afield as India. 'Felt terribly shaken and broken, and could not realise the dreadful fact.'[17]

Marie, who hated showing her feelings, remained in England for a while but gradually spent more and more time at her home in Tegernsee, Germany, away from memories of the past. Widowed at the age of only forty-six, she wore her usual drab clothes and became 'stout and elderly before her time'.[18]

* * *

As he had predicted, the tsar's proposed visit to Balmoral proved impossible and by the autumn of 1900 Nicholas was at Livadia, where he fell ill with typhoid. The queen recorded in her journal that the bulletins were favourable – but it was obvious that her own health was now failing. Worry about the war in South Africa had also taken its toll. One of the casualties was her grandson Prince Christian Victor of Schleswig-Holstein, who died from enteric fever on 29 October 1900.

One of the last entries in her journal regarding her Russian relatives was dated 24 November at Windsor. It read: 'Looked at some Shetland ponies, for me to give one to Alicky for her children.'[19]

There would be no more cosy reunions with the Romanovs. The queen went to Osborne for Christmas as usual but her sight was fading and she was often able to eat only a little. By the New Year it was obvious that it was only a matter of time.

In January she suffered a stroke and the family began to gather. Vicky was by now suffering from the cancer of the spine that would kill her later that year but her son Kaiser William hurried to the Isle of Wight.

Queen Victoria died at Osborne on 22 January 1901 surrounded by her family. Ten minutes later Superintendent Fraser of the Royal Household Police made the announcement of the queen's death from the steps of the lodge.

Outside the gates of Osborne House people stood in stunned silence. She had been on the throne for almost sixty-four years. Only the very elderly could remember a monarch other than Queen Victoria. The Duchess of York summed up the whole nation's feelings: 'The thought of England without the queen is dreadful even to think of. God help us all!'[20]

Journalists stampeded down the hill to Cowes on bicycles, yelling 'queen dead!' at the tops of their voices. Pressmen from all over Europe hurried to send the latest news home and messages of condolence arrived from around the world. During the next few days between fifty and sixty extra telegraphists were hired to cope with the additional burden of work at Cowes and East Cowes post offices.

As the news spread, church bells all over the island tolled and the flag at Carisbrooke Castle was lowered to half-mast. The Bishop of Winchester later held a short service in the queen's bedroom at which all the members of the royal family were present.

The Duchess of Coburg, recounting these momentous events to Missy, could not resist a dig at 'those foolish childish aunts', the queen's daughters, who had 'lost their heads and did not know what to do'. Particular venom was reserved for the malicious Princess Louise, Duchess of Argyll, who 'at times looks absolutely poisonous...' The royal household, Marie continued, also had no idea what to do, 'nobody had even ordered the coffin! They didn't even understand in the royal household that Bertie had to be called king at once and went on saying The Prince of Wales.' The hated kaiser, the duchess said, had been the most help, offering much practical advice. As for Queen Alexandra, who insisted that no one was to kiss her hand or treat her as queen until after they had left Osborne, Marie called her 'too naïve for words!... And I who had gone twice through such changes in my family [the deaths of Alexander II and Alexander III] could not cease wondering at this naïve and foolish sentimentality.'[21]

It was announced that the late queen's body would remain at Osborne until Friday 1 February. It would then be taken to Portsmouth on the royal yacht *Alberta*.

* * *

The tsar was still convalescing in the Crimea when news reached him of the queen's death. He and Alicky left immediately for the capital. The tsarina wanted to go to England with her brother Ernie, the Grand Duke of Hesse but had to be dissuaded. She was expecting another child (Grand Duchess Anastasia would be born in June) and her pregnancies were always difficult. She wrote to her sister Victoria, envying her because she would 'see beloved grandmama being taken to her last rest'. Continuing her letter, she added, 'I cannot believe she is really gone, that we shall never see her any more.'[22]

Although *The Times* correspondent reported on 24 January that Grand Duke and Duchess Sergei would be leaving for England on Saturday 26 January, for reasons that are unclear, Ella did not attend the funeral. Perhaps she decided to remain with her pregnant sister, or perhaps there were fears for the safety of Sergei, the unpopular Governor General of Moscow.

Nicholas did not attend the funeral either, deciding that he would be represented by his brother Michael.

The grand duke arrived in London on 1 February and was driven straight to Marlborough House to stay with King Edward VII and Queen Alexandra. *The Times* reported that Sergeant Michael Thorpe had been assigned to look after his safety.

Nicholas could hardly believe the queen had gone and he took the opportunity of his brother's journey to send a letter of condolence to the new monarch. 'She was so remarkably kind and touching towards me since the first time I ever saw her.' He had always felt so at home when he stayed at Windsor and Balmoral, he continued. 'I shall forever cherish her memory...'[23]

Over 400 visitors called to express their sympathy at the British Embassy in St Petersburg during the first two days after Victoria's death, but the reaction in the Russian press was mixed. Although the *Journal de St-Pétersbourg* said that 'In Russia especially, where the people's joys and sorrows are those of their imperial family, the grief caused by the death of a sovereign who was attached by so many ties to our own reigning house, will be deeply felt,' the general tone was different. On the whole, the press were 'quite unable to express sympathy with the British Empire in its great bereavement without introducing the subject of the South African war and attributing the death of the queen to the evil effects of that much-condemned enterprise,' wrote *The Times* correspondent on 25 January. After printing various comments from the Russian press against England and in favour of the Boers, *The Times* concluded by saying: 'Other papers curse and revile England as usual, which is not an exaggerated description of the remarks of such Russian journals in this hour of England's grief.'[24]

* * *

The queen's coffin arrived in London on 2 February. At Victoria Station it was placed on a gun carriage for a procession through the streets to Paddington Station, passing Buckingham Palace, the Mall, Piccadilly and Hyde Park along the way. Behind King Edward rode a column of crown princes and foreign royal representatives including Grand Duke Michael of Russia alongside Archduke Franz Ferdinand of Austria-Hungary and Grand Duke Ernest Louis of Hesse. As church bells tolled, artillery salutes thundered out and funeral marches were played by massed bands, the cortège wound its way to Paddington, where the coffin was placed on a funeral train.

At Windsor, with the gun carriage drawn by sailors after the horses bolted, the coffin was taken through the High Street and along the Long Walk to the castle. As the cortège wound its way along, minute guns fired a salute. The eighty-one shots marked each year of the queen's life. That night, surrounded by a guard of honour and countless wreaths, Victoria lay in state in the Albert Memorial Chapel.

Meanwhile, a memorial service was held in the English Episcopalian Church on the English Quay in St Petersburg. The tsar, tsarina, the dowager empress, her daughter Grand Duchess Olga, and Grand Duchess Ella were greeted at the church door by the ambassador Sir Charles Scott and his wife. Nicholas wore the Garter ribbon over his Russian uniform; Alexandra was in deep mourning and wore the Order of St Andrew. All the Embassy staff and the official world of Russia were present. After the service, which was conducted by the Reverend W. A. MacLeod, the tsarina and her sister were seen to be visibly affected. By the time they left the church the tsarina had quite broken down, something that the Russians, unused to such public displays of emotion by their sovereigns, did not appreciate.

* * *

On Sunday 3 February, Queen Victoria's coffin was carried into St George's Chapel for the funeral service, which was again attended by Grand Duke Michael and all the royal mourners. The following day, in bitterly cold weather and flurries of snow, the mourners followed the cortège through the George IV Gate and down the Long Walk to Frogmore. Here, Queen Victoria was finally laid to rest beside her beloved Albert in the mausoleum.

Grand Duke Michael left London on 9 February, having been awarded the Order of the Bath during his stay. The following year he would receive the Garter from King Edward VII.

Grand Duchess Xenia, who had met the queen in the south of France, summed up her impression in her diary: 'The queen was everything that was best about England; she was so much loved, and exuded such enormous charm.'[25]

As her sister-in-law Empress Alexandra wrote: 'England without the queen seems impossible.'[26]

* * *

The *New Zealand Herald* reported on 23 March that Queen Victoria left her wealth to her younger children to ensure they would be provided for. She left nothing to the Duchess of Coburg who already possessed a large fortune, and it is unlikely that she left more than a small memento to Alicky and Ella for the same reason. The Russians, she knew, already possessed everything they needed.

However, the queen left one final legacy to Nicholas II. His beloved Alicky proved to be a carrier of haemophilia, a blood-clotting deficiency transmitted by the mother usually only to male members of the family. Often called the 'Royal Disease', it had penetrated into the family through Queen Victoria, who passed it to her daughters Alice and Beatrice and thus to several of her descendants. Although females are carriers they rarely suffer from the disease and never know until they have children if any of their sons will be affected. When Tsarevich Alexei was born in 1904 it was discovered he had inherited this dreadful disease. There was no cure. Two-thirds of haemophiliacs died before the age of eleven, often in agonising pain from only a minor bump or scratch. Thus was put in train a set of circumstances that would end with the revolution in 1917. As the historian Sir Bernard Pares wrote: 'The nursery was the centre of all Russia's troubles.'[27]

Queen Victoria fortunately did not live to see her worst fears realised, when both Alicky and Ella were killed at the hands of the Bolsheviks. But in her own way, Victoria was partly responsible for the downfall of the dynasty she had always feared and distrusted.

Notes

Abbreviations
PRO – Public Record Office (now the National Archives), Kew.
RA – Royal Archives, Windsor.

Introduction
1. Massie, p 9.
2. Vorres, p 54.
3. Vorres, p 54.
4. Bainbridge, p 111. Fabergé refused but made the queen smaller and stouter and placed a crown on her head. The figure was later sold in London. It was the inspiration for Fabergé's hardstone Russian figures.
5. Fulford, *Dearest Child*, p 198.
6. Lord Mountbatten interview 1975, quoted in Van der Kiste, *Alfred*, p 9.
7. RA VIC/MAIN/QVJ (W), 1 November 1894.

Chapter 1
1. Mead Lalor, 'Poor Dear Aunt Julie.' In *Royalty Digest*, July 1996.
2. RA VIC/MAIN/QVJ (W), 6 October 1843.
3. Alexander, *Catherine*, p 320.
4. Beéche (ed), *Grand Dukes*, p 17.
5. Beéche (ed), *Grand Dukes*, p 17.
6. Beéche, *Coburgs*, p 14.
7. Mead Lalor, as above.

8. Alexander, *Catherine*, p 321.
9. Mead Lalor, as above.
10. Ashdown, p 26.
11. Beéche, *Coburgs*, p 14.
12. Ashdown, p 27.
13. Beéche, *Coburgs*, p 14.
14. Jackman, p 9.
15. *Russia. Art, Royalty and the Romanovs*, p 244.
16. Beéche, *Coburgs*, p 15.
17. Beéche, *Coburgs*, p 15.
18. Luise von Preussen, p 188; Laszlo Vajda, *Erläuterungen zu Alexander*. This child is not mentioned at all by Jacques Ferrand.
19. Ashdown, p 26.
20. Sotnick, p 13.
21. Wortman, p 251.
22. Ferrand, *Descendants Naturelle*, p 43; Mead Lalor, as above; Thornton, 'Prince Albert's Sister and Other Shady Coburgs'. In *Royalty Digest Quarterly*, No. 2, 2008.
23. www.G26.ch
24. www.Switzerlandisyours.com

Chapter 2

1. RA VIC/MAIN/QVJ (W), 19 July 1837. The queen's insignia was bequeathed to Princess Beatrice and is no longer in the Royal Collection. *See Russia. Art, Royalty and the Romanovs,* p 427.
2. RA VIC/MAIN/QVJ (W), 11 February 1838.
3. Longford, p 83.
4. RA VIC/MAIN/QVJ (W), 31 December 1838.
5. RA VIC/MAIN/QVJ (W), 10 July 1839.
6. RA VIC/MAIN/QVJ (W), 15 April 1839.
7. Benson, Vol. 1. p 154. 30 April 1839.
8. Quoted in *Russian Splendour*, p 91.
9. Quoted in Lincoln, p 215.
10. RA VIC/MAIN/QVJ (W), 4 May 1839.
11. Arapova, p 252.
12. RA VIC/MAIN/QVJ (W), 4 May 1839.
13. Jackman, p 288.
14. Benson, Vol. 1, p 172.
15. Radzinsky, *Alexander,* p 67.
16. *See* Tarsaidze, p 56 and footnote.
17. Pope-Hennessy, pp 29/30. There was no ballroom at Buckingham Palace until the queen added one in 1855.
18. Tarsaidze, pp 58/59.
19. Benson, Vol. 1. p 173.
20. Quoted in Tarsaidze, p 59.
21. Quoted in Tarsaidze, p 60.
22. Quoted in Tarsaidze, p 59.
23. RA VIC/MAIN/QVJ (W), 24 May 1839.
24. All quotations about the dinner and ball: RA VIC/MAIN/QVJ (W), 27 May 1839; for the graffiti at Frogmore Cottage *see The Times,* 1 December 2018.
25. RA VIC/MAIN/QVJ (W), 28 May 1839.
26. RA VIC/MAIN/QVJ (W), 29 May 1839.
27. Benson, Vol. 1, p 172; RA VIC/MAIN/QVJ (W), 29 May 1839.
28. Tarsaidze, p 64.
29. Longford, p 156.
30. Athlone, p 87.
31. RA VIC/MAIN/QVJ (W), 3 & 7 June 1839.
32. RA VIC/MAIN/QVJ (W), 17 June 1839.
33. Quoted in Lincoln, p 215.
34. RA VIC/MAIN/QVJ (W), 1 October 1839.
35. Quoted in Lincoln, p 217.
36. Lincoln, p 218.
37. Seaman & Sewell, p 90; RA VIC/MAIN/QVJ (W), 16 & 26 October 1839.
38. 17 September 1841. Ian Shapiro collection.
39. RA VIC/MAIN/QVJ (W), 18 September 1843.
40. RA VIC/MAIN/QVJ (W), 20 September 1843.
41. Benson, Vol. 1, p 492.
42. Benson, Vol. 1, p 494.

Chapter 3

1. Benson, Vol. 1, p 494.
2. RA VIC/MAIN/QVJ (W), 3 & 8 October 1843; *Russia: Art, Royalty and the Romanovs,* pp 242 & 248.
3. RA VIC/MAIN/QVJ (W), 4 October 1843.
4. RA VIC/MAIN/QVJ (W), 30 October 1843.
5. Benson, Vol. 2, p 501.
6. RA VIC/MAIN/QVJ (W), 6 October 1843.
7. Benson, Vol. 2, p 501.
8. Jackman, p 312.
9. RA VIC/MAIN/QVJ (W), 22 December 1843; *Russia. Art, Royalty and the Romanovs,* p 188.
10. RA VIC/MAIN/QVJ (W), 7 May 1844.
11. *Russian Splendour*, p 90; Seaman and Sewell, pp 82/83.

12. Fulford, *Your Dear Letter,* p 58; RA VIC/MAIN/QVJ (W), 30 May 1844.
13. Almedingen, *Alexander,* p 81.
14. RA VIC/MAIN/QVJ (W), 2 June 1844.
15. Quoted in Figes, *Crimea,* p 66.
16. Benson, Vol. 2, p 13.
17. Tarsaidze, p 68 footnote.
18. RA VIC/MAIN/QVJ (W), 3 June 1844.
19. All quotes Tarsaidze, p 68 footnote.
20. Magee, p 85.
21. RA VIC/MAIN/QVJ (W), 4 June 1844.
22. RA VIC/MAIN/QVJ (W), 5 June 1844.
23. Magee, p 85; Christie's New York. *Important English, Continental and American Silver and Gold.* Sale of 17 May 2011. Lot 143. The race reverted to the name of the Gold Cup when relations soured due to the Crimean War.
24. Quoted in Figes, *Crimea,* p 67.
25. Lincoln, p 222 quoting Stockmar's memoirs.
26. Quoted in Lincoln, p 223.
27. Quoted in Lincoln, p 331.
28. RA VIC/MAIN/QVJ (W), 6 June 1844.
29. Almedingen, *Alexander,* p 83.
30. Benson, Vol 2, p 14.
31. *Russia. Art, Royalty and the Romanovs,* pp 162, 164 & 171.
32. Jackman, p 312.
33. RA VIC/MAIN/QVJ (W), 9 June 1845.
34. *Russia. Art, Royalty and the Romanovs,* p 246.
35. RA VIC/MAIN/QVJ (W), 19 August 1845.
36. Ian Shapiro Collection.
37. RA VIC/MAIN/QVJ (W), 25 May 1847.
38. RA VIC/MAIN/QVJ (W), 1 June 1847.
39. RA VIC/MAIN/QVJ (W), 9 June 1847.
40. RA VIC/MAIN/QVJ (W), 17 June 1847.
41. RA VIC/MAIN/QVJ (W), 10 August 1847.
42. *Russia. Art, Royalty and the Romanovs,* p 243; RA VIC/MAIN/QVJ (W), 10 November 1847.
43. Benson, Vol. 2, p 166.
44. Quoted in Barber, p 143.
45. Benson, Vol. 2, p 449.
46. *Russia. Art, Royalty and the Romanovs,* p 175; RA VIC/MAIN/QVJ (W), 3 August 1853.
47. RA VIC/MAIN/QVJ (W), 8 August 1853.
48. Seaman and Sewell, p 54; RA VIC/MAIN/QVJ (W), 8 August 1853.
49. Strauss-Schom, p 239; Dolby, p 116.
50. Benson, Vol. 2, p 462.
51. Benson, Vol. 2, p 464. Translation from French.
52. RA VIC/MAIN/QVJ (W), 15 December 1853.
53. Weintrub, pp 232/33; Cadbury, p 75.
54. Benson, Vol. 3, p 26.
55. Lincoln, p 350. See Orlando Figes, *Crimea,* for the best discussion of the war.
56. Benson, Vol. 3, p 141.
57. RA VIC/MAIN/QVJ (W), 2 March 1855; *The Times,* 3 March 1855.
58. Benson. Vol 3, pp 112/3.
59. *Russia. Art, Royalty and the Romanovs,* p 173; information from Stephen Patterson, The Royal Collection Trust.

Chapter 4

1. RA VIC/MAIN/QVJ (W), 11 March 1856; Figes, *Crimea,* p 467.
2. Benson, Vol. 3, pp 252/3.
3. Figes, *Crimea,* pp 452/3.
4. Figes, *Crimea,* pp 452/3.
5. RA VIC/MAIN/QVJ (W), 29 April 1857.

6. RA VIC/MAIN/QVJ (W), 30 May 1857.
7. RA VIC/MAIN/QVJ (W), 31 May 1857.
8. Fulford, *Dearest Child,* pp 132/4.
9. Fulford *Dearest Child,* p 39.
10. Fulford, *Dearest Child,* p 198.
11. Fulford, *Dearest Child,* p 200.
12. RA VIC/MAIN/QVJ (W), 29 June 1859.
13. RA VIC/MAIN/QVJ (W), 11 August 1859.
14. *Russia. Art, Royalty and the Romanovs,* p 246; RA VIC/MAIN/QVJ (W), 17 August 1858.
15. Fulford, *Dearest Child,* pp 269/70.
16. Benson, Vol. 3, p 438.
17. The cemetery was closed in 1877 and Anna Feodorovna's grave was transferred to Schosshaldenfriedhof in Berne, which opened in 1878. Unfortunately, the grave is no longer there and her exact place of burial is unknown. A small stone against the wall with her name now commemorates Queen Victoria's aunt Julie. (Emails from Stefan Boller at the Staatsarchiv in Berne, and Simon Zwygart at Schosshaldenfriedhof in Berne.) Until 1917 the Russian Embassy in Berne paid for her grave which was, and still is, in the vicinity of the Russian Embassy. (*See* Vajda)
18. Fulford, *Dearest Child,* pp 134 & 277.
19. Fulford, *Dearest Child,* p 254.
20. Benson, Vol. 3, p 451.
21. Fulford, *Your Dear Letter,* p 366.
22. RA VIC/MAIN/QVJ (W), 7 November 1861.
23. Nicholas of Greece p 101.
24. Benson, Vol. 3, p 593.

Chapter 5

1. Benson, Vol 3, p 476.
2. Fulford, *Your Dear Letter,* p 27.
3. Fulford, *Dearest Mama,* p 54.
4. Fulford, *Dearest Mama,* pp 54/55.
5. Hibbert, *Letters,* p 168.
6. Almedingen, *Alexander,* p 197.
7. Almedingen, *Alexander,* pp 197/98.
8. Almedingen, *Alexander,* p 199.
9. Tarsaidze, p 98 footnote; *The Times,* 8 August 1864.
10. RA VIC/MAIN/QVJ (W), 26 August 1864.
11. Fulford, *Dearest Mama,* pp 341 and 345.
12. RA VIC/MAIN/QVJ (W), 29 June 1865.
13. Hibbert, *Letters,* p 196.
14. Almedingen, *Alexander,* p 214.
15. Weintraub, p 344.
16. Buckle, Vol. 1, p 370.
17. RA VIC/MAIN/QVJ (W), 7 June 1867; Fulford, *Your Dear Letter,* p 139.
18. Fulford, *Your Dear Letter,* p 153.
19. Fulford, *Your Dear Letter,* p 182.
20. RA VIC/MAIN/QVJ (W), 5 August 1869.
21. Fulford, *Your Dear Letter,* p 147.
22. Almedingen, p 250; Mosse, p 186; Taylor, pp 215/16.
23. RA VIC/MAIN/QVJ (W), 23 June 1871.
24. Gerladi, *Splendour,* p 33.
25. *Alice, Biographical Sketch...,* p 269.
26. Van der Kiste, *Alfred* p 80.
27. Abrash, p 390. Quoting from the Granville Papers in PRO 30/29.
28. Abrash, p 391. Quoting from the Granville Papers, PRO 31.
29. Fulford, *Darling Child,* p 68.
30. PRO 31, quoted in Abrash, p 391.
31. PRO 31, quoted in Abrash, p 392.
32. PRO 31, quoted in Abrash, p 393.
33. Fulford, *Darling Child,* pp 74/75.
34. Bolitho (ed), *Further Letters,* p 198.
35. Abrash, p 395.
36. Abrash, p 395.
37. Abrash, p 396.
38. Fulford, *Darling Child,* p 85.
39. Abrash, p 396.

40. Fulford, *Darling Child,* p 85.
41. Abrash p 396.
42. Fulford, *Darling Child,* p 88; *Alice, Letters....,* p 305.
43. Abrash, p 397. Quoting from RA S27/90. 7 June 1873.
44. Corti, p 214.

Chapter 6

1. Fulford, *Darling Child,* p 96.
2. Fulford, *Darling Child,* p 98.
3. RA VIC/MAIN/QVJ (W), 28 June 1873; *The Times,* 30 June 1873.
4. RA VIC/MAIN/QVJ (W), 1 July 1873.
5. Fulford, *Darling Child,* p 101.
6. RA VIC/MAIN/QVJ (W), 11 July 1873.
7. Fulford, *Darling Child,* p 102. Probably Nicholas, 4th Duke of Leuchtenberg (1843–1890). In 1863 he met Nadejda Sergeievna Akinfiyeva, who had left her husband and two daughters to become the mistress of Chancellor Gorchakov, some forty years her senior. She became pregnant by Nicholas and was sent abroad to avoid further scandal. Nicholas followed her and they went through a 'marriage' ceremony in Bavaria, where their sons Nicholas (born in 1868) and George (1872) grew up. Nicholas and Nadejda were officially married in 1878. The following year Alexander II recognised the marriage and created her Countess de Beauharnais.
8. Fulford, *Darling Child,* p 103; Fulford, *Your Dear Letter,* p 148 footnote.
9. Fulford, *Darling Child,* p 102.
10. Montefiore, p 421.
11. RA VIC/MAIN/QVJ (W), 14 July 1873.
12. Wilson, p 360.
13. Almedingen, pp 262/63.
14. Van der Kiste, *Alfred,* p 86.
15. RA VIC/MAIN/QVJ (W), 19 & 22 July.
16. Longford, pp 495/96.
17. Abrash, p 398.
18. Gerladi, p 40.
19. PRO 36, quoted in Abrash, p 399.
20. RA VIC/MAIN/QVJ (W), 29 July 1873.
21. RA VIC/MAIN/QVJ (W), 6 August 1873.
22. RA VIC/MAIN/QVJ (W), 9 August 1873.
23. Gerladi, pp 41/42.
24. Gerladi, p 41 estimates this as £2.7 million in 2011.
25. Van der Kiste, *Alfred,* p 90; *Russia. Art, Royalty and the Romanovs,* pp 364 & 379.
26. Hibbert, *Letters,* p 233; Fulford, *Darling Child,* p 120.
27. Wilson, p 360.

Chapter 7

1. Quoted in Abrash, p 400.
2. RA VIC/MAIN/QVJ (W), 18 January 1874.
3. RA VIC/MAIN/QVJ (W), 24 January 1874. The queen only received the letter after the wedding.
4. Both telegrams RA VIC/MAIN/QVJ (W), 23 January 1874.
5. Fulford, *Darling Child,* p 112.
6. RA VIC/MAIN/QVJ (W), 1 March 1874.
7. RA VIC/MAIN/QVJ (W), 7 March 1874.
8. RA VIC/MAIN/QVJ (W), 7 March 1874.
9. Quoted in Gerladi, p 41.
10. RA VIC/MAIN/QVJ (W), 12 March 1874.
11. Pope-Hennessy, p 76.
12. RA VIC/MAIN/QVJ (W), 18 April 1874.
13. Longford, p 507.
14. Elsberry, p 8.
15. Duff, *Hessian,* p 130.

16. Pakula, p 31.
17. Peacocke, p 10.
18. Pope-Hennessy, p 75; *Russia. Art, Royalty & The Romanovs,* p 226 and information from Stephen Patterson, The Royal Collection Trust. The iconostasis was moved to the Russian church in Darmstadt founded by Nicholas II and Alexandra Feodorovna in 1899. Prince Andrew of Greece and Princess Alice of Battenberg, parents of Prince Philip, Duke of Edinburgh, were married there in 1903. In April 1876, while visiting Baden Baden, the queen visited the Greek Chapel, where she was impressed by the beautiful chanting of the priests.
19. Pope-Hennessy, p 76; Van der Kiste, *Alfred,* p 116.
20. Duff, *Hessian,* pp 230/31.
21. St Aubyn, pp 411/12.
22. Van der Kiste, *Alfred,* p 116.
23. Lee, p 40.
24. Weintraub, p 413.
25. RA VIC/MAIN/QVJ (W), 13 May 1874.
26. RA VIC/MAIN/QVJ (W), 14 May 1874.
27. RA VIC/MAIN/QVJ (W), 17 May 1874.
28. Menus from the dinner at the Crystal Palace, the Guildhall, the Foreign Office and the programme of the review at Aldershot, all from the Ian Shapiro Collection.
29. Van der Kiste, *The Romanovs,* pp 67/68.
30. RA VIC/MAIN/QVJ (W), 29 August 1874.
31. RA VIC/MAIN/QVJ (W), 21 September 1874.
32. Corti, p 216; Van der Kiste, *Alfred,* p 98.
33. Mandache, pp 148/49.
34. RA VIC/MAIN/QVJ (W), 13 October 1874.

35. RA VIC/MAIN/QVJ (W), 16 October 1874.
36. Prince Bariatinsky to an unnamed French correspondent, 12 November 1874. International Autograph Auctions, 3 June 2017. Lot 481.
37. RA VIC/MAIN/QVJ (W), 16 November 1874.
38. RA VIC/MAIN/QVJ (W), 23 November 1874.
39. Klausen, *Alexandra,* p 238.
40. RA VIC/MAIN/QVJ (W), 23 November 1874; Klausen, *Alexandra,* p 239; Van der Kiste, *Alfred,* p 97.
41. RA VIC/MAIN/QVJ (W), 23 November 1874.
42. Fulford, *Darling Child,* p 229.
43. Gerladi, p 72; Pakula, p 33.
44. To Queen Marie of Romania, 27 October 1914. Charlotte Zeepvat, in *The Last Romanovs,* p 55.
45. *The Sussex Advertiser,* 1 May 1877; *The Daily Telegraph,* 25 September 2013; Catalogue of East Sussex Record Office; information from Barbara Merchant of Lewes History Group, Margaret Guyver and Marion Wynn. The monument was restored again in 1957 with help from the Soviet Embassy, and in 2013 in a Russian/Finnish initiative.

Chapter 8

1. *Russia. Art, Royalty and the Romanovs,* p 226.
2. *Alice, Biographical Sketch...,* p 343
3. RA VIC/MAIN/QVJ (W), 7 July 1876.
4. Wilson, p 377.
5. Wilson, p 378.
6. Quoted in Abrash, p 400.
7. Montefiore, p 429; Pakula, p 34; Corti, p 222.
8. Wilson, p 278; Van der Kiste, *Alfred,* p 103.

9. Memorandum in Hibbert, *Letters*, p 244; Graham, p 203.
10. RA VIC/MAIN/QVJ (W), 1 January 1877.
11. RA VIC/MAIN/QVJ (W), 24 April 1877.
12. Hibbert, *Letters,* p 245; RA VIC/MAIN/QVJ (W), 9 August 1877.
13. Fulford, *Darling Child,* p 253; Hibbert, *Letters*, pp 247/48.
14. Hibbert, *Letters* p 248.
15. Hibbert, *Letters,* p 250; RA VIC/MAIN/QVJ (W), 4 January 1878.
16. *Kejserinde Dagmar* Exhibition Catalogue, pp 131/32.
17. Corti, pp 242/243.
18. Barber, p 196.
19. Wilson, pp 384/85.
20. Hough, *Advice,* p 19.
21. RA VIC/MAIN/QVJ (W), 3 December 1879.
22. Hough, *Louis & Victoria,* p 96.
23. RA VIC/MAIN/QVJ (W), 24 February 1880; *Russia. Art, Royalty and the Romanovs,* p 73.
24. RA VIC/MAIN/QVJ (W), 16 March 1880.
25. RA VIC/MAIN/QVJ (W), 3 June 1880.
26. Graham, p 300.
27. RA VIC/MAIN/QVJ (W), 9 July 1880.
28. Ian Shapiro Collection.
29. RA VIC/MAIN/QVJ (W), 22 September 1880 & 18 January 1881.
30. Pares, *History,* p 441.
31. RA VIC/MAIN/QVJ (W), 13 March 1881.
32. RA VIC/MAIN/QVJ (W), 13 March 1881; Fulford, *Beloved Mama,* p 97.
33. RA VIC/MAIN/QVJ (W), 5 April 1881.
34. RA VIC/MAIN/QVJ (W), 19 March 1881.
35. *Russia. Art, Royalty and the Romanovs,* p 73.
36. Hamilton, pp 448/49.
37. *Russia. Art, Royalty and the Romanovs,* p 198.
38. Sir John Cowell to Mrs Pulleine, Clifton Castle, Bedale, 5 April 1881. Ian Shapiro Collection.
39. Queen Victoria to the Princess of Wales, 11 April 1881. Ian Shapiro collection.

Chapter 9

1. RA VIC/MAIN/QVJ (W), 1 April 1881.
2. Almedingen, *Romanovs,* p 272.
3. Harcave, *Witte,* p 92.
4. Seton-Watson, pp 461/63.
5. RA VIC/MAIN/QVJ (W), 8 April 1881.
6. RA VIC/MAIN/QVJ (W), 18 May 1881.
7. Alexander, *Once,* p 174.
8. Alexander, *Once,* p 174.
9. Marie of Romania, Vol 1, p 92; Alexander, *Once,* p 139.
10. Alexander, *Once,* p 151.
11. Vorres, p 54.
12. RA VIC/MAIN/QVJ (W), 24 September 1882; Fulford, *Beloved Mama,* p 126.
13. Montefiore, p 467.
14. RA VIC/MAIN/QVJ (W), 15 September 1883.
15. Warwick, p 54.
16. Duff, *Hessian,* p 195.
17. Warwick, p 77.
18. Zeepvat, *Romanov Autumn,* p 125.
19. Cadbury, p 42.
20. Hough, *Louis & Victoria,* pp 55/6.
21. Fulford, *Beloved Mama,* p 135.
22. Cadbury, p 79.
23. Cadbury, p 81.
24. Cadbury, p 83.
25. *Russia. Art, Royalty & the Romanovs,* p 314; Warwick, pp 82/83.
26. McClintock, p 157.
27. Hough, *Advice,* p 53.

28. Cadbury, p 84.
29. Arapova, p 255.
30. Hough, *Advice,* p 55.
31. Cadbury, p 85.
32. Warwick, p 84, quoting from the Hesse Archives.
33. Hough, *Advice,* pp 56/57.
34. Hough, *Advice,* p 48.
35. Fulford, *Beloved Mama,* pp 152/53.
36. Cadbury, p 85.
37. Zeepvat, *Romanov Autumn,* p 126.
38. Hough, *Advice,* p 57.
39. L. Millar, p 23. *See* Warwick pp 101/3 & Cadbury p 85 for Sergei's presents to Ella and the wealth loaded onto her. *See also* Irene's letter to the queen, Cadbury p 88.
40. Baddeley, p 227. *See* Warwick pp 131/32 for a discussion of Sergei's sexuality.
41. Warwick, p 131 footnote.
42. Zeepvat, *Romanov Autumn,* p 127.
43. Montefiore p 472, quoting Röhl, Vol. I, p 123.
44. Zeepvat, *Romanov Autumn,* p 127.
45. Telegram sent from Windsor on 30 March. Ian Shapiro Collection.
46. Hough, *Advice,* p 57.
47. Fulford, *Beloved Mama,* p 161; RA VIC/MAIN/QVJ (W), 17 April 1884.
48. RA VIC/MAIN/QVJ (W), 30 April 1884.
49. RA VIC/MAIN/QVJ (W), 21 May 1884.
50. L. Millar, p 24.
51. RA VIC/MAIN/QVJ (W), 21 May 1884.
52. Ian Shapiro Collection.
53. Ian Shapiro Collection; L.Millar p 27.
54. Ian Shapiro Collection.
55. Longford, p 602.
56. RA VIC/MAIN/QVJ (W), 15 June 1884.
57. Fulford, *Beloved Mama,* p 173.

Chapter 10

1. Montefiore, p 468 footnote.

2. Hough, *Advice,* p 73. Princess Alice was the mother of HRH The Duke of Edinburgh.
3. RA VIC/MAIN/QVJ (W), 23 April 1885; Fulford, *Beloved Mama,* p 188.
4. Fulford, *Beloved Mama,* p 188.
5. Taylor, p 300.
6. Hough, *Advice,* p 46.
7. RA VIC/MAIN/QVJ (W), 25 September 1885.
8. RA VIC/MAIN/QVJ (W), 1 November 1885.
9. Ramm, p 28.
10. RA VIC/MAIN/QVJ (W), 13 August 1886.
11. RA VIC/MAIN/QVJ (W), 25 August 1886; St Aubyn, p 466.
12. RA VIC/MAIN/QVJ (W), 27 August 1886.
13. RA VIC/MAIN/QVJ (W), 28 August 1886.
14. Ramm, p 43.
15. Gerladi, pp 112/13.
16. Hough, *Advice,* p 80.
17. Cadbury, p 92.
18. RA VIC/MAIN/QVJ (W), 30 April 1886.
19. RA VIC/MAIN/QVJ (W), 3 July 1886; Campbell, p 141.
20. Campbell, p 150.
21. Campbell, pp 151/52.
22. Campbell, p 195.
23. Annexed to RA VIC/MAIN/QVJ (W), 16 March 1887.
24. Campbell, p 210.
25. Campbell, p 228.
26. Campbell, pp 237 & 241.
27. Campbell, pp 242/43.
28. Martin, p 225.

Chapter 11

1. Cadbury, p 92.
2. L. Millar, p 43.
3. L. Millar, p 44.
4. RA VIC/MAIN/QVJ (W), 26 March 1888.
5. Massie, p 9.

6. Van der Kiste, *European Empires,* p 103; Montefiore, p 463.
7. RA VIC/MAIN/QVJ (W), 31 October 1888.
8. Alexander, *Once,* p 111; Montefiore, p 482 footnote.
9. Alexander, *Once,* p 112.
10. RA VIC/MAIN/QVJ (W), 14 May 1889.
11. Hough, *Advice,* p 112.
12. L. Millar, p 70.
13. Hall, *Little Mother,* p 152.
14. Warwick, p 149.
15. Hibbert, p 318.
16. Almedingen, *Unbroken,* p 40.
17. L.Millar, p 66.
18. RA VIC/MAIN/QVJ (W), 2 June 1892.
19. Hough, *Advice,* p 117.
20. Pakula, p 60.
21. Mandache, p 67.
22. Mandache, p 68.
23. RA VIC/MAIN/QVJ (W), 23 November 1892.
24. Warwick, p 171; L. Millar, pp 73/4.
25. RA VIC/MAIN/QVJ (W), 7 December 1892.
26. RA VIC/MAIN/QVJ (W), 12 December 1892.
27. Lee, p 150.
28. Churchill, p 183; Mandache, p 60.
29. Van der Kiste, *Alfred,* pp 133 & 151.
30. Ponsonby, *Letters,* p 438.
31. Brook-Shepherd, *Sunset,* p 190.

Chapter 12
1. Mandache, p 125.
2. Vorres, p 54.
3. RA VIC/MAIN/QVJ (W), 1 July 1893.
4. Bing, p 70.
5. Maylunas & Mironenko, p 28.
6. RA VIC/MAIN/QVJ (W), 5 July 1893.
7. *Russia. Art, Royalty and the Romanovs,* p 190.
8. RA VIC/MAIN/QVJ (W), 29 September 1893.

9. RA VIC/MAIN/QVJ (W), 3 October 1893.
10. RA VIC/MAIN/QVJ (W), 10 October 1893.
11. Quoted in Zeepvat, *Romanov Autumn,* p 199.
12. L.Millar, p 77.
13. Montefiore, p 479.
14. Hough, *Advice,* p 120.
15. Mandache, p 146.
16. Mandache, p 172.
17. Mandache, p 163.
18. Mandache, p 169.
19. Maylunas & Mironenko, p 45.
20. RA VIC/MAIN/QVJ (W), 20 April 1894.
21. Massie, p 21.
22. RA VIC/MAIN/QVJ (W), 21 April 1894.
23. Maylunas & Mironenko, p 51.
24. RA VIC/MAIN/QVJ (W), 4 July 1894; Basu, p 122.
25. Arapova, p 276.
26. Maylunas & Mironenko, p 67.
27. Cadbury, p 254.
28. Arapova, p 276.
29. Pakula, p 96; Mandache, p 123.
30. Pakula, p 98.
31. Hough, *Advice,* pp 125/26.

Chapter 13
1. Timms, 'Princess Alix of Hesse's Visit to Harrogate.' In *Royalty Digest Quarterly,* No. 1, 2018.
2. Buxhoeveden, p 38.
3. RA VIC/MAIN/QVJ (W), 25 June 1894.
4. Maylunas & Mironenko, p 78.
5. RA VIC/MAIN/QVJ (W), 29 June 1894; Ramm, p 169.
6. Maylunas & Mironenko, p 78.
7. Bing, p 82.
8. RA VIC/MAIN/QVJ (W), 4 July 1894.
9. RA VIC/MAIN/QVJ (W), 8 July 1894.
10. Maylunas & Mironenko, pp 78/79.
11. RA VIC/MAIN/QVJ (W), 11 July 1894.

12. Nicholas II, *Journal Intime*, p 77.
13. RA VIC/MAIN/QVJ (W), 22 July 1894.
14. RA VIC/MAIN/QVJ (W), 23 July 1894.
15. Maylunas & Mironenko, p 89.
16. RA VIC/MAIN/QVJ (W), 18 October 1894.
17. Hough, *Advice*, pp 126/27.
18. RA VIC/MAIN/QVJ (W), 28 October 1894.
19. RA VIC/MAIN/QVJ (W), 1 November 1894.
20. Ramm, p 172.
21. RA Z499/79. Translation from German. Quoted in Hall, *Little Mother*, p 164.
22. RA Z106/67. Translation from German. Quoted in Hall, *Little Mother*, p 172.
23. Maylunas & Mironenko, p 301.
24. L.Millar, p 85.
25. Warwick, p 179.
26. The telegrams sent from the Prince of Wales in Russia to Queen Victoria between 24 October/5 November 1894 and 18/30 November 1894 are in the Ian Shapiro Collection and used here by kind permission. The Prince gives the dates as N.S.
27. RA VIC/MAIN/QVJ (W), 15 November 1894.
28. Hough, *Advice*, pp 127/28.
29. Maylunas & Mironenko, p 107.
30. RA VIC/MAIN/QVJ (W), 19 November 1894.
31. Prince Hans of Glücksburg to Sir Hugh MacDonell, 6 November 1894. Ian Shapiro Collection.
32. Ramm, p 173; Ella's letter and the sketches are in L. Millar, pp 82/84.
33. RA VIC/MAIN/QVJ (W), 26 November 1894.
34. Maylunas & Mironenko, p 113.
35. *Russia. Art, Royalty and the Romanovs*, pp 258 & 427.
36. RA VIC/MAIN/QVJ (W), 6 December 1894.
37. Carter, p 143.
38. RA VIC/MAIN/QVJ (W), 21 December 1894.
39. Lee, p 179.

Chapter 14
1. RA VIC/MAIN/QVJ (W), 1 April 1895.
2. RA VIC/MAIN/QVJ (W), 23 April 1895.
3. Van der Kiste, *European Empires*, p 143.
4. Hough, *Advice*, p 133.
5. RA VIC/MAIN/QVJ (W), 15 November 1895.
6. RA VIC/MAIN/QVJ (W), 6 April 1896.
7. RA VIC/MAIN/QVJ (W), 8 April 1896.
8. Belyakova, *Maria*, p 230.
9. RA VIC/MAIN/QVJ (W), 9 April 1896.
10. RA VIC/MAIN/QVJ (W), 10 April 1896.
11. RA VIC/MAIN/QVJ (W), 22 April 1896.
12. RA VIC/MAIN/QVJ (W), 26 April 1896.
13. Bing, p 113.
14. Frankland, pp 202/204; Buckle, Vol. 3, pp 45/6.
15. RA VIC/MAIN/QVJ (W), 27 May 1896.
16. RA VIC/MAIN/QVJ (W), 4 June 1896.
17. Warwick, pp 193/94.
18. RA VIC/MAIN/QVJ (W), 25 June 1896.

Chapter 15
1. Maylunas & Mironenko, p 151.
2. Longford, p 685.
3. *Russia. Art, Royalty and the Romanovs*, p 328.
4. Duff, *Highlands*, p 221.
5. RA VIC/MAIN/QVJ (W), 21 September 1896.

6. Welch, p 11.
7. Bing, pp 117/18.
8. Reid, p 124.
9. Duff, *Highlands,* p 221.
10. RA VIC/MAIN/QVJ (W),
    22 September 1896; Bing, p 118.
11. King, *Twilight,* p 174.
12. All quotations about Nicholas and
    Toria are from Bokhanov, *Romanovs,*
    p 28.
13. RA VIC/MAIN/QVJ (W),
    24 September 1896.
14. RA VIC/MAIN/QVJ (W),
    26 September, 1896.
15. RA VIC/MAIN/QVJ (W),
    26 September, 1896.
16. St Aubyn, p 577.
17. Welch, p 57; RA VIC/MAIN/QVJ
    (W), 27 September, 1896.
18. Bing, p 120.
19. Welch, p 58; RA VIC/MAIN/QVJ
    (W), 28 & 29 September 1896.
20. Ramm, p 196; Lady Lytton's Court
    Diary. In *Royalty Digest,* May 1993,
    p 338.
21. RA VIC/MAIN/QVJ (W), 2 October
    1896; Hough, *Advice,* p 138.
22. Reid, p 125.
23. Bomann-Larsen, p 118.
24. RA VIC/MAIN/QVJ (W),
    30 September 1896.
25. Seating plan in the Ian Shapiro
    Collection; Reid, pp 124/25.
26. Welch, p 72; RA VIC/MAIN/QVJ
    (W), 1 October 1896.
27. RA VIC/MAIN/QVJ (W), 2 October
    1896; Nicholas's Diary, 20 September
    OS 1896. Translated by the Reverend
    Terence A. McLean Wilson. In
    Royalty Digest, September 1996, p
    69.
28. RA VIC/MAIN/QVJ (W), 3 October
    1896; Wynn, 'What am I Supposed
    to Do?' in *Royalty Digest Quarterly,*
    No. 1, 2006.
29. Reid, pp 124/25.
30. Buxhoeveden, p 73.
31. Bing, p 120; *Russia: Art Royalty and
    the Romanovs,* p 75.
32. Buxhoeveden, p 73.
33. Seton-Watson, p 577.
34. Maylunas & Mironenko, p 153.
35. RA VIC/MAIN/QVJ (W),
    24 November 1896.
36. RA VIC/MAIN/QVJ (W),
    20 December 1896. Sultan Abdul
    Hamid was deposed in 1909 and
    deported to Salonika.
37. *See* de Guitaut, p 237.
38. *See* de Guitaut, pp 14, 104, 110 &
    208; Habsburg & Lopato, p 242.
39. Welch, p 86.
40. Quoted in Figes, *A People's Tragedy,*
    p 26.

Chapter 16

1. Duff, *Victoria Travels,* p 342.
2. RA VIC/MAIN/QVJ (W), 19 March
    1897.
3. RA VIC/MAIN/QVJ (W), 19 &
    29 March 1897.
4. Trevelyan, p 207.
5. RA VIC/MAIN/QVJ (W), 25 April
    1897.
6. RA VIC/MAIN/QVJ (W), 26 April
    1897.
7. RA VIC/MAIN/QVJ (W), 3 May
    1897.
8. RA VIC/MAIN/QVJ (W), 10 June
    1897; Hough, *Advice,* p 139.
9. Pakula, p 118; Mandache, pp 301 &
    303.
10. Pope-Hennessy, p 335.
11. RA VIC/MAIN/QVJ (W), 21 June
    1897; *Russia. Art, Royalty and
    the Romanovs,* pp 402 and 414;
    Warwick, p 196.
12. RA VIC/MAIN/QVJ (W), 21 June
    1897.
13. RA VIC/MAIN/QVJ (W), 22 June
    1897.
14. RA VIC/MAIN/QVJ (W), 27 June
    1897.
15. Mandache, p 307.
16. Mandache, p 308.

17. Poore, p 224.
18. RA VIC/MAIN/QVJ (W), 7 February 1898.
19. RA VIC/MAIN/QVJ (W), 7 February 1898.
20. RA VIC/MAIN/QVJ (W), 18 February and 29 November 1898.
21. Ramm, p 219.
22. RA VIC/MAIN/QVJ (W), 25 April 1898.
23. RA VIC/MAIN/QVJ (W), 23 November 1898.
24. *Russia. Art, Royalty and the Romanovs,* p 75.

Chapter 17

1. Hibbert, pp 337/38.
2. Maylunas & Mironenko, p 183.
3. Maylunas & Mironenko, p 184.
4. RA VIC/MAIN/QVJ (W), 12 March 1899.
5. Duff, *Victoria Travels,* p 336.
6. RA VIC/MAIN/QVJ (W), 1 May 1899.
7. Mandache – 'dear & kind', pp 438, 394 & 433; 'influence & interference,' p 146; 'telegraph & agitate,' p 298.
8. RA VIC/MAIN/QVJ (W), 10 July 1899.
9. Hall, *Little Mother,* p 186.
10. Maylunas & Mironenko, p 187.
11. Vorres, p 33; RA VIC/MAIN/QVJ (W), 8 October 1899.
12. Maylunas & Mironenko, p 191.
13. Bing, p 142; RA VIC/MAIN/QVJ (W), 17 January 1900.
14. Sotheby's catalogue, Russian Sale June 2018 and information from Darin Bloomquist.
15. Maylunas & Mironenko, p 197.
16. Buxhoeveden, p 90.
17. RA VIC/MAIN/QVJ (W), 31 July 1900.
18. Van der Kiste, *Alfred,* p 185.
19. RA VIC/MAIN/QVJ (W), 24 November 1900.
20. Longford, p 706.
21. Quoted in Gerladi, pp 172/73, from the Romanian National Archives.
22. Buxhoeveden, p 90.
23. Carter, p 269.
24. *The Times,* 26 January 1901.
25. Carter, p 269.
26. Buxhoeveden, p 90.
27. Pares, *Fall,* p 16.

Bibliography

(The place of publication is London, unless otherwise stated.)

Alexander, Grand Duke of Russia. *Once a Grand Duke.* (Cassell, 1932)

Alexander, John T. *Catherine the Great. Life and Legend.* (Oxford University Press, 1989)

Alice. Biographical Sketch and Letters. Preface by Princess Christian. (John Murray, 1884)

Almedingen, E. M. *Alexander II.* (The Bodley Head, 1962)

Almedingen, E. M. *An Unbroken Unity.* (The Bodley Head, 1964)

Almedingen, E. M. *The Romanovs: Three Centuries of an Ill-Fated Dynasty.* (Bodley Head, 1966)

Arapova, Dr Tatiana & others. *Nicholas and Alexandra. The Last Imperial Family of Tsarist Russia.* (Booth-Clibborn Editions, 1998)

Aronson, Theo. *Heart of a Queen.* (John Murray, 1991)

Aronson, Theo. *Victoria and Disraeli.* (Cassell, 1977)

Ashdown, Dulcie M. *Victoria and the Coburgs.* (Robert Hale, 1981)

Athlone, HRH Princess Alice, Countess of. *For My Grandchildren.* (Evans Brothers, 1966)

Bainbridge, Henry Charles. *Peter Carl Fabergé. His Life and Work.* (Spring Books, 1949)

Baddeley, John F. *Russia in the Eighties.* (Longmans, Green & Co., 1921)

Baird, Julia. *Victoria. The Queen.* (Blackfriars, 2016)

Barber, Noel. *Lords of the Golden Horn.* (Macmillan, 1973)

Basu, Shrabani. *Victoria and Abdul.* (Stroud: The History Press, 2010)

Beéche, Arturo E. *The Coburgs of Europe.* (California: Eurohistory.com, 2013)

Beéche, Arturo E. (editor). *The Grand Duchesses.* (California: Eurohistory.com, 2004)

Beéche, Arturo E. (editor). *The Grand Dukes.* (California: Eurohistory.com, 2010)

Belyakova, Zoia. *Grand Duchess Maria Nikolayevna and her Palace in St Petersburg.* (St Petersburg: Ego Publishing,1994)

Belyakova, Zoia. *Honour and Fidelity.* (St Petersburg: Logos Publishers, 2010)

Bibliography

Benson, A. C. (ed). *The Letters of Queen Victoria.* 3 Volumes. (John Murray, 1908)

Bergamini, John. *The Tragic Dynasty.* (Constable, 1970)

Bing, Edward J. (ed). *The Letters of Tsar Nicholas & Empress Marie.* (Ivor Nicholson & Watson, 1937)

Bokhanov, Alexander & others. *The Romanovs. Love, Power & Tragedy.* (Leppi Publications, 1993)

Bolitho, Hector (ed). *Further Letters of Queen Victoria.* (Thornton Butterworth, 1938)

Bomann-Larsen, Tor. *Kongstanken – Haakon & Maud.* (Norway: J W Cappelens Forlag, 2002)

Boulay, Cyrille. *La France des Romanov.* (France: Editions Perrin, 2010)

Brooke-Shepheard, Gordon. *Royal Sunset.* (Weidenfeld & Nicolson, 1987)

Buckle, G. E. (ed). *Letters of Queen Victoria, Second Series.* 3 Volumes. (John Murray, 1926–1928)

Buxhoeveden, Baroness Sophie. *The Life and Tragedy of Alexandra Feodorovna, Empress of Russia.* (Longmans Green, 1930)

Cadbury, Deborah. *Queen Victoria's Matchmaking.* (Bloomsbury, 2017)

Campbell, Christy. *The Maharajah's Box.* (Harper Collins, 2000)

Churchill, Lady Randolph (Mrs George Cornwallis-West). *The Reminiscences of Lady Randolph Churchill.* (Edward Arnold, 1908)

Corti, Count Egon. *The Downfall of Three Dynasties.* (Methuen, 1934)

Cowles, Virginia. *The Russian Dagger.* (Collins, 1969)

de Guitaut, Caroline. *Fabergé in the Royal Collection.* (Royal Collection Enterprises, 2003)

Dolby, Karen. *My Dearest, Dearest Albert.* (Michael O'Mara Books, 2018)

Duff, David. *Albert and Victoria.* (Frederick Muller, 1972)

Duff, David. *Hessian Tapestry.* (Frederick Muller, 1967)

Duff, David (ed). *Queen Victoria's Highland Journals.* (Webb & Bower, 1980)

Duff, David. *Victoria Travels.* (Frederick Muller, 1970)

Elsberry, Terence. *Marie of Romania.* (Cassell, 1973)

Fabb, John. *Victoria's Golden Jubilee.* (Seaby, 1987)

Figes, Orlando. *Crimea.* (Allen Lane, 2010)

Figes, Orlando. *A People's Tragedy.* (Jonathan Cape, 1996)

Frankland, Noble. *Witness of a Century.* (Shepheard-Walwyn, 1993)

Fulford, Roger (ed). *Dearest Child.* (Evans Brothers, 1965)

Fulford, Roger (ed). *Dearest Mama.* (Evans Brothers, 1968)

Fulford, Roger (ed). *Your Dear Letter.* (Evans Brothers, 1971)

Fulford, Roger (ed). *Darling Child.* (Evans Brothers, 1976)

Fulford, Roger (ed). *Beloved Mama.* (Evans Brothers, 1981)

Gerladi, Julia. *From Splendour to Revolution.* (St Martin's Press, 2011)

Gillen, Mollie. *The Prince and His Lady.* (Sidgwick & Jackson, 1970)

Graham, Stephen. *The Life & Reign of Alexander II.* (Ivor Nicholson & Watson, 1935)

Hall, Coryne, *Little Mother of Russia. A Biography of the Empress Marie Feodorovna, 1847–1928.* (Shepheard-Walwyn, 1999)

Hamilton, Lord Frederick. *The Vanished World of Yesterday.* (Hodder & Stoughton, 1950)

Harcave, Sidney (ed). *The Memoirs of Count Witte.* (New York: M E Sharpe, 1990)

Hibbert, Christopher. *Queen Victoria in her Letters & Journals*. (John Murray, 1984)

Hough, Richard (ed). *Advice to a Granddaughter*. (Heinemann, 1975)

Hubbard, Kate. *Serving Victoria*. (Chatto & Windus, 2012)

Jackman, S. W. (ed). *Romanov Relations*. (Macmillan, 1969)

Kejserinde Dagmar, Exhibition Catalogue. (Copenhagen: The Royal Silver Room, 1997)

King, Greg. *The Last Empress*. (New York: Birch Lane Press, 1994)

King, Greg. *Twilight of Splendour*. (John Wiley, 2007)

Klausen, Inger-Lise. *Alexandra af Wales. Prinsesse fra Danmark*. (Copenhagen: Lindhardt og Ringhof, 2001)

Lambton, Anthony. *The Mountbattens*. (Constable, 1989)

Lee, A. G. (ed). *The Empress Frederick Writes to Sophie*. (Faber & Faber, 1955)

Lincoln, W. Bruce. *Nicholas I. Emperor and Autocrat of All the Russias*. (Allen Lane, 1978)

Longford, Elizabeth. *Victoria R.I.* (World Books, 1969)

McClintock, Mary Howard. *The Queen Thanks Sir Howard*. (John Murray, 1945)

Magee, Sean. *Ascot. The History*. (Methuen, 2002)

Mandache, Diana (ed). *Dearest Missy*. (Sweden: Rosvall Royal Books, 2011)

Marie, Queen of Roumania. *The Story of My Life. Volume I.* (Cassel, 1934)

Martin, Ralph G. *Lady Randolph Churchill*. Vol. 1, 1854–95. (Cassell, 1969)

Massie, Robert K. *Nicholas & Alexandra*. (Gollancz, 1968)

Maylunas, Andrei; and Mironenko, Sergei. *A Lifelong Passion*. (Weidenfeld & Nicolson, 1996).

Millar, Lubov. *Grand Duchess Elizabeth of Russia. New Martyr of the Communist Yoke*. (California: Nikodemos Orthodox Publishing Society, 1991)

Montefiore, Simon Sebag. *The Romanovs. 1613–1918*. (Weidenfeld & Nicolson, 2016).

Nicholas II, Tsar of Russia, *Journal Intime de Nicolas II*. (Paris: Payot, 1923)

Nicholas, Prince of Greece. *Erindringer fra et Halvt Aarhundrede*. (Denmark: Gyldendal,. 1929)

Noel, Gerard. *Princess Alice*. (Constable, 1974)

Pares, Sir Bernard. *A History of Russia*. (Jonathan Cape, 1949)

Pares, Sir Bernard. *The Fall of the Russian Monarchy*. (Jonathan Cape, 1939. Cassell paperback, 1988.)

Payne, Peter L. (ed), John S Smith and Aberdeen University Library. *George Washington Wilson and Royal Deeside*. (Aberdeen: AUL Publishing. 1995)

Peacock, Marguerite D. *The Story of Clarence House*. (Pitkin Books, n.d. but c. 1950)

Ponsonby, Sir Frederick (ed). *Letters of the Empress Frederick*. (Macmillan, 1929)

Poore, Judith. *The Memoirs of Emily Loch*. (Kinloss: Librario Publishing Ltd, 2007)

Pope-Hennessy, James. *Queen Mary*. (George Allen and Unwin, 1959)

Radzinsky, Edvard. *Alexander II. The Last Great Tsar*. (N.Y.: Free Press, 2005)

Ramm, Agatha. *Beloved & Darling Child*. (Stroud: Alan Sutton, 1990)

Reid, Michaela. *Ask Sir James*. (Hodder & Stoughton, 1987)

Russia: Art, Royalty and the Romanovs. (The Royal Collection Trust. Exhibition Catalogue, 2018.)

Russian Splendour. Sumptuous Fashions of the Russian Court. (N.Y.: SkiraRizzoli, in Association with the State Hermitage Museum, St Petersburg, 2014.) Translated by Antonina W. Bouis.

Bibliography

Seaman, W. A. L., & Jewell, J. R. (ed). *The Russian Journal of Lady Londonderry 1836–37*. (John Murray, 1973)

Seton-Watson, Hugh. *The Russian Empire 1801–1917*. (Oxford University Press, 1967)

Sixsmith, Martin. *Russia*. (BBC Books, 2011)

Sotnick, Richard. *The Coburg Conspiracy*. (Ephesus Publishing, 2008)

Taylor, A. J. P. *The Struggle for Mastery in Europe, 1848–1918*. (Oxford: Oxford University Press, 1954)

Strauss-Schom, Alan. *The Shadow Emperor. A Biography of Napoleon III*. (Stroud: Amberley Publishing, 2018)

St Aubyn, Giles. *Queen Victoria. A Portrait*. (Sinclair-Stevenson, 1991)

Tarsaidze, Alexandre. *Katia, Wife Before God*. (Macmillan, 1970)

The Last Romanovs. Archival and Museum Discoveries in Great Britain and Russia. Various authors, edited by Maria Harwood. (Pindar Press, 2018)

Trevelyan, Raleigh. *Grand Dukes and Diamonds*. (Secker & Warburg, 1991)

Troyat, Henri. *Alexander of Russia*. (Sevenoaks: New English Library, 1984)

Van der Kiste, John. *Alfred. Queen Victoria's Second Son*. (Stroud. Fonthill Media, 2013)

Van der Kiste, John. *Queen Victoria and the European Empires*. (Stroud: Fonthill Media, 2016)

Van der Kiste, John. *The Romanovs, 1818–1959*. (Stroud: Sutton Publishing, 1998)

Van der Kiste, John. *Sons, Servants and Statesmen. The Men in Queen Victoria's Life*. (Stroud: Sutton Publishing, 2006)

von Habsburg, Geza & Lopato, Marina. *Fabergé. Imperial Jeweller*. (Thames & Hudson Ltd, 1993)

von Preussen, Königin Luise. *Briefe und Aufzeichnungen 1786–1810*. (Germany: Deutscher Kunstverlag, 2010)

Vorres, Ian. *The Last Grand Duchess*. (Hutchinson, 1964)

Warwick, Christopher. *Ella: Princess, Saint and Martyr*. (Chichester. John Wiley, 2006)

Weber, Berchtold. *Historisch-Topographisches Lexikon der Stadt Bern*. (Berne, 2016)

Welch, Frances. *Imperial Tea Party*. (Short Books, 2018)

Williams, Kate. *Becoming Queen*. (Hutchinson, 2008)

Wilson, A N. *Queen Victoria. A Life*. (Atlantic Books, 2014)

Woodham-Smith, Cecil. *Queen Victoria, Her Life & Times. Vol. 1. 1819–1861*. (Hamish Hamilton, 1972)

Wortman, Richard. *Scenarios of Power*. (Princetown: Princetown University Press, 1995)

York, HRH The Duchess of, & Stoney, Benita. *Travels with Queen Victoria*. (Weidenfeld & Nicolson, 1993)

York, HRH The Duchess of, & Stoney, Benita. *Victoria and Albert. Life at Osborne House*. (Weidenfeld & Nicolson, 1991)

Zeepvat, Charlotte. *Romanov Autumn*. (Stroud: Sutton Publishing, 2000)

Articles

Abrash, Merritt. 'A Curious Royal Romance. The Queen's Son and the Tsar's Daughter.' In *The Slavonic and East European Review, No. 109*. July 1969, pp 389–400.

Brown, Dr Catherine. 'Henry James and Ivan Turgenev'. In *Literary Imagination*, 22 February 2013.

Goliczov, Roman Ilmar. 'Grand Duchess Marie Alexandrovna and Music.' In *Royalty Digest,* January 1997.

Hall, Coryne. 'Dear Aldershot'. In *Royalty Digest,* November 1997.

Mead Lalor, William. 'The Grand Duchess Anna Feodorovna. Poor Dear Aunt Julie.' In *Royalty Digest,* July 1996.

Mosse, W. E. 'The End of the Crimean System. England, Russia and the Neutrality of the Black Sea, 1870–1871'. In *The Historical Journal,* Volume 4, No. 2. 1961.

Thornton, Richard. 'Prince Albert's Sister and Other Shady Coburgs.' In *Royalty Digest Quarterly,* No. 2, 2008.

Timms, Elizabeth Jane. 'Princess Alix of Hesse's Visit to Harrogate.' In *Royalty Digest Quarterly,* No. 1, 2018.

Wynn, Marion. 'The Romanovs in Nice.' In *Royalty Digest Quarterly,* No. 2, 2008.

Wynn, Marion. 'What Am I Supposed To Do?' In *Royalty Digest Quarterly,* No. 1, 2006.

Archives & Collections

Ian Shapiro collection.

Balliol College, Oxford. Mallet Family Papers V. Papers of Marie Constance Mallet née Adeane (1861–1934)

Internet

Queen Victoria's Journals online. www.queenvictoriasjournals.org/ (Princess Beatrice's copies.)

www.G26.ch Plattform für kunst kultur und gesellschaft. Anna Feodorovna and Elfenau.

https://archive.org/.../ErlauterungenAlexanderDE15Aug/Ërlauter... Laszlo Vajda. Erläuterungen Zur Geschichte von Grossfürstin Anna Feodorowna (Prinzessin Julian von Sachsen-Coburg-Saalfeld) und Ihr erster Sohn.

www.rbth.com/arts/2013/10/02 Monument in memory of Crimean War prisoners of war restored in Britain – by Denis Voroshilov.

Newspapers & Journals

The Daily Telegraph.

The European Royal History Journal.

The Isle of Wight County Press

The Sussex Advertiser.

The Times.

Royal Russia.

Royalty Digest.

Royalty Digest Quarterly.

Sotheby's auction catalogue. Russian sale, June 2018.

Index

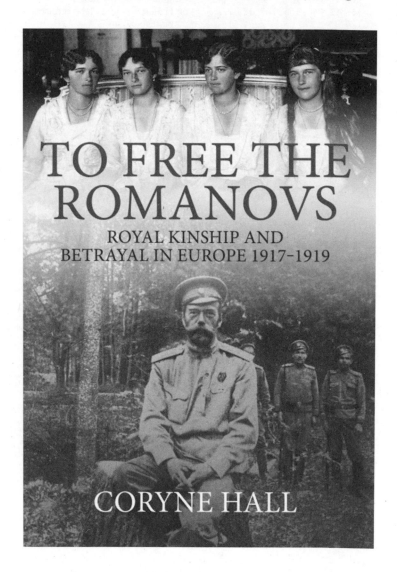